Legends Beneath the Waves Volume I

Truk Lagoon

By

Andrew Marriott

In partnership with

Kimiuo Aisek Memorial Museum

Legends Beneath the Waves Volume 1: Truk Lagoon
A Fata Morgana by Andrew Marriott Publication

First Edition - November 2016

Published by
Fata Morgana by Andrew Marriott Publications
03 Golden Eagle Road, Santa Fe, New Mexico USA

ISBN Number: 978-0-9983537-0-8

All color photographs and text are by Andrew Marriott
Historic photographs are sourced as indicated, all are public domain

Lengends Beneath the Waves, Legends Beneath the Waves Volume 1: Truk Lagoon and any other in the Legends Beneath the Waves series of books are trademarks of Fata Morgana by Andrew Marriott Publishing

Fata Morgana by Andrew Marriott, Fata Morgana by Andrew Marriott Publishing and their associated logos are trademarks of Andrew Marriott who maintains full ownership of these entities

The Blue Lagoon Resort and The Kimiuo Aisek Memorial Museum are trademarks owned by the Aisek Family of Chuuk, Federated States of Micronesia

The author and publisher has made every effort to make the information on the dive sites as accurate as possible. However it cannot be guaranteed accurate and they accept no responsibility for any loss, injury, or inconvenience sustained by any person using this book. This book is not meant to be a comprehensive dive guide or planning tool. Dives in Chuuk are serious business; always dive responsibly and within your limits.

All rights reserved. No part of this publication may be reproduced, stored in a retrieval system or transmitted in any forms by any means electronic, mechanical, photocopying, recording or otherwise, except in brief excerpts for the purpose of review, without the written permission of the publisher and copyright holder.

All images in this book are available for licensing or purchase. To inquire please contact: amarriott@fata-morgana.net
or visit the website: www.fata-morgana.net
or Fata Morgana by Andrew Marriott on Facebook

Manufactured in China and the USA
all rights reserved

Table of Contents

Map of the Pacific Theatre of Operations in World War Two	4
Map of Truk Lagoon/Chuuk Using Historic Names	5
Introduction	6
Author's Notes	8

Combined Fleet and Repair Anchorages — 10

Fumizuki	12
Futagami	24
Hanakawa Maru	28
Heian Maru	34
Hoyo Maru	46
I-169	52
Kensho Maru	62
Kiyosumi Maru	72
Patrol Boat 34	82
Sapporo Maru	88
Shinkoku Maru	90
Yamagiri Maru	102

Fourth Fleet Anchorage — 112

Aikoku Maru	114
Fujikawa Maru	126
Fujisan Maru	136
Hoki Maru	144
Kikukawa Maru	152
Momokawa Maru	158
Nippo Maru	164
San Francisco Maru	172

Southwestern Anchorage & Aircraft — 178

Amagisan Maru	180
Gosei Maru	188
Hino Maru No. 2	194
Rio de Janeiro Maru	200
Sankisan Maru	210
Unkai Maru No. 6	220
Yubae Maru	228
G4M Betty	236
H8K Emily	240
B6N Jill	244
A6M Zero	246

Other Wrecks	248
Notes on Sources	252
About the Author	253
Want to see More?	254

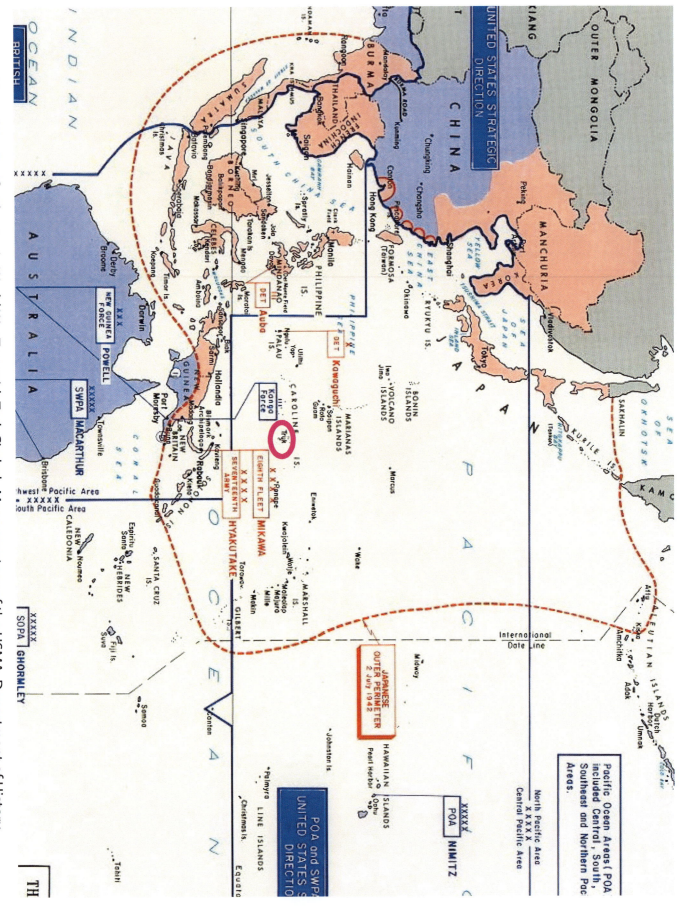

Map of the Pacific Theatre in World War Two with Truk Circled. Maps courtesy of the USMA, Department of History

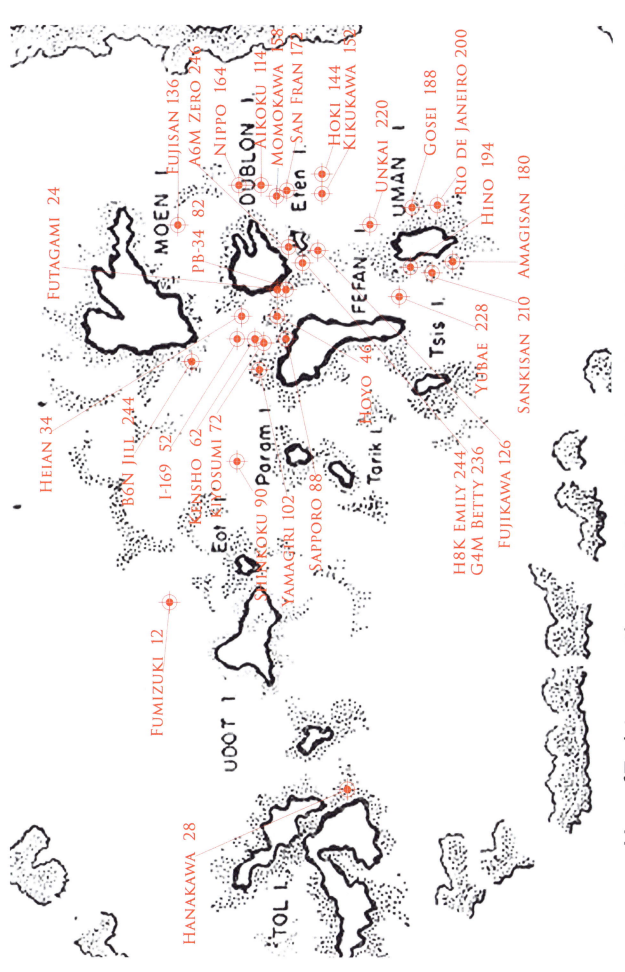

Map of Truk Lagoon Showing Relative Ship Locations and Page Number
Original map is from US Army Air Corps and ship locations are by the author.

INTRODUCTION

Every year roughly 2,000 divers and tourists make the long and difficult journey to Chuuk. They come mostly from the United States, Japan and Australia; the three countries that most heavily battled it out in this remote part of the world. These travelers spend huge amounts of money and often spend several days in airports just to make this journey. For some it is to memorialize those lost, or to spend time camping on a remote tropical island with just a dozen palm trees for company; but for most it is to dive the most incredible collection of shipwrecks in the world. As the license plates on the cars say, this is "Diver's Haven".

The wrecks located in this pristine atoll are without parallel anywhere in the world and diving Truk Lagoon is near the top of most divers bucket lists. For days on end divers repeat the cycle of waking, eating, diving, eating, diving, drinking, eating and finally sleeping. They see a seemingly unending stream of massive ships covered in incredible marine life in every color of the rainbow. There are bombs, bullets, tanks, trucks, boots, bottles and even bones. When asked, divers will have a hard time saying whether the wrecks, or the reefs they have become, are more spectacular. Often they cannot even remember the names of the ships at the end of the day. This is called getting "Maru'd".

With all this amazing and adrenaline pounding adventure it is easy to lose track of where you really are. Truk Lagoon is a massive battlefield and one of the most important locations in all of World War Two. For almost two years young men from farms, small towns and big cities were brought to this place by titanic forces well beyond their control. Caught in the current of the greatest war in history, these men from Japan, the United States and even Great Britain were thrust into gun turrets, engine rooms, cockpits and kitchens and thrown into mortal combat. They came to battle in massive warships, lethal submarines, old tramp steamers, sleek former passenger liners and small cramped aircraft. On an almost daily basis these men did their best to kill each other and on three occasions huge attacks from aircraft carriers left these idyllic islands a smoking ruin with thousands of boys sent home in caskets or consigned to a watery grave.

For 28 years this now largely empty lagoon was one of the great Japanese naval bases with huge installations on land and dozens of ships at anchor. At one point almost every major warship in the Imperial Japanese Navy came through Truk and for long stretches of time the area just south of the Blue Lagoon Resort was full of everything from super battleships to big fleet aircraft carriers to whole squadrons of submarines. In between this vast concentration of killing power were the cargo ships, tankers, tenders and auxiliary ships. In the warm tropical air overhead the sky was full of hundreds of the most famous planes of all time like the A6M Zero and G4M Betty. On land massive guns were dug into the mountains and large cement buildings sprang up out of the jungle, while thousands of Japanese civilians worked in tea houses, stores and schools. It was like a small part of Japan had transported itself to this hot tropical paradise.

When war came there were a few good years, but then over two days of apocalyptic battle the islands of Truk became a living hell. The aircraft had been brutally knocked from the skies, their crumpled forms littering the land and sea alike. The big warships had fled, but their smaller destroyer and submarine compatriots put up a valiant fight against overwhelming odds and paid the ultimate price. Their shredded wreckage also went to the bottom. The dozens of big auxiliary tenders and transports, still packed with men and equipment, could only stoically accept their fate. Whether that was to slowly go down after two days of pounding and wreathed in flames, or to simply vanish in a single instant with a monstrous thunderclap and mushroom cloud;

these proud ships also went to the bottom. Finally there were all the smaller craft that were vital to the functioning of the base. They were strafed, rocketed and bombed to the bottom of the sea. Thousands of men went down with these ships that today delight divers.

These ships are so much more than markings on a map and a mountain of rusting metal; they all once sailed in the light of day on the open sea and helped chart the fate of a nation. Over the course of all those years these ships accomplished incredible feats and were witnesses to some of the most significant moments of the 20th Century. There were ships that had set speed records, circumnavigated the globe and once hosted guests in luxurious accommodations. Some of these ships fought in two wars and were built at the end of the Victorian Era, while others barely had their paint dry before circumstance placed them in Truk Lagoon. There are raiders that conducted daring boarding operations right out of the age of piracy and even some of their victims. The lone submarine was at Pearl Harbor and saw the *USS Arizona* explode and one transport had some of the very first Japanese casualties at the battle of Midway. These ships were at Pearl Harbor, the Philippines, Coral Sea and Midway; while others carried supplies to fight Rommel in North Africa and others fought in the bloody battles around Guadalcanal. The entire Japanese experience in the Pacific War is represented in the wrecks of the ships in Truk Lagoon.

The life and times of the ships beneath the waves of Truk Lagoon are fascinating and knowing them adds tremendously to the experience of actually visiting them. Stand where the captain stood as he went down with his burning ship. Look down the barrels of anti-aircraft guns towards the attacking planes of long ago with spent shell casings scattered on the deck below. Swim through the massive hole that broke the back of a proud ship and sent her to the bottom, or float over the missing forward half of a legendary merchant raider where over 600 men were killed in the blink of an eye. Equipped with these stories it is possible to experience the true essence of these warriors and to have them turned into memories that will last a life time. These are the legends beneath the waves. This is Truk Lagoon.

Evening view of Chuuk today from the best bar in the world.

Author's Notes

First a little bit about what this book is and is not. It is not intended to be a dive guide, nor is it a definitive historical reference. Instead it is meant to tell the stories of these incredible ships in a manner that is both educational and entertaining to read. My many experiences talking to divers in Chuuk led to the creation of this book. People wanted a book they could read over breakfast that would tell them the story of the ship they were about to go visit. The focus was the STORY and not the actual wreck or dive and it is something that people could read in thirty minute single sittings. For anyone interested in a tremendous hard core history and wreck guide, I highly recommend World War 2 Wrecks of the Truk Lagoon by Dan Bailey. It is an indispensable reference and I call it my "Bible".

The other thing that people were looking for was a book that had pictures that captured the essence of what they had seen in their minds eye during their dives. Most divers remember Chuuk as a mix of dark and dramatic interior spaces and explosively colorful reefs outside. I have done a number of magazine articles on just this theme and the photos resonated well with divers. They felt like they could return home and show them to friends and say, "See this is what I saw!" To compliment the current wreck photos I also wanted to include photos of the ships in life when they proudly sailed the seas, and finally attack photos of when they met their end.

Apo celebrating the end of our last long session in the museum.

I still felt like there was something missing. It was when the Kimiuo Aisek Memorial Museum opened at the Blue Lagoon Resort that the final photographic piece fell into place. Over the course of many evenings at the greatest bar in the world at Blue Lagoon the concept for this book came together. This last piece was to incorporate the museum and the artifacts into the book. So on a follow up trip we spent many hard hours in the great museum setting up a temporary studio where we shot archival style shots of every object there. These pictures were the final piece of the puzzle and you will find them throughout this book.

This book was a true partnership with the great people at the Blue Lagoon Resort. I can't do enough to express my deepest thanks to Gradvin, Tryvin, Advin, Rich and Isiro; plus all the amazing staff who know me by name and laugh when I walk back in the front door. Also a big high-five to the greatest guides on earth. Men like Rio, Estos and Kieren who have taken me through so many wrecks. Mostly though I have to thank my constant guide Apo.

Apo and I hunting wrecks in paradise.

We've done hundreds of dives together and he was a great sport putting up with the needs of my photo shoots. He even managed to find the Yubae for us, but not the Taiho!

When researching the story of Japanese ships there are many difficulties, not the least of which is language. Additionally many of the primary sources who took part in these events either died in the war or never spoke of them in the long years after. There were many holes to fill in when it came to the Japanese record and I did my best to fill them accurately, however there are cases where I had to simply make my best estimate of what happened. For example the reason for the big shells in the *Yamagiri Maru*. For cases where actions and events are described I sometimes had to use a technique used by documentary film makers (thanks Tom Roberts!) and that is to find a source who was in a very similar situation and then transpose that on the story I am telling. For example the descriptions of crew reactions to air attacks and being hit by torpedoes. I used these literary devices as little as possible, and only in the interest of making the story more complete.

Finally a note about place names and photos. All names used in the stories are written as they were at that time, for example I call Sri Lanka "Ceylon". Also for Chuuk, I use that name when talking about the present country. The lagoon is always called Truk Lagoon and I use "Truk" when writing about past events. Photos that appear in full color shot on the wrecks or in the museum are all shot by myself or my wife, Dalice Marriott. I have not indivually credited these photos.

The Japanese fleet under attack in the Repair Anchorage. The large colum of smoke to left is the submarine base. (US Navy)

The massive super battleships Yamato and Musahi at achor in the Combined Fleet Anchorage. (Japanese Navy)

Combined Fleet & Repair Anchorages

The Combined Fleet and Repair Anchorages in Truk Lagoon are centrally between the islands of Dublon, Moen and Fefan. During the golden days of the Imperial Japanese Navy this stretch of water was known as Uola Roads and it was the home of the massive striking power of the Kido Butai. When the sun rose on this stretch of water there could be over a hundred ships riding at anchor including the massive battleships Yamato and Musashi and the menacing flat topped carriers such as Shokaku and Zuikaku. The Combined Fleet Anchorage was the home of the battleships, carriers, cruisers, destroyers, submarines and assorted tenders that made the Japanese Navy the most fearsome striking force on earth at the beginning of the war.

Over time the power of the Imperial Navy began to wane and fewer ships rode at anchor in Uola Roads, but in between Dublon and Fefan the Repair Anchorage began to grow. This sheltered area was just offshore of the facilities of the 4th Shipping Repair Department and it included a floating dry dock. This area was where ships came for emergency repairs before being sent back to real shipyards in Japan for more substantial work. Most of these ships had been torpedoed by US Navy submarines.

Ironically this was also where the Japanese 6th Submarine Fleet was based. Ships badly mangled by submarines rode at anchor next to the lethal hunters themselves. Just north of the repair base was the 85th Submarine Base, on the northwest side of the island. This base was further bolstered by the presence of submarine tenders that anchored just offshore, like the *Heian Maru*. Often many of the crewmen on the submarines were ashore when they were in port and shore based work parties would be aboard performing maintenance and repairs.

This combination of submarine, repair and warship anchorages creates a very unique collection of ships for the diver to explore today. Aside from the standard cargo ships there is a submarine, submarine tender, destroyers, tankers, merchant raider, tug boats and even a fishing trawler. The sheltered location of the anchorage tends to mean visibility on these sites is not as good, but they make up for it be being very close and easy to reach. Dives here also are not as deep as elsewhere and all the wrecks are accessible to experienced recreational divers. Today it is hard to picture the sprawling bases along the shore and the constant shuttling of small harbor craft back and forth. The bases have been reclaimed by the jungle and the ships mostly lie on the bottom. The calm and quiet of the area today is a shadow of the past when this area was home to the most potent naval striking force on the planet.

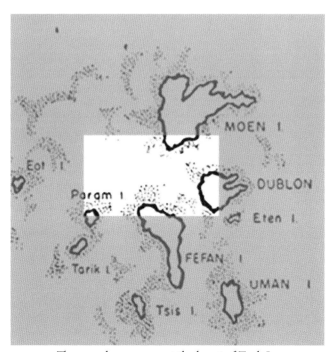

These anchorages are at the heart of Truk Lagoon.

A Mutsuki class destroyer conducting high speed manuevers before the war. (Japanese Navy)

The stern gun on the Fumizuki; still menacing even covered in colorful sponges.

Fumizuki

The *Fumizuki* was part of a construction program that took place throughout the 1920's that sought to field a new force of destroyers capable of operating in the newly acquired Mandated Islands. In 1926 she joined the new Mutsuki class and spent the first 15 years of her service as one of the modern destroyers that formed the back bone of the Japanese fleet. However as war in the Pacific neared the Mutsuki class was showing its age and the *Fumizuki* and her sister ships were being re-rated as fast escorts and transports. Some of their heavier weaponry around the stern was removed, but they still remained a potent ship with two 4.7-inch main guns, ten 25-millimeter anti-aircraft machine guns, six 24 inch torpedo tubes and 36 depth charges on four throwers. Extra equipment was also added to allow fast unloading of troops and cargo carried on the deck. The *Fumizuki* was still a deadly ship to most foes as the war began.

When the curtain went up in the Pacific on December 7, 1941, the *Fumizuki* was with Destroyer Division 22 assigned as escorts for the invasion ships headed towards the Philippines. The first landings took place in rough weather around Aparri in the far north of Luzon and were unopposed except for a single air attack by two American B-17's on the second day. The attacks were the first time the crew of *Fumizuki* saw their foe and they joined the other escorts and fired away at the attackers far above; ultimately shooting down one B-17. This was the famous plane flown by Captain Colin Kelly who radioed that he had severely damaged the battleship *Haruna* before he became the first kamikaze of the war by flying his stricken bomber into the ship. In fact the battleship was not even in the area and the damage done was very minor to the light cruiser *Natori*. This was a case of early war American propaganda looking for heroes amidst the many early defeats in the war. The crew of *Fumizuki* would have been shocked if they heard American newsreel reports of their first taste of battle.

An early model B-17 like the one flown by Colin Kelly. (US Army Air Corps)

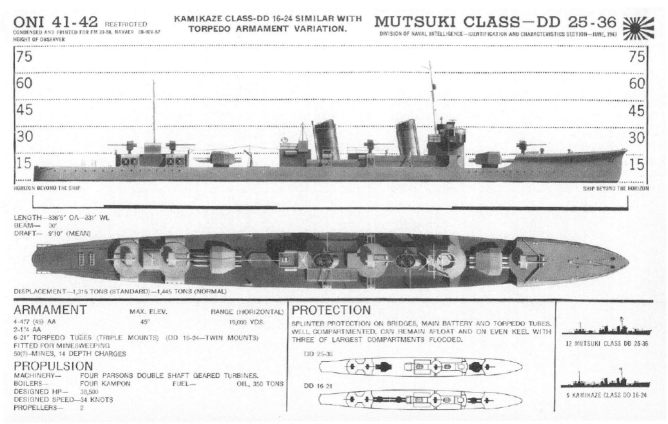

A ship indentification card for a Mutsuki class destroyer used by the US Navy. (US National Archives)

Following the Aparri landings the *Fumizuki* joined the invasion force headed for Lingayen Gulf in central Luzon. Once again the weather was foul with wind and rain lashing the decks. On December 22, 1941, the crews on the transports struggled to unload in the heaving waves, while the destroyers watched for any air or submarine attacks. The landings were ultimately successful and the end game began in the Philippines. In the aftermath the *Fumizuki* conducted routine troop transport operations for the invasion of western Java in late February 1942 and ultimately spent the rest of the spring and early summer escorting the constant stream of troop convoys that moved through the East Indies securing vital sources of oil. Finally as the campaign there died down the *Fumizuki* returned to Japan to have improved submarine detection gear installed.

The *Fumizuki* remained in port through August before finally being ready to return to duty with her new sound gear in early September. She joined a convoy headed towards Formosa and the crew prepared themselves to return to war following the all too short time spent at home. The crew would see home much sooner then they realized as the *Fumizuki* collided with the transport *Kachidoki Maru* and suffered heavy damage to her hull. She entered port in Mako for a month of emergency repairs before heading back to Japan and more substantial repair work in dry dock.

The time spent in port was long as repairs were made and then further refitting was done to modernize the older destroyer. The crew enjoyed their time and visited their families when they could get leave from training duties. Finally in late January 1943 the *Fumizuki* would leave Japan, but now she would head to where the war was really heating up in the Solomon Islands. The *Fumizuki* arrived at her new home in the Shortlands located in the far north of the string of islands that make up the Solomon Islands chain. On the southern end was where the battle was raging on Guadalcanal. The lane of water that ran between these two became known as "The Slot" and it was one of the most contested stretches of water in the world. The Slot was a deadly place for all sides as ships battled each other at close range at night and planes roamed the skies during the day.

By February 1943 it was mostly American planes that did the hunting and the numbers of American ships was growing, despite some stunning early victories in the area by the Japanese Navy. There were so many ships sunk in this area that it was nicknamed "Iron Bottom Sound"

The battle for Guadalcanal had been raging for five months by this time. Over this time the US Marines had dug in an area around the main airfield and defended it against nonstop Japanese attacks. The Japanese attackers never fully understood that they were fighting a bigger and heavily dug in force and for many months they threw unit after unit into battle on the island piecemeal. Finally they had reached the breaking point and the strategy changed to evacuating the thousands of soldiers left on the doomed island so that they could fight another day. The fast convoys that ran down the famous "Slot" at night to resupply the men on the island were nicknamed the Tokyo Express by the Americans. *Fumizuki* joined this famous action as the focus shifted to evacuation and not resupply.

The *Fumizuki* entered the Slot for the first time on a troop evacuation mission on the night of February 1 and for this mission she would be part of the covering force detailed to screen against enemy ships trying to interfere with the troop loading operations. There had been a successful night attack by Japanese Betty torpedo bombers on the American forces defending the Slot the prior night and the path appeared wide open for the next major evacuation mission. That morning twenty Japanese destroyers left the Shortlands and headed at high speed down the Slot.

The timing of their departure was designed to give them the maximum amount of darkness to conduct the evacuation operations, but it left them in the open during the afternoon as the sun slowly sank towards the horizon. The men of *Fumizuki* were confident heading down the slot as this was an impressive force to behold. As the sun very slowly began to creep down in the sky an American patrol plane was spotted while north of Vella Lavella and the crews of the destroyers went to action stations. On the *Fumizuki* the anti-aircraft machine guns were checked one last time and extra ammunition was brought up. It was not long before the Americans arrived and their numbers came as a shock to the *Fumizuki* as the only other enemy planes they had seen were the two B-17s in the very first days of the war.

This time they had kicked a hornet's nest and nearly a hundred American warplanes came roaring up the Slot. The men opened fire with everything they had as the planes came in from all directions and altitudes. The cacophony of heavy machine guns was deafening as the destroyers juked back and forth to avoid attack, all while trying to maintain formation and keep pressing south. Planes came in low with machine guns blazing and dropping bombs as they swooped overhead. The men of *Fumizuki* watched as the nearby *Makinami* was bracketed by a pair of bombs and she soon began to slow. The *Fumizuki* was detailed to assist and closed the distance and protectively pulled alongside, all while blasting away at any planes that came too close. Lines were passed to the *Makinami* and she was taken under tow. The two ships turned north and a third destroyer peeled off to provide cover to the slowly moving duo. Finally darkness fell and the gun barrels finally cooled off after a long afternoon of intense combat.

A bugle used on Japanese ships of the day.

That night the ships returned to Shortlands and were on hand to welcome the rest of the force when it returned. Twelve destroyers had made it through the gauntlet of planes and PT boats to pick up the soldiers waiting on the beach. The sight of the gaunt and emaciated soldiers shocked the crew on deck as they watched them disembark. In the end almost 5,000 men were picked up that night.

There was little time for the shock of combat and seeing the surviving Army soldiers to wear off before the *Fumizuki* joined the other destroyers and headed back down the Slot on February 4th. This run was not nearly as eventful and the ships loaded almost 4,000 men for the return trip. *Fumizuki* did not load any, as she was a used as a picket to look out for PT boats and bigger enemy warships. She would pick up her first soldiers on the final run to Guadalcanal on February 7, when the flotilla would pick up almost 2,000 more men. The sight of the emaciated and diseased men on deck was a sober reminder to the crew that the war was not going as planned. Overall Operation KE was a success as over the three nights the destroyers had pulled over 10,000 men out of the place they called "Starvation Island".

The old destroyers were proving their worth as fast transports in the narrow waters around the Solomon Islands and New Guinea. They had the ability to handle the PT boats sent to harass them and were hard to hit from the air. Even bigger warships had to respect them and their Long Lance torpedoes that could sink any ship that they hit. The tempo of operations for the men on *Fumizuki* was frantic in the two months following the success of Operation KE. Rarely a day went by when they weren't racing between islands to deliver reinforcements where it was anticipated the Americans might land next. Places like Rekata and Gasmata were often visited while home was usually Rabaul or Kavieng.

At the end of March 1943 operations had shifted to New Guinea and the *Fumizuki* was ordered to transport troops from Kavieng to the base of Finschhafen. The troops were needed their as the Australians were moving towards that area through the dense and unforgiving jungle. The four destroyers in the convoy were spotted by enemy aircraft and it did not take long for land based planes to appear on the horizon. These planes came in low and the destroyers swerved and fired their main guns as they approached. The army troops on the deck could only try and make themselves as small as possible when the planes swooped in with guns blazing. The men on *Fumizuki* returned the heavy machine gun fire and tracers zipped across the waves in a deadly dance. Several times planes made passes and the sound of bullets hitting metal and ricocheting off tried the courage of even the bravest soldier on deck. The damage was very minor but the intensity of the attacks just increased and finally the ships turned around and aborted the mission before all the men on their decks were slaughtered.

Japanese destroyer under attack during Operation Hailstone. (US Navy)

Two days later on April 2nd they tried once more, and again the enemy planes quickly found them and pounced. This time the *Fumizuki* was unable to dodge the bombs falling and skipping across the waves and one landed close aside and knocked the ship to the side with a sharp blast and a cascade of water. Down below the alarms were raised that there was flooding in the boiler room. This was serious and the crew responded with urgency to get the flooding under control before it caused the ship to lose power. Once again the air attacks were too much and the ships turned back. The damage to the boiler room would require the *Fumizuki* to head to Kavieng and then Truk for repairs.

The *Fumizuki* was not to remain long in Truk; it had been decided to perform her repairs in Japan and to upgrade her anti-aircraft armament at the time. *Fumizuki* bid goodbye to Truk and headed for Japan escorting the *Heian Maru*, one of her nearest neighbors on the bottom of Truk Lagoon today. The ship was to get a number of newer and heavier machine guns to fight off the near constant air attacks they encountered. The crew were happy to find out they would be home for the entire summer of 1943 as the ship underwent her refit in Sasebo. For the men at home in Japan it was a happy time, but they were haunted by the thoughts of their fellow destroyer crews in the southern seas facing daily battle and death. The list of destroyers sunk and friends killed continued to grow. The feeling when the ship left Japan to return to battle was that they would never see home again. The departures were hard and in this case they were right, the *Fumizuki* would never see Japan again. In fact every single ship in her class would be sunk in battle.

The remains of the Fumizuki's superstructure.

Spent small caliber bullet casings from the battle in Truk Lagoon on February 17-18, 1944.

Rabaul was not exactly a welcome sight when the *Fumizuki* arrived in September 1943. She was immediately pressed into service to once again rescue badly needed soldiers from an isolated island. This time the evacuation runs were to Kolombangara, an island halfway between Guadalcanal and Shortlands. In the months the *Fumizuki* was home the American air and surface forces had grown considerably and every mission was fraught with almost unbearable tension. The destroyers made two successful runs to Kolombangara dodging constant air patrols and PT boats. On October 6 the objective was changed to pick up troops on Vella Lavella. These were the very same waters where *Fumizuki* had encountered the massive air attack on their first ever Slot run ten months prior.

There were 600 soldiers remaining on the island and the *Fumizuki* joined the other destroyer transports *Matsukaze* and *Yunagi* as the ships designated to pick these men up. They were joined by six much more modern destroyers who would act as a screen. The nine ships slipped down the slot and at 22:30 local time they neared the pickup point. Suddenly out of the dark three American destroyers were spotted charging towards them. The six escorts raced towards them to engage, while *Fumizuki* and the other transports could only watch as guns flashed and explosions bloomed on the water. It was all over in ten minutes with one Japanese destroyer sunk and the three Americans crippled and burning. Victory was seemingly in hand when lookouts on the transports spotted what appeared to be three American cruisers heading towards them. It appeared this was part of a much larger force and the evacuation mission was aborted.

It seemed Vella Lavella was too dangerous to evacuate and the focus now shifted back to reinforcing the next islands in the path of the Americans. The first of these missions was to Buka at the most northern point in the Solomon Islands. Not only was the front moving north quickly, but the strength of the Americans in the air was nearly overwhelming. With bases in the central and southern Solomons, American planes could easily attack any ships operating around Rabaul. This was painfully obvious on the mission to Buka when the *Fumizuki* was again bombed and several near misses dented her hull.

October 1943 was spent ferrying men from Rabaul to forward islands under almost constant air attack. On November 1st the *Fumizuki* set out with a deck full of soldiers bound for nearby Bougainville but had to abort when word reached her that a massive invasion force was attacking the island at that very moment. The *Fumizuki* turned around and returned to Rabaul to await the opportunity to make her next run. In port she found a very inspiring sight. Ten cruisers and a similar number of destroyers had come down from Truk with the intention of attacking the American landings at Bougainville. The crew of *Fumizuki* was thrilled by this concentration of power and so were the American planes who quickly spotted them.

On November 2nd an amazing nine squadrons of American B-25's escorted by six squadrons of P-38's appeared over Rabaul to attack this very inviting target. *Fumizuki* was stuck in the middle between 72 bombers, 80 fighters and the heavy cruisers they were sent to sink. Japanese planes rose to the challenge and tangled with the P-38's while the B-25s came in for low altitude bombing attacks. The entire harbor exploded in massive waves of gun and artillery fire as every gun in the fleet and on the surrounding hills opened fire on the attack planes. The anti-aircraft fire was ferocious and the *Fumizuki* contributed her guns to the cause as well, her twin barreled heavy machine guns targeted any plane that got to low or close. The low altitude of the attacks meant the return fire was deadly effective and seventeen American planes were shot out of the sky.

The attacks by the land-based aircraft were largely ineffective against the ships, but they were still deadly to men exposed on deck. Many of the B-25's were modified to include a battery of heavy machine guns in a fixed position pointed forward. One of these bombers zeroed in on the *Fumizuki* and commenced a deadly attack blanketing the ship with heavy .50 caliber bullets as it zoomed by. The effect on board was chaotic as some of the heavy bullets were able to punch through the decks causing a fuel leak and leaving six dead and four injured men bleeding on the decks.

Wreckage in the stern area now the site of a pretty reef.

At the end of the day holes were patched up across the harbor and preparations were still made to go hit the American invasion force at Bougainville.

A porthole cover closed in watertight configuration.

The attack would be made in conjunction with a counter landing on the night of November 5/6. The US Navy was in no mood to wait and in a prelude to Operation Hailstone the fast carriers moved quickly in range of Rabaul hidden by bad weather on November 4th and launched a full deck attack off the big old carrier *Saratoga* and the smaller light carrier *Princeton*. It was a bold attack and took the Japanese off guard, every plane was launched with none left to protect the fleet. At daybreak the 97 planes from the two carriers joined 27 B-24's and 58 P-38's in hitting the fleet still in Simpson Harbor. This attack was much more effective and the cruiser force was mauled with six of the seven cruisers left heavily damaged and burning. The *Fumizuki* was busy loading soldiers for the counter landing and could only contribute sporadic fire from her guns to the fight. She was lucky and not damaged during the attack this time.

Amazingly the decision was made to go ahead with the counter landing and *Fumizuki* answered the call with three other destroyers loaded with soldiers even as the fires in the harbor still burned. In an amazing feat of seamanship the old destroyers threaded their way through the vast fleet assembled offshore and then through swarms of PT boats and successfully delivered their cargo in the early morning hours of November 7. This success was small consolation to the crew as they endured yet another air attack back in Rabaul that day launched off the deck of another group of carriers. At this point Rabaul was finished as a major base, but she would still serve as a stopover point for destroyers making transport runs out to other islands.

The nonstop troop runs continued through December and January. On many occasions the transports were attacked by aircraft and the old *Fumizuki* was damaged by strafing attacks and near misses from bombs on several occasions. The constant running about at high speed and the damage from the air attacks were taking their toll on men and machine alike. Men had seen their friends and passengers gunned down on deck, while below the plates of the hull took repeated poundings and the engines reached the point where they were in desperate need of maintenance. Despite all this the *Fumizuki* continued to make her runs.

The last straw came on January 31, 1944, when American B-24 bombers hit Rabaul in one of their now regular attacks. By this point the thrill of battle was long gone and the novelty of seeing the enemy overhead was replaced by a resignation that soon it would be their time. On this day it was their time and the bombs fell close aside the *Fumizuki* badly damaging her already battered hull and engines. The engineers reported they could barely make steam and the ship could only get underway at very slow speeds. Her time as a fast transport was done and finally she joined a convoy of damaged ships and headed north very slowly towards Truk Lagoon.

Once in Truk she was anchored in the Repair Anchorage and immediately she was prepared for an overhaul. During the first two weeks of February the ship was totally opened up, which made some of the guns unusable. In addition most of the ammunition was taken off as it was only a hazard during the repair work. Her turbines and boilers were broken down and a total refurbishment commenced. Finally *Fumizuki* was getting the service she so badly needed even before the last attack.

When dawn broke with the roar of engines and explosions of anti-aircraft fire the crew new exactly what was happening. They had already survived two attacks like this in Rabaul, or so they thought. As they watched the number of planes swarming overhead they realized this was not like the Rabaul raids from back in November, this was much bigger. The *Fumizuki* herself could not have been in a more helpless position with her engines disassembled and her ammunition mostly gone. As the fighter battle raged and the first dive bombers began to go after the big ships in the Repair Anchorage the engineering crew scrambled to reassemble the engines and boilers. Above decks the gun crews grabbed what ammunition they could and began to return fire in a vain attempt to save the other helpless ships under repair nearby.

As the chaos of the first attack wave died down the men on deck watched the nearby *Hoyo Maru* burn furiously and then turn turtle and sink. Below them the engineers had performed a small miracle and had gotten a boiler and single engine back in action, but nowhere near full power. Some power was better than none and the ship pulled up the anchor and got underway, but very slowly. The *Fumizuki* headed away from the bigger targets in the Repair Anchorage and headed for the open water west of Moen to allow room to maneuver. On the way she passed the *Shinkoku Maru*, miraculously still afloat and in the fight. Then the next wave arrived and the battle began all over again.

An array of colorful fish now make the Fumizuki their home.

The *Fumizuki* was found by planes which were reacting to reports of warships making for the North Pass. On the old warrior the gun crews began to fire their remaining ammunition and the helmsmen valiantly twisted and turned the ship as attackers made their passes. On deck strafing attacks began to take their toll on the gunners returning fire and they sold their lives dearly defending their ship to nearly the last bullet. One attacker dropped a 500-pound bomb with a short delay fuse and this hit just off the port side of the ship. The bomb hit the water and went beneath the waves before detonating. This directed the force of the explosion into the water and it slammed into the side of the *Fumizuki* in exactly the same place the B-24s had already damaged. The repairs in the engine room gave way and the plates in the hull buckled unleashing a torrent of water into the engine room. What little speed the *Fumizuki* had was quickly gone and she glided to a halt with water pouring in. The crew below tried everything they could trying to dam up the flow of water. They battled bravely surrounded by dead and wounded comrades, but in the end the sea would win.

As the last attacker departed the *Fumizuki* was dead in the water with a serious flood in the engine room that was causing her to settle in the water and list to port. As the sun set she dropped her anchor to prevent her from running aground and then stopped dead in the water above her final station on the west side of Moen Island. Her heroic evasive maneuvers had taken her a long way from her berth in the Repair Anchorage; which would make her very hard to find in later years. The night of February 17, 1944, though she was still afloat and a tug boat was called to pull her back to safer waters. When the tug arrived she found the ship in very bad shape, but lines were still secured and towing operations commenced. The tug tried hard to pull the *Fumizuki* to safety, but no matter what she tried she couldn't get the sinking ship to budge. Finally the decision was made to abandon her and the men were transferred to the tug, leaving 29 of their comrades who were already dead behind. What nobody realized in that moment was the ship was still anchored, so of course she could not be towed.

On board the last surviving crew were evacuated and the Emperor's portrait was taken down and carried to safety by the three most senior officers. As the tug began to pull away the crew's downcast eyes were drawn up by colored flares being fired and soon thereafter the roar of airplane engines. Above them big TBF Avenger torpedo bombers from the *USS Enterprise* powered overhead using radar to hunt for targets. The planes were clearly visible by their engine exhausts which glowed with blue flames in the night. This was the first night carrier attack in US Navy history, but for the men of *Fumizuki* it was the night their ship died. As the tug crossed the lagoon the men could see the bow of the *Fumizuki* sticking into the air, lit by flames and explosions from the night attack. The proud old warrior settled upright but with a modest list to port on the lagoon below, still at anchor.

The grave of the *Fumizuki* is in 125 feet of water. Descending on to the bow of the wreck the forward 4.7 inch main gun is very prominent and truly is a moment trapped in time. Around the gun are boxes of shells, some ready to be loaded and some empty. There are even more spent shell casing lying about nearby, leaving little doubt that this gun was in heavy use during the attacks. This gun was fired in anger all across the Pacific, from the Philippines to Solomon Islands, and is an incredible monument to the war. Just behind the gun is the forward torpedo launcher. It can be slightly hard to visualize, but the triple mount can be made out clearly when the viewer is correctly oriented.

The bridge area is now heavily damaged, but this is mostly not due to battle. Instead it is the result of greed and an attempted salvage gone horribly wrong. There are still some artifacts around including many 25-millimeter bullets which were used for the heavy anti-aircraft machine guns. Behind the bridge is the entrance to the engine room, which is pretty cramped as one would expect on a destroyer. It is interesting to look inside and see this area of so much drama that would ultimately seal the fate of the warship. Behind the engine room is the second 4.7 inch gun, which in this case appears to be stowed. It was likely placed this way so that it was out of the way of the repairs being conducted below in the engineering spaces. The area around the stern has a very interesting depth charge launcher. This device was used to throw depth charges to a set distance behind the ship which maximized the explosive force of the blasts underwater. On the starboard side the hull is bent in what appears to be damage from a bomb near miss, but the overall hull damage in the stern is more likely the result of the ship impacting the ocean floor when it sank. The *Fumizuki* is a unique wreck with an amazing story. It is one of the few warships in the lagoon, which combined with the fact the depth is not excessive makes this an excellent dive. There is a lot of action frozen in time on the *Fumizuki* and she is still has the looks of a warrior.

Sake bottles, bones and other miscellaneous items on the deck of Fumizuki.

Looking into the bridge of the Futagami from the bow.

The helm and engine telegraph inside the bridge of the Futagami.

Futagami

The *Futagami* was a salvage tug, perhaps one of the most unglamorous jobs in the Navy. Nonetheless an interesting story and a really fun wreck to dive. For starters *Futagami* is not a "Maru", she was a navy ship from the beginning. Secondly she is perhaps the only Imperial Japanese Navy ship in the lagoon to actually survive the war but still end up as a wreck in Truk. The *Futagami* was launched in 1939 as a 600 ton salvage tug. She was everything one would expect in a tugboat, basically strong winches and towing lines built over massive engines. In the early days of the war she performed standard tug boat functions in Kure Harbor, maneuvering and docking many of the other ships that now lie on the bottom of Truk Lagoon. As the initial victorious years gave way to the constant grind in the southern theatre the services of the *Futagami* were needed in Truk.

Starting in April 1, 1943, *Futagami* helped in the tow and repair of many of her neighboring wrecks in the lagoon. She would have been there to help the badly mangled *Kiyosumi*, the nearly sinking *Yamagiri*, the horribly fire ravaged *Hoyo* and the *Kensho*. When the attacks of February 17, 1944, began the *Futagami* could only act as a spectator as she was unarmed. However her services were sorely needed as the attacks took place and in their immediate aftermath.

As the attacks entered their second day on the morning of the 18th the crew of *Futagami* was in for another long day of watching their friends and comrades die and wondering when it would be their turn. Fortune favored them during that long hot day as they were never singled out for serious attack. As the day wore on the tug was desperately busy trying to help with repairs to damaged and sinking ships. Thanks to efforts of ships like the *Futagami* not every ship in the lagoon sank during the attacks. The strong lines and powerful engines were sorely needed in the aftermath of the attack, especially on April 4 and 5th.

April 4th began like any other morning on Truk Lagoon. Just after breakfast an incoming raid of American B-24's was spotted, but even this was starting to become routine. The submarines replenishing off the nearby submarine base on Dublon submerged to ride out the attack on the bottom, but one of them failed to surface after the attack. Something had happened to the *I-169*. The *Futagami* and the floating crane were dispatched to help after divers had determined that there were survivors in the bow area, but the flooded stern was quiet. The officers on the surface came up with a plan to use the crane and the *Futagami* to lift just the bow section to the surface like a lever, allowing the trapped crew to escape and make further salvage operations feasible.

Engine telegraph from the Futagami.

The two salvage ships rigged a hoist on the bow and began to lift, but a loud bang announced to all that the cable had snapped and the operation failed. After taking a break due to another air raid, rescue operations resumed on April 5. This involved sending down divers to drill holes and in the ballast tanks and to secure air hoses to float the submarine. However these efforts were to be in vain as the crew inside was unable to open the valves to the ballast tank; they had suffocated just hours before.

April 1944 also saw a return of the US carriers on the 29 and 30th. It is unclear if the *Futagami* was around for these attacks, but there are many reports of numerous smaller craft around the islands and a few of them were sunk. It is likely that the tug was again simply ignored by the attackers, especially as they were heavily focused on attacking land targets during this raid. The objective was to put the airfields out of action and destroy the ability of aircraft to effectively use Truk as a base. In this they were successful.

Futagami next appears in September 1944 on Puluwat Island, which is west of Truk, in the company of a few small harbor minesweepers. Puluwat hosted a garrison of almost 3,000 men who by this point were starving. The decision was made to evacuate two thirds of these soldiers of the 11th Mixed Regiment back to Truk to bolster its defenses and to prevent their certain death on Puluwat. Ironically the food situation on Truk wasn't much better. During this operation the small ships crammed with soldiers were attacked by American B-25 medium bombers and one of the smaller craft was beached to prevent sinking. The *Futagami* reportedly sustained damage in this attack, but it would have been minor as there is no evidence of damage on the wreck today and there were no resources to repair any damage she would have sustained.

The final fate of *Futagami* is shrouded in mystery. In September 1945 she was one of the few Navy ships still in Truk Lagoon that was in serviceable condition. She had survived the Pacific War nearly unscathed despite two massive carrier raids, one smaller carrier raid by the Royal Navy and a huge number of heavy bomber attacks. With the surrender of Imperial Japan the flag was lowered on *Futagami* and she surrendered to American forces when they entered the lagoon. At some point she moved back to the former Repair Anchorage and was scuttled. Who deliberately sank the vessel, or for what reasons will probably never be known. Despite surviving the war she ended up on the bottom near the ships she had fought hard to save.

The engine room is still in amazing condition.

The bridge is small, but packed with an amazing amount of artifacts.

The *Futagami* today is a fantastic wreck as she is completely intact and generally upright. Most dives start on the bow as she sits on a steep slope and that is the deepest spot at roughly 85 feet. The bridge is small, but is one of the best preserved bridges on any of the wrecks. The helm and one engine telegraph are still in place, the other telegraph is in the Kimiuo Aisek Memorial Museum. Also intact are an amazing array of valves, switches and speaking tubes. Leaving the bridge, divers often head to the engine room which is also still in pristine condition. The conditions are very cramped and silt can be a problem, but the entire area looks like it could be restarted today. The final stop on a dive are the two big three-bladed propellers at the stern that are often shrouded in schools of small fish. Being a simple salvage tug, the *Futagami* is often overlooked by divers and history buffs in favor of the bigger, more famous ships nearby, but given the opportunity divers should jump at the chance to explore this easily divable wreck and appreciate her unique history and contribution to the war.

Hanakawa Maru

The *Hanakawa Maru* is the youngest member of the museum beneath the waves in Truk Lagoon. She was put in service on October 25, 1943, and therefore only had a little over 100 days of active service before the attacks of Operation Hailstone sank her. The ship is 367 feet long and weighed 4,793 tons and was part of the Standard B class. These were very simple ships that were being produced to fill the void in shipping caused by US submarines. These ships were coal-powered and ran on a single 2,000 horsepower turbine, which allowed them to cruise at 10 knots and perhaps reach 15 knots under full steam on a calm day.

The first time the *Hanakawa* hit the open seas was on October 30 when she joined a huge convoy leaving Japan headed for Formosa. There were 17 cargo ships of all types, including the *Shinkoku Maru*, and only two light escorts. The escorts thought they detected a submarine and spent time hunting this phantom menace on the morning of November 2, but nothing ever came of this. The *Hanakawa* would stay in Formosa and return to Japan as part of another convoy on December 11, which again saw the single light escort attack a phantom submarine. It was obvious to the crew of *Hanakawa* that these really were submarine infested waters, but it was not totally clear if they had ever actually been attacked by one.

On their return to the chilly waters of Tokyo Bay, the *Hanakawa* was loaded with basic construction supplies and aviation fuel bound for Saipan and then on to Truk. Five days out of Tokyo Bay the small convoy of *Hanakawa*, *Reiyo* (also sunk in Truk) and *Tamashima Marus* and escorted by the coastal defense ship *Hirado* was 400 miles north east of Pagan in the far Northern Mariana Islands. Finally the *Hanakawa* would encounter a real American submarine, in this case the *USS Spearfish* which attacked the convoy midmorning on January 30. Despite claiming hits on all three ships, the *Spearfish* succeeded in only striking the *Tamashima* amidships on the starboard side. The ship was carrying almost a thousand Imperial soldiers plus their equipment so every effort was made to get the men off the ship as it slowly flooded. The escort *Hirado* charged after the submarine and subjected it to a terrific pounding of almost 50 depth charges, which bought the *Hanakawa* and *Reiyo* time to offload the soldiers. As darkness came the *Spearfish* returned and put a final torpedo into the *Tamashima* sinking her, but the rest of the ships escaped to Truk.

The emergency helm in the stern is in amazing condition.

Opposite: Life explodes on the mast of the Hanakawa.

A shallow wreck rarely visited by man.

COMBINED FLEET AND REPAIR ANCHORAGES

The masts on Hanakawa Maru.

Descending into the cargo hold full of oil barrels.

The ships entered the calm, safe waters of Truk Lagoon on February 12 and the *Hanakawa* headed to Tol Island where she was to offload the soldiers she had picked up and her cargo of fuel and construction supplies. On February 17, 1944, she found herself empty of soldiers but still full of extremely volatile aviation fuel in her cargo holds. From far off Tol the crew on board could make out the smoke and hear the distant blasts from massive explosions as the battle raged, but otherwise the *Hanakawa* went unmolested on the first day of the attack.

Hanakawa Maru may not have been attacked that first day, but she was noticed. On the morning of February 18 a flight of TBF Avenger torpedo bombers off the *USS Bunker Hill* came for her. The first pilot dropped his torpedo, followed soon by the other three planes in the flight. The last three planes need not have bothered as the first torpedo hit the *Hanakawa* in the starboard side and blasted a gaping hole in the forward holds. This explosion set off a massive secondary explosion and fire as the blast from the torpedo set off the aviation fuel still awaiting unloading. The entire front and amidships of the *Hanakawa* erupted in an inferno as a huge cloud of smoke and debris boiled high into the air. By the time the pilots could pull out of their attack runs and look back all they could see was a huge burning lake of aviation fuel on the surface and towering pall of smoke.

The *Hanakawa* burned fiercely but not for very long. The huge hole in her side set loose a torrent of water that rapidly flooded the ship and pulled her to the shallow bottom. On the surface the fire continued to burn as the slick of aviation fuel made its way to shore; where the flames set fire to the mangroves in the area and spread into nearby structures. The career of *Hanakawa Maru* was very short and her destruction was very swift. There are no records of any survivors from amongst the crew and any Army soldiers remaining on board were also swiftly drowned or cremated in the roaring flames.

The wreck of the *Hanakawa* is in stark contrast to her violent and flame-filled end. Today she is overgrown with one of the top five reefs on any ship of Truk Lagoon. Her entire structure is covered in an amazing rainbow of soft corals and the volume of fish is stunning. It is very apparent that this wreck is rarely visited by humans. Part of this is due to her history of causing nasty skin burns to anyone who came into contact with the remains of her former cargo. The chemicals that cause the burns are mostly gone now, but the years of isolation only served to make *Hanakawa* even more beautiful.

Hanakawa sits upright in fairly shallow water, the deepest parts being only a little over 100 feet down. Most of the decks, structures and masts are much shallower at around 50 feet or less. This allows a lot of natural light to illuminate the wreck, even inside the cargo holds there is always a blue glow from the outside. There is not much to see inside the wreck anymore except a large number of fuel drums, which are still best avoided due to their potentially toxic nature. The superstructure area has evidence of severe fire damage, but it still very atmospheric to explore with the shafts of natural light penetrating in. Towards the stern there is a very interesting deck gun, which is small and so completely covered in marine life as to be almost unrecognizable. Below the poop deck there is a small cabin that contains a very nice lantern and a second helm for emergencies or manual control of the rudder. This helm is in excellent condition, perhaps the best of any in the entire lagoon. Overall the *Hanakawa* does not have much of a history, but the wreck itself is well worth the long trip out to Tol Island to explore.

Storage containers found on the wreckage.

The Heian Maru in her heyday.   (City of Vancouver Archives)

Passengers and luggage unloading in Vancouver after crossing the North Pacific Ocean.   (City of Vancouver Archives)

Heian Maru

The title of biggest wreck in the lagoon belongs to the massive *Heian Maru*, weighing in at a little over 11,600 tons and stretching 510 feet from bow to stern across a sandy bottom. The *Heian Maru* was built in 1930 and put into service with the Nippon Yusen Kaisha, or NYK line. *Heian* was the last of three sister ships, the other two being the *Hie* and *Hikawa*, that were designed to service the company's routes across the North Pacific Ocean. The *Heian Maru* was a fast and beautiful ship, both inside and out and her interior was the height of fashion at the time. Passengers travelled in comfort and style across the North Pacific between Yokohama, Japan and Seattle and *Heian* wouldn't have looked out of place amongst the famous liners plying the legendary Atlantic routes.

The *Heian Maru* was famous on both sides of the Pacific and for a time in the 1930's was seen as a symbol of hope for peace in relations between the United States and Japan. On *Heian's* first Pacific crossing in 1931 she set a company speed record and was warmly welcomed in Seattle by over 10,000 people that came to tour her. These visitors marveled at the fine English style interior spaces and cabins; in addition to the very impressive twin 8 cylinder Burmeister and Wain diesel engines that turned the two massive propellers. *Heian* serviced the route across the North Pacific for ten years carrying hundreds of passengers on every trip and thousands of tons of cargo. As the clouds of war grew in the Pacific the era of the Trans Pacific steamships slowly drew to a close. For the ship that was so welcomed in 1931 that end came on the 16th of August, 1941, as the *Heian Maru* pulled away from the dock in Seattle for the last time. She would be the last Japanese ship to visit Seattle before war erupted less than four months later.

The Imperial Japanese Navy recognized the value of a ship like the *Heian Maru* and she was requisitioned on October 3, 1941. Her time as a civilian was over, the *Heian Maru* was a warrior now. Her conversion took place at the shipyards in Kobe, where her luxurious interior and promenade were stripped out and four 6-inch guns and a pair of machine guns took their place. It took until the end of 1941 to complete her conversion, but on the last day of the year she departed Japan as a submarine tender assigned to the Sixth Fleet. Her mission was to rearm the lethal Japanese submarines known as "I" boats that were operating in the around the Hawaiian Islands. Leaving Japan on New Year's Eve 1941 her bow no longer pointed east towards Seattle as it had done so many time before; now it pointed south on a course to Kwajalein Atoll and war.

It did not take long for *Heian Maru* to get her first glimpse of battle. As dawn broke over Kwajalein on the first day of February 1942 the normal routine of day to day operations was shattered by US Navy planes flying off the carrier *USS Enterprise*.

A phone found on the Heian Maru.

Heian was lucky that day as she was merely a spectator, but a number of Japanese ships were not so lucky and they remain on the bottom of the lagoon in Kwajalein to this day. With the conclusion of the operations around Hawaii, the *Heian Maru* weighed anchor and returned to Japan and out of harm's way.

As spring gave way to summer in 1942 there was an increase in Japanese activity in the area of New Guinea and the Solomon Islands, and these operations would pull in the *Heian Maru*. These voyages would take advantage of the size and speed of the *Heian*, as the objective was to move as many men into the theatre of battle as quickly as possible. Leaving Japan in August she was full of supplies needed for operations in the southern theatre, and for the first time she entered the waters of Truk Lagoon while heading to the major base at Rabaul. *Heian* made the run between Japan and Rabaul several times, her once fine rooms now full of soldiers destined for battle and all their equipment in the cargo holds. It would not be until the end of 1942 that she would finally resume her role as a submarine tender beneath the brooding volcanoes in Simpson Harbor, Rabaul.

Heian Maru seemed to have a knack for arriving at new forward operating bases just when they came within range of US aircraft. Her first actual taste of combat took place in Simpson Harbor on New Year's Day 1943 as big four engine American B-17 and B-24 bombers blasted Rabaul. For the bombardiers high above the huge ship anchored in the middle of the harbor made an inviting target and they lined up for their chance to drop their big 500 and 1000-pound bombs on her. The gunners on *Heian* defended themselves furiously, firing thousands of rounds at the bombers droning high overhead. On this day the bombs fell harmlessly away from the ship, and the gunfire in return was just as ineffective. The bombers took a day off, but returned with a vengeance just after dawn on January 3 quickly going after the *Heian* again. On the deck of the former luxury liner the guns opened fire on the bombers high above as the bombs fell. Explosions rocked the water near the ship, sending

The view of the Heian from off the bow.

COMBINED FLEET AND REPAIR ANCHORAGES

huge columns of water high in the air ultimately to come crashing down on the deck. When the water and smoke cleared the *Heian* still gently rocked in the waves, unscathed with only the thousands of spent brass cartridges from her machine guns littering the deck. Her luck still held.

The American and Australian advance up the Solomon Islands and across New Guinea placed Rabaul within range of an increasing armada of bombers and fighters. Such a valuable asset could not be left that close to the front, so *Heian* found herself back in the safety of Truk Lagoon. She stayed there over the spring, but events were in motion on the far side of the ocean that would again draw her into the spotlight. In the frozen far north of the Pacific the Japanese had invaded the Aleutian Islands in Alaska the previous year and in May 1943 the United States launched an offensive to retake these cold, bleak and barren islands. The Japanese, in a rare case of preserving their troops, decided to undertake an operation to evacuate their remaining forces from these islands, and for this they needed the abilities of the *Heian Maru*. So the *Heian* joined with the destroyer *Fumitzuki* and left Truk headed back to the site of her former glory; the North Pacific Ocean. Nobody on the two ships knew that in less than a year the two ships would share a watery grave near each other in Truk Lagoon.

A vase from the Heian Maru.

As the long days of June arrived the *Heian* dropped anchor in her new base of operations in Paramashiro, part of the Kurile Islands in the far north of Japan. This was the closest Japanese base to the Aleutians and *Heian* returned to resupplying submarines that were conducting operations in the area around Alaska. During this time the *Heian* also recaptured some of her former glory by acting as the headquarters for Rear Admiral Koda, the commander in charge of the operation to evacuate Kiska Island in the Aleutians. For the long days of the summer months *Heian* flew the admiral's flag and played an important role in the successful evacuation of Japanese forces; troops that would soon desperately be needed elsewhere as back in the South Pacific the Americans had been busy.

Back in the Solomon Islands, the US Marines had pushed halfway to Rabaul from their starting point on Guadalcanal and in New Guinea US Army and Australian forces were on the brink of capturing the critical bases of Lae and Salamaua. These two operations were like a pincher clearly designed to lead to the final objective of Rabaul. To counter this the Japanese Army desperately searched for troops and the ships to move them to this critical area. *Heian Maru* was a perfect choice for this operation, being fast and having the ability to carry a large number of troops and equipment. So *Heian* left the chilly waters of the North Pacific for the last time and headed to Shanghai to join a large convoy that was to ferry the Army's 17th Division to Rabaul so

Heian (second from left) during the operations in the Aleutian Islands.

that it could join the climactic battle that Imperial Headquarters believed was imminent.

In Shanghai the *Heian Maru* joined convoy "Te No. 2" which placed her in the company of the *Kiyosumi Maru*, *Gokoku Maru*, *Akitsushima* and the destroyers *Hibiki*, *Makanami* and *Yamagumo*. Almost 2,000 Army soldiers embarked with their equipment onto *Heian* and again she returned to her designed role as a fast and efficient mover of people and cargo. With her quarters jammed full of men in the tropical heat *Heian* finished loading up by taking on a cargo of torpedoes and the convoy increased speed and left the teeming and war weary city of Shanghai behind them. Convoy Te No. 2 entered Truk Lagoon through the North Pass on October 2, 1943, and the sight in the anchorages before them was awe inspiring.

Gathered in their long time base were the big ships of the *Nihon Kaigun*. Heading towards the dock on Dublon the *Heian* passed the massive super battleships *Yamato* and *Musashi* and the only slightly less imposing battleships *Nagato*, *Kongo* and *Haruna*. The carrier fleet had been badly reduced in battle with

A drinking water filter in almost perfect condition.

the US Navy; but the sight of the old Pearl Harbor veterans *Shokaku* and *Zuikaku* was still impressive. Their long flat decks dwarfed those of their smaller cousin, the light carrier *Zuiho*. Also present on that day long ago were ten heavy cruisers and a large host of smaller destroyers.

The convoy did not stay long to enjoy the spirit-raising site of the entire fleet at anchor in Truk Lagoon. Torpedoes were quickly offloaded while the soldiers in their quarters sweated in the tropical heat, and the next day they resumed their journey south. Rabaul had changed since *Heian* had last visited; the Allies were closing in and the base was taking a near daily pounding from the air. Few Japanese planes were left to defend the ships unloading and the convoy was quickly sighted by a reconnaissance plane as it entered Simpson Harbor. There was a sense of urgency as the men of the 17th Division scrambled off the decks and back on to land, for everyone knew the swarms of bombers would soon be coming. Unloading continued through the wet and sticky night of October 5; the crew drenched in sweat as they worked frantically to offload all the desperately needed troops and supplies. As the sun rose, the fear of bombers rose with it. The fear only began to subside as the two big diesel engines roared to life and *Heian Maru* and her convoy left beleaguered Rabaul behind shortly after breakfast. The *Heian Maru* was still a lucky ship.

Heian and submarine during the Aleutian campaign.

COMBINED FLEET AND REPAIR ANCHORAGES

The war had changed since *Heian Maru* had originally been converted to wartime use and she was badly in need of an update to help defend against the twin menaces of submarine and air attack. So with this in mind, *Heian* left her convoy in Truk and returned home to Japan. As the ship entered the yards for her overhaul many of the crew took the chance to return home and visit families they had not seen in several years. The *Heian Maru* was a different looking ship when the crew returned. Gone were the ineffective guns of the early war, replaced by two big 12-centimeter multipurpose guns and a pair of twin anti-aircraft machine guns. To deal with the submarine threat a sonar was installed and a depth charge rack added to the stern. It is very likely that *Heian* also sported a new dazzle style paint scheme at this point. To man the extra armaments crew were added and 242 men boarded the *Heian Maru* as she joined a convoy headed back to Truk. As Japan slowly disappeared in the haze behind them nobody would know it would be the last time the *Heian Maru* and many of her crew would ever see the land of the rising sun.

It did not take long for the war to find the *Heian* after her time home in Japan. On November 16, 1943, her lookouts spotted an American submarine stalking them but it quickly disappeared and for the next two days the crew was on high alert well aware that they were being hunted. Their hunter was the *USS Dace* and her commander had chosen the biggest ship in the convoy as his primary target, that honor of course belonged to the *Heian Maru*. On the morning of the 19th lookouts screamed a warning as torpedoes were spotted streaking into the convoy aimed at *Heian*. The *Dace* was a new boat on her first patrol and the torpedoes missed the big *Heian* but almost struck the bow of the escort *Oki* as she turned to engage the threat. *Heian* was still lucky and she turned on her sonar to find the threat with payback in mind. *Heian* briefly joined the hunt for the sub using her new gear and at one point depth charges fell from her racks in an attempt to kill the threat beneath her. After a short hunt the convoy gave up the search and continued south. They entered the protected waters of Truk Lagoon four nervous days later. *Heian Maru* would never feel the open ocean again.

The war was closing on Truk and it was a very busy time for the submarine fleet as they sought American targets for their deadly torpedoes, which brought the *Heian Maru* back to her primary role as a submarine tender. Day after day the crew toiled in the heat swinging their big and deadly cargo across the decks and into the waiting holds of the sleek submarines. One of her regular customers was the *I-169*; another of her future partners in a watery grave. The months in Truk were long and strenuous; but also peaceful in the protected waters.

On the morning of February 17, 1944, *Heian Maru* was anchored in her usual place on the western side of Dublon Island and on board was Vice Admiral Takagi and his entire staff for the Sixth Fleet. The large and relatively comfortable quarters of the ship were always popular with the senior officers and made her a good choice as a headquarters ship.

Submarine periscopes inside the wreck.

Her neighbor that fateful morning was her sister ship the *Hikawa Maru* which had been converted to a hospital ship and was painted bright white with big red crosses. The sister ships were a long way from the glamor and luxury of their days crossing between Japan and Seattle. As the crews of the two ships began their morning routines in the early dawn a huge armada just over the horizon was launching hundreds of aircraft to come and put an end to Truk as a fleet base.

Warnings sounded across the lagoon joined shortly after by the roar of engines as US Navy F6F3 Hellcat fighters swooped in, shattering the early morning calm. The alarm roused the crew of *Heian* to action and the anti-aircraft guns were manned and even rifles were passed out to crew without any other job at the time. The admiral and his staff watched the air battle overhead as a huge fur ball of fighters tangled for control of the air, but most of the wreckage that fell flaming and smoking from the sky bore the red *hinomaru* of Japanese planes. It did not take long for American fighter pilots to begin looking for other targets and a few Hellcats picked *Heian Maru* for their deadly attention. The Hellcats roared in low

The Heian burning fiercely during Operation Hailstone. (US Navy)

over the water with their six M2 .50 caliber blazing. The big heavy bullets from these guns ripped across the *Heian* sending men diving for cover as others furiously returned fire from the twin machine gun mounts and even from the rifles passed out shortly before. The deadly exchange of fire between fighters and the *Heian* crew continued for several passes, but there was little the fighters could do to actually damage the ship and they left.

As the morning attacks continued it seemed the *Heian Maru* would continue to be lucky as the fighters that had been attacking her left. Then the bombers arrived overhead. The crew of the two big 12-centimeter guns took aim and began to blast away as the bombers began their deadly dives above the sitting ducks below them. Across the ship the roar of engines could be heard above the din of all the guns in Truk blazing away at the attackers. Two ungainly looking SB2C Helldivers from *USS Bunker Hill* took aim at *Heian* and began their dives. The first of the bombers, nicknamed "Beast", released a single big 1,000-pound bomb but this only hit open water and the crew breathed a sigh of relief. The second Beast came shortly after from the stern and it released two bombs at the end of its dive. A pair of simultaneous blasts rocked the massive ship as the bombs impacted very close to the stern of *Heian*. The explosions were so powerful they ruptured the No. 6 cargo hold, started fires near the stern and even damaged one of the huge propeller shafts. Even as the crew battled the fires and worked to seal off the flooding cargo hold they knew they were lucky as the bombs had actually missed. Had they hit the damage would have been much worse.

Somehow the *Heian* survived the long violent day without attracting any more attention, which allowed her crew to fight to extinguish the fires in the stern. Finally as the sun went down and fires burned across the shattered lagoon the crew felt safe for the moment. They had been lucky on the 17th as the ship was still full of highly explosive torpedoes which if set

Opposite: Fire gutted interior of the bridge.

off would have likely destroyed the ship in a single cataclysmic explosion similar to others the crew had seen around the lagoon that day. To address this threat the ship moored at the submarine base on Dublon and began to unload torpedoes under the cover of darkness. Admiral Takagi and his staff also said their goodbyes to *Heian* and disembarked. All too soon dawn came on the 18th of February, the last time *Heian* would great the rising sun above the waves.

The wreck is full of beautiful porcelain dishes like these.

The crew had not had time to finish unloading the torpedoes in Hold 1 and this weighed heavily on the mind of Captain Tamaki as the increasing light brought waves of American dive and torpedo bombers. A flight of four SBD Dauntless dive bombers from the *USS Yorktown* launched from their carrier at 5 am and as the dawn broke they arrived over the *Heian Maru*. The exhausted crew manned their guns and opened fire on the attackers as they plunged down on the ship with their deadly cargo of 1,000-pound general purpose bombs. The first bomb plunged down and hit the water off the stern blasting the already battered hull with a shockwave and a torrent of sea water. The crew had no time to react before three more bombs hit in quick succession, *Heian's* luck had finally run out. The first bomb hit the water just a few feet off the stern and the next two slammed into the *Heian Maru* above the engine room causing massive damage and starting serious fires. Flames roared as crews fought to battle the blazes amidst the twisted metal of the area that had once held fashionable first class cabins.

Amidst the chaos, carnage and destruction the crew fought for the next two hours to save their ship. The fire above the engine had spread forward and the captain was forced to leave the bridge as it was engulfed in the roaring inferno. His most serious concern was to prevent the flames from reaching the torpedoes sitting in the first hold, but the US Navy didn't give the crew a break as more Dauntless dive bombers arrived overhead. These planes were from the *USS Enterprise* and mostly focused their attention on the undamaged *Yamagiri Maru* nearby, but a three-plane division broke away and chose the smoking *Heian* as their target. The planes plunged down and dropped their 1,000-pound bombs, two of which impacted close off the bow. As debris was blasted off the ship by the force of the blasts the crew held their breath, but the expected torpedo explosions never came. Unfortunately for the crew of the bow gun they were likely instantly killed in the blasts and their gun flung high in the air and into the smoke towards the stern. The hull and structure had been further damaged by the shockwaves, but the cargo hold remained intact.

The burned out shell of the bridge.

The *Heian Maru* had been well built and she remained afloat even after all the repeated hammering of shockwaves on her hull. The superstructure of the ship though was a single mass of flames and efforts to fight the blaze had been a failure. Captain Tamaki realized his ship was doomed as the flames would eventually reach the high explosives in the first hold. In this moment of supreme crisis as attacking planes continued to tear apart the ships in the lagoon the captain ordered the flag lowered and gave the order to abandon ship. The crew obeyed his command and took to the water, making their way to the submarine base close by. Sixteen of their shipmates and one construction worker didn't survive, killed in the explosions and flames that doomed their ship. On shore the crew could only watch as flames continued to consume the *Heian Maru*, but she did not sink.

The final blow fell later in the day when TBF Avenger torpedo bombers from the *USS Bunker Hill* arrived on the scene to finish off any ships still floating in the lagoon. Once again the big *Heian Maru* proved a tempting target and the planes came in just over the waves and dropped their torpedoes at the now abandoned ship; a silent blazing pyre with her guns silent. At least one and possibly two massive explosions sent huge columns of water skyward as the torpedoes ripped into the port side of the ship. All the crew could do was watch from afar as at 2:08 pm on February 18, 1944, the once lucky *Heian Maru* rolled onto her port side and slid beneath the waves.

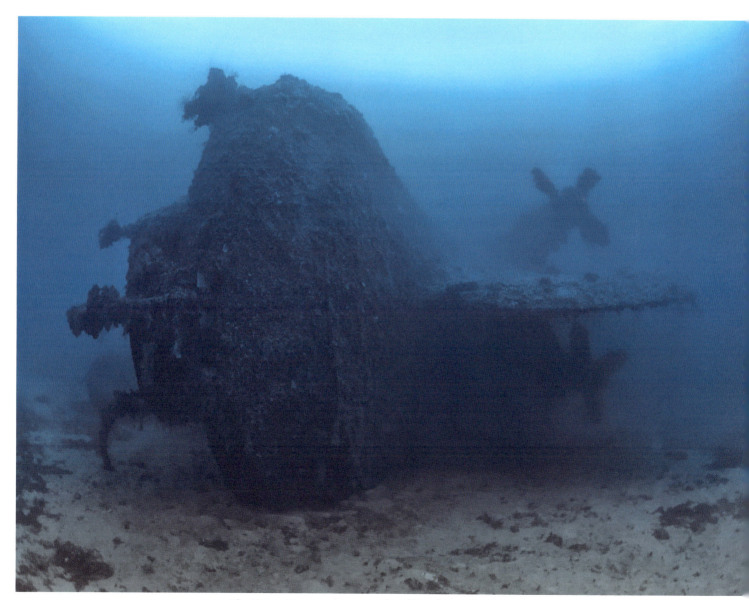

The Heian Maru as she rests today. View from off the stern.

The propeller on a 53-centimeter torpedo now encrusted in colorful marine life. Once one of the most feared weapons of the war.

The *Heian* came to rest on the bottom about 130 feet below the surface, laying on her stricken port side. Her long graceful lines and powerful presence make for a spectacular wreck and diving *Heian* requires multiple dives due to her massive size. Even on days where visibility is great, when descending on the wreck it is impossible to see the entire ship as she extends hundreds of feet in both directions into the gloom. To this day she is still a sub tender, full of all the machinery and parts that made her so valuable to the Japanese Navy so long ago.

Starting on the bow the name of the ship is still clearly visible in big Romanized letters and also the associated kanji characters, "HEIAN MARU". Below the name, on what would have been the deck, is the big platform where one of the 12-centimeter anti-aircraft guns could be found. The gun is gone, likely blown off when the *Enterprise* SBD's dropped their bombs close off the bow. While the gun may be gone, there are still shell casings from it strewn about below providing a tangible link to the ferocity of the struggle to defend *Heian Maru*. Also in the area is an engine telegraph, still ready for use many decades later. Heading astern from the bow is the No 1 cargo hold. Deep inside the dark hold now there are still 12-centimeter shells for the deck gun stacked and ready for use. A little further in lie almost a dozen 53.3-centimeter torpedoes which were destined for use on submarines. These are the torpedoes that were never unloaded the night after the first attack, and whose presence caused so much concern. These lethal weapons are over twenty feet long and the twin propellers on some are still visible. These implements of war were the reason for the *Heian Maru's* modifications and the special equipment to move and transport them to submarines is still in evidence.

Continuing towards the stern divers come across the superstructure area and the stark evidence of the fires that consumed the ship and ultimately spelled her doom. One area of interest is the promenade deck and the companionway where passengers once strolled and admirals conducted discussions with their staffs. In this area there are a number of submarine periscopes lying about, the area was transformed into a make-shift storage area for them. The periscopes are long and narrow with the eye piece and handles clearly visible.

Heading down into the bridge area there is an area where china can still be seen, lying in stacks and shattered having fallen off its shelf when the ship rolled over. There is not much left of the bridge, but the wide open space and twisted metal provides testament to the heat of the fire that swept through here.

Behind the bridge area the bomb damage from the two 1,000-pound high explosive bombs dropped by *Yorktown* Dauntless dive bombers is clearly evident. This entire section of the ship is just a mess of torn steel and sharp twisted edges. The only recognizable object is the huge funnel that has broken off and is laying against the seabed. The entire area is dangerous to enter and most divers swim past, paying silent testimony to the damage around them. Swimming on to the rear cargo areas of the ship the deck guns can be found. The near miss on the bow must have blasted the gun high into the air and flung it all the way across the flame drenched superstructure to its current resting place. A likely candidate for the stern gun lies nearby as well. Past the guns there are several more cargo holds and finally the stern. The name of the ship is still visible here as well. The most impressive sight here though is to head just off the stern and look back on the ship while floating mid water. From here the two massive propellers loom in the blue water. So long ago these propellers and the engines that drove them amazed the Americans that came to see them in Seattle and they continue to inspire awe in those who visit them today.

The name "HEIAN MARU" is still legible on the hull.

An indentical sister ship of the Hoyo Maru in civillian colors. (Nippon Shosen)

A cross-section of the curving hull showing the area where Hoyo split in half.

Hoyo Maru

The thirst for oil was a major cause of the Pacific War, just as it has remained a source of conflict in the many years since. Japan had no substantial domestic sources of oil, so she needed to import it from overseas and that created a constant demand for more oil tankers to service the long routes to the United States and the Dutch East Indies. To help meet this demand an 8,691 ton and 475 foot long merchant tanker was laid down on October 15, 1935, at the Mitsubishi Heavy Industries shipyard in Yokohama. This huge tanker was launched at the end of August 1936 and named the *Hoyo Maru*. Her story did not get off to an auspicious start and she almost never saw anything beyond the Japanese coast. In January 1937 she was at sea in Ariake Bay on the island of Kyushu when heavy weather moved in. During the storm the big new tanker ran aground, causing serious damage to her hull and leaving her stuck on the rocks. It would take many months of salvage and repair operations to get her off the rocks and back into service.

Following this early debacle, the ship was soon taken into the service of the Imperial Japanese Navy and some modifications were made to allow her to refuel other ships. These were basic modifications and the ship was not one of the high speed fleet oilers like *Shinkoku Maru*. Interestingly the *Hoyo Maru* returned to civilian cargo service after being requisitioned. This was a simple testament to the desire to import as much oil as possible before the war began and supplies were cut off. During the last months of peace in 1941 the *Hoyo Maru* made several trips to San Francisco and the Dutch East Indies to haul oil back to the home islands. The people who saw her dock in San Francisco Bay had no idea the simple looking tanker loading oil was actually a member of the Imperial Navy and the oil was going to be used to fuel the very ships which were to attack the United States in December. Like so many other Japanese merchant ships she was formally taken into service in August 1941 and went into dock for conversion to a naval auxiliary ship. In this case it meant minor modifications and the addition of a bow and stern deck gun.

Hoyo's conversion was completed just before the Pacific War began and she was reassigned to the Fourth Fleet based in Truk. On November 21, 1941, she departed Japan for her new wartime home. During the first month of the war *Hoyo Maru* completed several local operations hauling oil to forward bases for use in the early expansion of the Japanese Empire. This changed on January 17, 1942, when she was tasked with supporting her first combat operation. This was Operation R, the invasion of Rabaul and Kavieng.

The support *Hoyo Maru* rendered to the invasion was very distant, she was never too close to the front as she was not really equipped nor trained for underway resupply. Mostly she carried oil to resupply ships after the key port of Rabaul had fallen and she did this over the course of several weeks.

A small decorative statue.

The highlight of this time was refueling the light carrier *Shoho* while in Truk Lagoon. During these first three months of 1942 she moved repeatedly between Truk, Rabaul, Kavieng and Tokyo moving fuel and resupplying ships in port. This routine of resupply operations was broken by one bizarre occurrence on March 31, 1942.

In the dark of night the *Hoyo Maru* was in a convoy out of Truk headed for Rabaul. Not far north of Rabaul the lookouts on the *Hoyo Maru* spotted a submarine on the surface. Suddenly alarms rang throughout the ship and the gun crew sprang into action. The crews took aim on the submarine and opened fire, the deck guns flashing in the night, sending shells screaming downrange. The men even reported return fire from the submarine, but nothing hit the ship. The battle raged in the night and finally the submarine slipped beneath the waves as the gun crews cheered. Shortly after the jubilant crew was officially awarded with a submarine kill, which was a rare honor for a tanker especially this early in the war. There is something off about this fish tale though. There were no submarines belonging to any nation sunk, nor in that area at the time of the battle. The closest anything can found to a submarine sinking in that area did not happen until later in 1944, well after the *Hoyo Maru* was sunk in Truk Lagoon. It is more likely the crew simply outgunned a poor whale that they mistook for a submarine.

Following the mysterious battle, the *Hoyo Maru* stayed in the area around Truk moving fuel to more nearby bases like Kavieng and Palau. In late April she received a new captain and the crew hoped that maybe their strange fortunes would change. Shortly after things looked up when *Hoyo* joined her first, and ultimately last, task force that was taking part in significant operations. On May 4 she joined Operation MO, the invasion of Tulagi and Port Moresby as part of the Transport Force. This taskforce carried the army invasion forces for the attack on Port Moresby. The *Hoyo* proudly steamed with this force as they neared the Jomard Pass and the turn west towards Port Moresby, but unknown to them the world's first all-carrier battle had just taken place nearby. The Battle of the Coral Sea resulting in the sinking the big US carrier *Lexington* and several support units. On the Japanese side the light carrier *Shoho* was sunk and the big *Shokaku* and *Zuikaku* were damaged and their air units badly depleted. It seemed a victory for Japan, but the *Hoyo Maru* and her force aborted the operation and turned north, as they now lacked any air cover for the invasion.

The carrier Shoho, refueled by the Hoyo just before she was sunk in the Coral Sea. (Japanese Navy)

That would be the high point of 1942 for *Hoyo Maru* as for the rest of the year she resumed her routine duties with the Fourth Fleet in the area around Truk, with the occasional stops in Singapore and even Kure back in the home islands. On December 19 her strange story took another unusual turn. While steaming through the area around Saipan enroute to Truk the watch was interrupted by a strong explosion. The crew raced to battle the damage while the gun crews scanned the ocean looking for the offending submarine. However there was no submarine and the cause of the damage was never determined. In Truk she went into the Repair Anchorage for three months of repairs. Perhaps it was a whale seeking revenge that caused the damage.

The engine room is full of machinery and gauges, but all upside down!

In February another new captain arrived and again there was hope the strange fate of the *Hoyo Maru* would change. Yet nothing changed and the ship managed to sustain further damage while in port in Truk, which necessitated a return to Japan and three more months of repairs in Osaka. Before resuming her duties in bringing fuel to Truk and other bases the Hoyo Maru received yet another captain. Perhaps the ship really was cursed. By this point it was October 1943 and the might of the Combined Fleet was gathered in Truk Lagoon. The Japanese high command believed that an American attack on Wake Island was imminent and the entire striking power of the navy set forth to meet them in a decisive battle. The men aboard *Hoyo Maru* watched the super battleships, battleships, heavy cruisers and remaining aircraft carrier weigh anchor and leave the lagoon headed for battle. The men were enthusiastic when they were ordered to help support this huge task force; finally they could make a meaningful contribution. The *Hoyo Maru* followed the big ships, full of oil for the coming battle. As she could not keep up with the warships, nor refuel them underway, the *Hoyo* instead headed to Eniwetok and waited there to refuel them after the battle. Instead there was no battle and the fleet only churned up empty ocean. The fleet returned to Truk and the *Hoyo Maru* followed arriving a day later.

The *Hoyo Maru* returned to Truk dejectedly and resumed her regular duties. Her first trip was to head to Palembang and Singapore to load up with more oil and bring it to Truk, very routine. Fate would again intervene one day out of Truk on November 6, 1943. The convoy was steaming at night when it was sighted by the *USS Haddock* in the dark. The submarine closed on the surface in the dark and fired all six bow torpedoes at the tankers *Hoyo Maru* and *Genyo Maru*, she then quickly turned around and fired all four stern tubes at the escorting destroyer *Yakaze*. The torpedoes missed, and the convoy turned on all their searchlights and manned their guns. Without a firm sighting the gun crews enthusiastically blazed away while the ships began to rapidly zig zag to dodge any other torpedoes. All this excitement, firing and zig zagging led to the *Genyo* turning in front of the *Yakaze*, which promptly ran into her.

The confusion and damage slowed the convoy and the *Haddock* moved off into the dark and reloaded for another attack. As the men on the damaged ships worked to keep them in the action, the submarine slipped in on the surface again and closed with the *Hoyo*. From 3,000 yards she fired another spread of torpedoes and this time one of them found their mark. As the explosion blasted the stern of the *Hoyo Maru* it was cold comfort to the crew that at least they could be sure what had caused the damage this time. The engine room is really the only place a tanker can be hit that can cause her to sink quickly as there is no way to seal it off like the fuel storage holds. The torpedo tore a hole into the engine room and it quickly flooded, pulling the ship down by the stern as she drifted to a stop as fires began to rage in the aft superstructure area.

There were now two burning tankers and one escorting destroyer with a mangled bow on the scene. Luckily for them the *Haddock* was out of torpedoes and had set course for home. As the *Hoyo* settled in the water and burned Captain Hojo ordered her abandoned. The *Yakaze* came alongside, twisted bow and all, and took off the 90 men plus their Captain leaving the ship to burn. Two of the crew of *Hoyo Maru* died at this time from injuries sustained in the explosion and fire. To assess the situation further the light cruiser *Nagara* was dispatched from Truk to investigate. Six hours after the crew had abandoned ship, the *Nagara* found *Hoyo Maru* still afloat! She was very low in the water by the stern and there were still fires burning out of control in that area. The crew of *Nagara* sprang into action and battled the flames from their ship, ultimately extinguishing them. The tanker was just too valuable to leave and the crew of the *Nagara* believed she could be saved, however all the flooding made her too heavy for the light cruiser to pull. A radio call went out to Truk and the *Kinjo Maru* was sent to tow the *Hoyo* back to port.

The smoldering and badly wounded *Hoyo Maru* was towed into Truk Lagoon on November 10, 1943, and placed in the Repair Anchorage near the repair ship *Akashi*. Her captain and crew sheepishly returned to the vessel they had given up on and began the task of repairing her; once again the story of *Hoyo Maru* had taken a strange turn. It would be the last of her story though as she was still undergoing repairs when the planes of Task Force 58 arrived to finish her off on February 17, 1944.

Like the other ships in this area it would be planes from the *USS Enterprise* who would draw first blood. The men of *Hoyo Maru* were still hard at work repairing their ship of the fire and flooding damage in the stern when the dive bombers began their attack. The big and immobile tanker made for a prime target and it wasn't long before a 1,000-pound bomb slammed into her just aft of the bridge superstructure and the resulting explosion caused severe damage to this area and weakened the hull. There was no time to react to this destruction before a second half-ton bomb hit her just in front of the aft superstructure. This area was already very weak from the torpedo attack months before and was also full of men working on repairs. The explosion killed six men and blew out the side of the weakened hull in this area. Once again the stern area was wreathed in flames and destruction, but this time the *Hoyo Maru* could take no more. She gave her crew very little time to escape into the warm water as she turned turtle and capsized.

A diver exploring the hard coral reef that covers the Hoyo today.

COMBINED FLEET AND REPAIR ANCHORAGES

The water in the lagoon is very shallow where she came to rest and she came to rest on top of the mid-ship superstructure with the bow on the bottom. This left her stern to stick up above the waves. The *Hoyo Maru* even sank in an unusual way, a fitting end to her often bizarre career. The weakened area from the first bomb strike would eventually give way and the hull would break in two, with both bow and stern underwater. The mid-ship area with the broken hull as its highest point stuck up like a small mountain from the bottom. This area of the *Hoyo Maru* is easily visible from the surface today, but in no way does this look like a ship. The wreck is completely upside down and the bottom of the hull has grown an incredible hard coral reef that covers the entire ship. The only clue that this is not a natural reef comes when divers swim towards the stern and reach what appears to be a natural cave, which reveals itself to be the hole from the bomb blast that sank her only when entered.

Once inside the wreck divers find themselves in a spacious, if badly damaged engine room. This is the area of the ship that was blasted not once but twice before she sank. It is unclear what damage is from the November 6 torpedo attack and what is from the bomb strike that sunk her. The damage is amazing as sheets of metal and piping is strewn everywhere and the engines are knocked from their mounts. In addition it is possible to see evidence of the two fires that engulfed this area as many objects appear to be melted together. Aside from the engine room there is little of interest wreck-wise on the *Hoyo Maru*. On the other hand she is a very nice hard coral reef, which is different from other wrecks in the lagoon. Exploring the reef after a brief penetration into the engine room area makes for an easy second or even third dive of the day. Even as a dive the *Hoyo Maru* is anything but usual, which pretty much sums up her entire story.

It is possible to swim under and through the Hoyo in several locations.

I - 169

The story of *I-169* begins in September 1936 in Kobe, Japan, where she was built as part of the KD6 class of submarines. The submarines of this type were designed to range far from their forward bases and attrite the US Navy as they made their way across the Pacific for the decisive battle. The war of course did not follow this neatly laid out plan. The submarines of this class were over 340 feet long and displaced 1,422 tons on the surface. *I-169* could make 23 knots on the surface and had a range of 14,000 nautical miles. For weapons she had four bow torpedo tubes and two stern tubes that fired the excellent 21-inch Type 89 torpedo. On deck she carried a single 3.9-inch dual-purpose gun and one heavy and one light machine gun. Overall these were excellent submarines which did much damage to their enemies.

I-169 didn't begin her career with that designation, instead she was the *I-69*. Like all the ships of her class she had the extra "100" added later in the war. In the years before the war she operated like all ships in the peacetime navies of the world and spent her time on training exercises. During one of these in May 1941 she collided with her sister ship *I-70* and would spend the last few peacetime months getting her bow repaired. This was just the first case of the misfortune that would plague the submarine and her crew throughout the war. When war came, though, she was ready and her crew had been trained to a very high level, ready to fight and die for the Emperor.

The war began for *I-69* when she departed from her forward base at Kwajalein on November 23, 1941, destined for Oahu in the Hawaiian Islands. Even though no bombs had yet fallen, the ship was on a war footing and all weapons were armed and she operated on the surface only at night time. Once on station she met her sister ship *I-68* and they both proceeded to the entrance of Pearl Harbor early on the morning of Sunday December 7th. *I-69* would literally witness the most famous, or infamous day, in US Navy history.

As the sun rose *I-69* was operating at periscope depth, her mission was to retrieve midget submarine crews. The midget subs were two-man submarines launched from much bigger submarines that were trying to make their way inside the harbor to launch their two torpedoes. The captain, Lieutenant Commander Watanabe, waited and watched through his periscope as the first planes swooped in. From the conning tower of *I-69* he watched the attack on Pearl Harbor, able to describe for his anxious crew the action as it unfurled. At one point he said, "a massive explosion in Pearl Harbor. There are several explosions, followed by high columns of fire. This must have been some capital ship sunk by our midget submarines!"

It is likely he witnessed the destruction of the *USS Arizona* by a bomb dropped by a B5N Kate bomber. The explosion is well documented and there is little doubt the crew cheered the success of their comrades

The USS Arizona explodes at Pearl Harbor. (US Navy)

Opposite: Fish swarm outside the stern torpedo tubes.

A type KD6 I-Boat, in this case the I-173. There are no known pictures of the I-169. (Japanese Navy)

even as they grew concerned over the fate of the midget subs. As the morning of the attack wore on no sign was detected of the midget submarines and the men came to realize they were not coming back. When darkness fell a destroyer was spotted coming out of Pearl Harbor, likely to hunt submarines that had earlier been detected. *I-69* was hungry for action and took aim, but a destroyer is a difficult target. A single torpedo was fired but it was sighted before it could strike and the destroyer turned away to dodge it. This turn allowed *I-69* to begin her escape as the destroyer came charging back ready for vengeance for the destruction inside the harbor. The crew could feel the sub vibrate and hear the dull booms of the depth charges being dropped, but they were already out of danger.

The submarine waited one more day for the midget subs, but the only thing they spotted that day was pillars of smoke still rising over the American fleet in Pearl Harbor. Finally on the 9th they decided to hunt for American ships and were quickly rewarded when they found a cargo ship being escorted by a destroyer heading for Pearl Harbor. The crew took careful aim and fired a spread of torpedoes, but they missed. The destroyer though had seen the attack and charged over and began to viscously depth charge the submarine as it tried to escape. Suddenly *I-69* lurched to a halt and the captain ordered her to sit still and silent until the destroyer left. After what seemed like forever the destroyer left, but the *I-69* was still stuck. The fortunes of the submarine had turned and the crew was now in mortal peril as the periscope and conning tower had become fouled by an anti-submarine net. For 39 long hours the submarine tugged and pulled, all the while running dangerously low on air. Finally she freed herself when her periscope bent and released the net. They were out of action for the time being and so returned to Kwajalein for a new scope.

The attack on Pearl Harbor had been a spectacular success, at least tactically, and *I-69* had been there to see it happen. On the other hand her contribution had been disappointing as she had fired on two American ships and the only thing to show for it was nearly running out of air while getting stuck on a net. The crew's blood was up and they spent a long two weeks returning to Kwajalein, followed by another two weeks having a new periscope put in place. Finally on January 12, 1942, she left the anchorage on her second war patrol.

Her mission this time was to reconnoiter Midway Island in anticipation of future operations in that area. It took nine days to reach the area and the submarine quietly hid beneath the waves on arrival. As the days passed the officers of the watch could only watch as American patrol planes left on their long patrols, plus the occasional flight by pairs of single seat fighters. Three weeks were spent watching and studying the base and its defenses.

Finally the crew reached the point where they couldn't stand just watching the planes sitting beside the runway anymore. After so much time sitting cramped up beneath the waves and doing nothing they craved action and after much pleading the captain finally gave into the desire for battle and surfaced the sub in broad daylight. The deck gun crew rushed out and manned the single gun and took aim at the American facilities ashore. They cheered as they finally opened fire. The shelling of the island soon brought the old United States Marine Corps F2A Buffaloes based there. These were single seat fighters that were hopelessly obsolete by this point, but their four .50 caliber machine guns could still pack a punch against the thin skin of a submarine. The Marine planes dove in with guns flashing and *I-69* soon felt the sting of their bullets. As the marines lashed the brazen sub with heavy machine gun fire, the crew on the subs machine guns gamely returned fire. In the end though this was not a battle the submarine should have ever been in and the captain regained his senses and submerged. The sub had done very little damage ashore and had been holed many times in return. The crew turned their leaky boat back to Kwajalein.

I-69 was only in Kwajalein very briefly to get her holes patched before she headed out again on her third patrol. This patrol was largely uneventful, with most of the time dedicated to hunting the *USS Lexington* which had been spotted. With no carrier to be found the submarine returned to Japan for a refit. The month spent in Kure between March and April resulted in the submarine getting an improved deck gun and having the holes from the Buffaloes finally fixed. In mid-April she left Japan on another uneventful patrol in a patrol line near Wake Island. Unlike the US and German navies who gave their submarines areas to roam and hunt merchant ships, the Japanese navy deployed their submarines in picket lines in attempts to find warships. While this did result in the occasional spectacular warship sinking, it mostly minimized the value of the Japanese sub fleet. After several uneventful weeks near Wake she returned to Kwajalein.

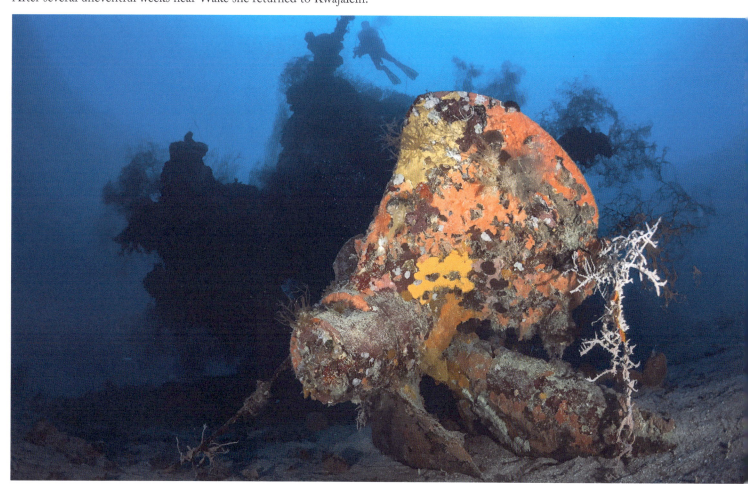

One of the propellers on the wreck of I-169.

The SS Tjinegara, the only ship sunk by the I-169. (US Navy)

Upon arrival in Kwajalein she officially became *I-169* on May 20, 1942, and four days later she joined Submarine Squadron 3 which was to take part in the upcoming Midway operation. The group went out and formed the standard picket line and waited for the US carriers to come to them, but while they waited in position the US carriers had simply sailed around them and ambushed the Japanese fleet. For all the fighting at Midway, Subron 3 did not see any action and retuned to Kwajalein.

On July 9, 1942, the now *I-169* headed out on her sixth war patrol which would take her south for the first time and would allow her freedom from the unsuccessful picket lines she had been taking part in. The mission was to scout New Caledonia in preparation for a potential invasion and the submarine spent the rest of July scouting Allied bases and watching for ship traffic. On the 25th of July her normal recon duties were interrupted when a big freighter suddenly was spotted by lookouts. The freighter was the 9,227 ton *Tjinegara* and was actually Dutch but being used by the US Army as a troopship. The crew was anxious as they took up battle stations and silently moved into position. The memories of their failed attacks at Pearl Harbor hung heavily over them as they plotted the torpedo attack. Finally when all was ready the order to fire was given and the submarine shook as the compressed air blasted the torpedoes out of their tubes. This time the aim was true and several tense minutes later the men were rewarded with the distant sounds of explosions rumbling through the water. It did not take long for them to hear the terrible sound of twisting metal and collapsing bulkheads as the big ship plunged to the bottom of the sea. Banzai!

The submarine remained around Noumea and then headed north to Efate to search for prey and do recon work. The only ships she found there were a pair of destroyers that chased her away from the port of Port Vila on the night of August 4th. Three days later the US Marines landed on Guadalcanal and everything was to change. I-169 was ordered home as the invasions that she was scouting for had been cancelled, the fight was now in the Solomons. The submarine made the long journey back to Japan for maintenance; she would need to be in top shape for the coming battles.

By the time I-169 arrived in Truk to take part in the Guadalcanal campaign the nature of the operations there were changing. The Japanese Navy had valiantly tried to cut the Marines off, but had failed. Over time the American airpower at Henderson Field had grown and their Navy offshore grown much more powerful. Now the focus was on getting supplies to the

Japanese Army on the island that was beginning to be called "Starvation Island". On November 16, 1942, Admiral Komatsu met with his sub captains and informed them that they would join the destroyer force and become cargo transports hauling desperately needed supplies to the isolated island. A warship no longer, the *I-169* instead make repeated stealthy runs carrying limited cargoes of food to Guadalcanal. The submarine was designed as a hunter and had very little room for cargo, but the crew tried their best. Overall though the transition to cargo ship was hard on morale and the men were not disappointed when they were ordered back to Japan in January 1943.

In Japan the men learned that they would need to break out their cold weather gear. Gone were the days of the sweltering tropics in the Solomon Islands, *I-169* was headed north to take part in operations in the Aleutian Islands. The sub would again be hauling supplies to an isolated garrison, but there was some hope for opportunities to hit enemy warships. *I-169* took on a full load of Army soldiers, loaded up their torpedo tubes and even placed a Type A midget sub on the stern deck. The sub would make several trips like this to Kiska and the only time she ever sighted the enemy was when she approached an American cruiser, but was driven away by a destroyer and a flurry of depth charges.

These cold and tension filled missions lasted through March and April. *I-169* brought a continuous trickle of men and supplies to the barren rocky islands, with only an occasional patrol line to break up the routine. Even the patrol duty was monotonous as the enemy was never engaged. In May 1943 the Americans invaded nearby Attu Island and the decision was made to abandon Kiska and the Aleutian Islands. For the submarine all this meant was that the men they had transported over the prior months had to now be picked up and brought home. The frustration level was extremely high.

During these chilly summer months of tedium the submarine operated from the sub tender *Heian Maru* and the two ships would be constant companions between missions, just as they would be very near each other the following year on the bottom of Truk Lagoon. *I-169* had been operating as a glorified troop transport for almost an entire year by this point, so the crew was elated to learn they would be heading south again with a return to the role of a hunter. Enroute to the South Seas she stopped in Japan for an overhaul after a year of grueling operations in severe weather. *I-169* set sail for Truk on September 25, she and most of her crew would never see home again. In Truk the men were happy to see the familiar sight of the *Heian Maru* again and during the coming months they would spend a lot of time moored together while the *Heian* performed minor repairs and resupplied the ship. When news came that the Americans had been spotted in a huge taskforce south of Hawaii headed west spirits on the sub soared as the subs based in Truk sortied to intercept.

This taskforce was part of Operation Galvanic, the American invasion of the Gilbert Islands to the east of Truk. There were 200 ships in the force, including 13 battleships and 11 carriers! There was to be good hunting indeed and the crew were excited to finally be heading to honorable battle again. As was normal, the submarines formed a picket line and waited to see if the Americans would steam over it. On December 1, 1943, the lookouts on deck screamed a warning as an American plane was sighted. The men below scrambled as alarms rang throughout the ship. The submarine dove and escaped and while below

I-Boat on patrol in the Aleutian Islands. (Japanese Navy)

Submarine torpedo in storage. (Australian War Memorial)

her sound gear began to pick up very heavy noise contacts. The enemy had actually stumbled over their picket line!

For hours the captain, Lieutenant Commander Toyama, desperately tried to break through the escorting screen of destroyers to get at the big ships he could hear just beyond. All the time of frustration as a transport drove him and the men hard. In the end despite many white knuckled hours, *I-169* was never able to get in a good shot at this huge target. Throughout January and into February *I-169* was part of constant patrols and picket lines in operations in the Gilberts and Marshalls, but there is no report of her ever making contact with enemy surface forces.

On February 15, 1944, she received a new commanding officer, Lieutenant Shinohara Shigeo, and departed on another patrol in search of American ships to sink. Little did the crew know that they sailed right through the same waters a massive American force would occupy less than 48 hours later. *I-169* was heading to her patrol zone when Operation Hailstone hit Truk Lagoon, sending her close compatriot the *Heian Maru* to the bottom along with many other ships. The patrol was again fruitless.

When *I-169* returned to Truk on March 11, 1944, it was a shock to the men to see the damage. The shore facilities were a shambles and the airfields pockmarked wastelands full of the skeletons of planes. Most striking was the fleet, or the lack thereof for it was almost completely gone. The waters of Truk Lagoon were empty for the first time in anyone's memory. The mood was very somber as the *I-169* anchored just off the badly battered submarine base on the northwest side of Dublon. From the deck the men could see the oil bubbling up from the wreck of the *Heian Maru* almost beneath them. It still occasionally bubbles up to this day.

The submarine would make one more brief patrol during the third week of March, searching for a phantom fleet that intelligence was convinced was headed towards Truk for another attack. Nothing was found and the submarine returned to resupply and receive some minor maintenance. The work was slow going without a tender to help and with badly damaged facilities ashore and with the days stretching on the captain and twenty of the crew moved ashore to create room for workmen and some Army soldiers pressed into service.

A type KD6 submarine returning from patrol. These lethal weapons were often misused by Japan. (Japanese Navy)

At 9 am local time on April 4, 1944, the work was continuing when the air raid sirens began to wail across the lagoon. Standard procedure for submarines was to simply submerge and rest on the sandy bottom until the attack was finished and then surface. It was a simple process and very effective at preventing air attacks. As the first PB4Y (the Navy designation for the B-24) appeared the officer of the watch ordered an immediate dive and the diving alarms sounded. The captain and other experienced crew could only watch from shore as the sub began to descend, they would never see their proud ship again. Aboard the submarine there was much confusion with the workers and army support crew onboard and the main induction valve was left open, along with the deck hatches. The moment the submarine began to descend she was immediately flooded in the stern compartments. As the water poured in unchecked a last desperate attempt to surface was made, but it failed and *I-169* came to rest on the bottom 125 feet below the surface.

Onshore the captain took cover from the raid, but it was hammering the airfields again and he and his men soon emerged and waited for *I-169* to surface. Long after the bombers disappeared the submarine was still submerged and it was realized that she was in trouble. Late in the afternoon a diver in a helmet was sent down to find the submarine and make contact. The Japanese Navy diver would be the first of many to visit this wreck, but when he arrived he could hear banging on the hull from the forward sections of the submarine. The men inside had sealed off the flooded stern and the survivors were in the bow.

The open hatch cover that contributed to the sinking of the I-169.

An immediate order went out for a crane and the tug *Futagami* to head to the scene and try and raise the submarine, or failing that at least get the bow up so that the crew could escape. The submarine was over 300 feet long, so raising the bow up just a few degrees would get it to the surface. It took precious hours to locate the submarine again, and when it was finally found it took even more hours to rig the hoist. Finally in the afternoon of April 5 the crane turned on and the sub began to inch off the bottom, but suddenly there was a huge crack and the submarine fell back to the bottom with a massive thud. The line had broken and time was running out. More divers went in the water and holes were drilled in the ballast tanks and air hoses rigged to pump in air. Suddenly the air raid sirens began to wail again and the repairs had to be suspended for the night. When divers returned the next morning no response could be heard from the crew; they had suffocated. At Pearl Harbor two and half years earlier the sub had survived 39 hours snagged on the net, but in Truk Lagoon almost 48 hours had passed.

Over the rest of April divers removed the remains of 32 men from the bow areas of the ship, while captain Shinohara could only watch in torment. In May 1944 it was expected that Truk would be invaded any day by the Americans and the decision was made to destroy the intact submarine instead of letting it fall into enemy hands. Carefully a patrol boat lined up on the bow area and began to blast the submarine below, destroying the bow and conning tower area. Care was taken to preserve the stern where more bodies remained entombed. *I-169* was part of some of the most momentous moments of the 20th century. She personally witnessed the attack on Pearl Harbor, one of a very few Japanese to see the destruction of the *USS Arizona*. After that she was at Midway, Guadalcanal, Aleutians, Gilberts and finally Truk Lagoon. There may not be much of the wreck left today, but to visit her with this history in mind is a profound experience.

The wreck of the submarine *I-169* is one of the rarest wreck dives. During the Pacific War almost all the Japanese I boats were eventually sunk, most of them in deep and unknown graves. To actually have one that is within recreational dive limits and is very close to dive facilities is unique. So while the wreck may not be the most spectacular in the lagoon, for the serious history buff this is one dive not to be missed! The remains of *I-169* are not far from her comrade the *Heian Maru*.

The I-169 today is home to several beatiful anemones and their often fiesty anemone fish guardians.

COMBINED FLEET AND REPAIR ANCHORAGES

Her shape is a mass of destruction on the bow and it takes time to sort out the layout of the conning tower. This is where the captain witnessed Pearl Harbor and where the final order to submerge was given. Towards the stern the submarine is intact and her lines are clearly identifiable. Perhaps the most impressive area is the stern where the two propellers that drove her across the Pacific remain intact. The wreck is a silent place now, home only to some anemonefish who make their homes near the stern hatch. The stern hatch is there, but it is NOT recommended to enter the submarine. The human remains were removed to Japan and cremated in 1973, but other divers have died inside these confined spaces since. The spirits of the men of *I-169* can be found at the Yasukuni Shrine in Tokyo, where the ships bell is proudly on display.

The two stern torpedo tubes lit up from within. These tubes were in action at Pearl Harbor on December 7, 1941.

Kensho Maru

The *Kensho Maru* was laid down in the years just before the war began and in June 1938 was for service in the Inui Kisen line. She was designed as a combination cargo and passenger ship and measured 384 feet long and weighed in at 4,862 tons. She would only serve a brief time in the civilian role her builders intended as she was requisitioned by the Navy in September 1940. Her induction into the Navy did very little to change the routine duties and cargo runs the *Kensho Maru* made. Before fighting started she was used in the mundane role of hauling men and supplies to the Marshall and Caroline Islands. The men onboard the *Kensho* learned they were at war while unloading supplies onto small boats for transport ashore in the bright sunny lagoon of Kwajalein Atoll.

In sports, every team needs players who do the dirty work. They are not famous and nobody remembers them for great plays or stirring victories. On the other hand, without them the team would fall apart and there would be no glory for the stars. The *Kensho Maru* was one of these types of players, doing all the dirty work in anonymity. In the first six months of the war the *Kensho* was a site often seen on the fringes of the Empire in the Marshall Islands. She came and went repeatedly from Tarawa, Kwajalein, Wotje, Roi-Namur, Marcus and even Wake Island. The trips were not elegant as she was often hauling livestock in one of her holds with the wooden cargo hatches open to let the smell out. Besides pigs and chickens, she usually was packed full of construction material, rice, beer and basic supplies. There was never much sign of the war to the men aboard and the *Kensho* didn't even have a gun!

The Kensho Maru during her brief civillian career. (City of Vancouver Archives)

Opposite: The wide open engine room.

In the summer of 1942 the *Kensho Maru* entered the shipyards in the comfort of Japan and modifications were made that reflected the changing course of the war. For starters, she finally got a small deck gun on the bow and a few more Navy crewmen to fire and maintain it. The more substantial changes took place in the cargo holds. Gone were the wooden hatch covers and steel plating was added in the tween deck areas. This newly enclosed space was now home to a small infirmary and sick bay and even an X-ray machine came aboard. The ships complement grew even more as a number of doctors and 20 orderlies made their home in the former passenger quarters. The ship wasn't the only thing that changed, the cargo changed too. Gone were the pigs and chickens; now replaced by ammunition, explosives, construction material and food. Also on the return journeys to Japan the *Kensho* now carried sick, infirm and wounded. The crew still never actually saw combat, but as the months passed they increasingly carried the human evidence of heavy fighting not far away. Her holds now echoed with the cries of the wounded instead of the clucking of chickens.

For the remainder of 1942 and almost all of 1943 the *Kensho Maru* continued her supply runs from Japan to the Marshall Islands in peace. She came and went dozens of times and the fact that she never saw the enemy in this entire time is incredible. Aside from the wounded and sick she carried home to Japan her life was spent traversing the endless blue seas of the Pacific Ocean in peace. Nothing would indicate that anything was going to change when she entered the familiar waters of Kwajalein on December 19, 1943, as part of a small convoy consisting of herself and the *Shoei Maru* and escorted by the small subchaser *CH-29*.

The ships entered the lagoon and dropped anchor as whistles blew and men began to prepare the boats and cranes to begin unloading cargo. There was barely time to get the cargo hatches open before men began to point up into the sky where high above a formation of planes appeared between the broken clouds. Those with binoculars swung them skyward to discover that these planes had four engines and they were big. Suddenly it dawned on the men of *Kensho Maru*, these were American planes! Finally the hated enemy was before them, but there was little they could do but watch as the planes headed straight for them.

The two fat cargo ships in the lagoon made inviting targets for the bombardiers looking through their bomb sights in the nose of the big B-24 Liberator bombers. On command the crews released their bomb loads and turned back to their bases far to the south. The 500-pound bombs fell in strings towards the helpless ships below where relief mixed with horror as the bombs missed the *Kensho* but then blanketed the *Shoei*. The lagoon reverberated with the thundering blasts of the general purpose bombs as they tore the *Shoei Maru* apart. Flames and smoke erupted into the air and debris rained down, splashing into the water like rain.

A microscope found in excellent condition.

COMBINED FLEET AND REPAIR ANCHORAGES

Opposite: Rainbow of colors on the Kensho's mast.

The *Kensho Maru* had finally met the enemy. Darkness came to Kwajalein and the crew worked frantically to unload their cargo, lit by the flames of the nearby *Shoei*. Finally the flames disappeared with a loud hiss and darkness reigned as the *Shoei* slipped beneath the waves. Unloading work continued into the morning and with the rising sun came 16 more big Liberator bombers to finish the job. This time the squadron of bombers had only one target and they calmly lined up overhead to finish what they had started the previous day.

A full extended range loadout on a B-24 would have been five or six 500-pound bombs in each plane. That meant that the crew of the *Kensho Maru*, who had only just seen the enemy for the first time, had to watch as roughly 80 deadly bombs fell towards their vulnerable ship. The impact in the lagoon of this huge amount of ordinance produced utter chaos around the *Kensho*. Bombing ships from high altitude in level bombers was difficult even when the ship was stationary and 98% of the bombs dropped that day missed, but that left a single bomb unaccounted for. This bomb hit the *Kensho* just behind the superstructure in the area around the fourth cargo hold and it couldn't have been aimed any better.

The force of the explosion smashed into the engineering spaces and the machinery of the engines. The engines took the full force of the impact and gears were knocked off, rods bent and even the propeller shaft was badly damaged. Aside from the fact that the *Kensho* was now paralyzed; fires began to rage in the engineering spaces and water began to seep into the stern holds. Men from across the ship raced to scene to battle the blazes and fight the flames, but it seemed they were fighting a losing battle. The captain shook off his daze from the blast and soon realized that *Kensho Maru* was in serious danger of sinking. He yelled orders for anchors to be raised and with the small amount of power the engines could give him he plowed his ship into a nearby reef. Normally this is how a captain loses his ship, but in this case he saved *Kensho Maru* from a watery grave in Kwajalein Atoll. Unfortunately it also spelled doom for the engines and propeller shaft.

A sink from one of the heads on the Kensho Maru.

The amazing spectacle that is the reef on the superstructure of the Kensho today.

A sake bottle inside the cavernous engine room.

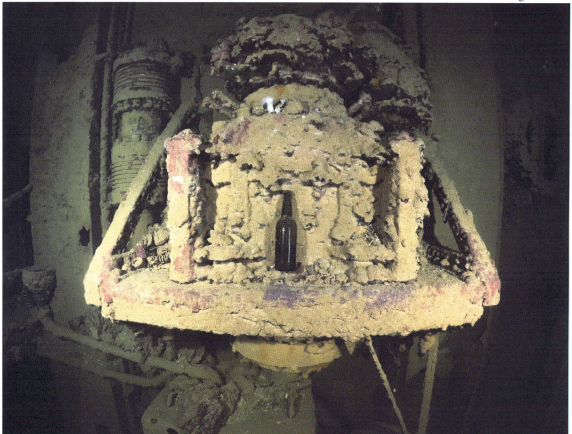

KENSHO MARU   67

The *Kensho* was alive, but her situation was grave as the bombers could return at any time. In addition she was unable to generate her own propulsion. On the plus side, her crew had heroically battled the fires and fixed the flooding and the ship was no longer in danger of sinking. The Navy had to get them out of Kwajalein if there was to be any hope for *Kensho Maru*. First she would need emergency repairs in the Marshall Islands; just enough for her to get to Truk. Once there she would be given enough repairs to allow her to make it back to Japan for a total refit. On the 3rd of January, 1944, the *Kensho* was pulled off the reef and towed to nearby Roi-Namur for the first round of repairs. She spent three weeks in the punishing sun of Roi-Namur undergoing temporary repairs to ensure that she wouldn't sink in the open ocean. Finally on January 29 the *Momokawa Maru* arrived and took her under tow. The two ships proceeded across the open water to Truk, the voyage taking six long days. On February 4th the two ships entered Truk Lagoon and the *Kensho* was promptly placed in the Repair Anchorage. Unfortunately for the *Momokawa Maru* her rescue of the *Kensho* placed her back in Truk Lagoon at a very bad time.

The crews of the *Kensho* and the repair ship *Akashi* sprang into action, beginning the laborious process of getting the ship seaworthy and underway to Japan. Men labored in the heat and sun for two weeks and on February 17, 1944, the crews began to wake for another day of hard work. Then all hell broke loose. *Kensho* was almost totally helpless as the attack began. The men tried to clear the decks and do what they could but the fact was the ship was completely out of commission. Not only could she not move or defend herself, she was full of flammable material used in the repairs. For a brief time things seemed like they would be alright as the fighters battled overhead, but then dive and torpedo bombers began to appear and they fell on the ships like vultures. The captain knew his ship was a perfect target and there was nothing he could do. In a gesture of humanity towards his crew he ordered all the watertight doors closed and then put the crew in the boats and took them ashore to watch the fate of their ship from the beach.

The first wave to hit the ships in the Repair Anchorage were Dauntless dive-bombers off the *USS Yorktown* with 1,000-pound bombs slung beneath their fuselages. The bombers fell on the ships and one of them planted its big bomb on the stern of the *Kensho Maru*. The bomb hit the extreme stern and blasted a hole in the poop deck and shattered the steering gear.

The emergency steering gear in the stern.

The next planes to attack came off the *USS Essex*. These were more SBD Dauntless dive-bombers and they too found the *Kensho Maru* an inviting and easy target. One pilot reported hitting the *Kensho Maru* amidships, but there is no evidence on the wreck of a bomb explosion anywhere in this area. It's possible the bomb actually hit in the area of the forward cargo holds. The final indignity to the defenseless ship came when an F6F Hellcat fighter swooped in and the pilot dropped his half full external fuel tank on the ship, helping to feed the fires burning on the ship.

The crew ashore could only watch as the *Kensho Maru* smoldered in the night, the ship lit up by the glow of small fires in the bow and stern. When dawn returned so did the American planes. The morning torpedo strike by the TBF Avengers from the *Bunker Hill* came first, and for several ships in the area this strike would be fatal. A single Avenger lined up on the inert *Kensho Maru* and hit her neatly in the bow with an air dropped torpedo. The force of the blast near the first cargo hold literally bent the ship and metal beams and plates buckled. In a single instant the torpedo explosion broke the back of the ship and she quickly settled by the bow and slipped beneath the waves.

Thermometer still in good shape.

The *Kensho* settled on the bottom in a graceful manner, sitting almost perfectly upright on the sandy bottom. The wreck is in very good condition even after decades on the bottom, with plenty of marine growth due to the shallow depth and runoff from nearby Fefan Island. This runoff also leads to a lot of silt and algae growth, so colors are not quite as explosive as some of the other shallow wrecks. What the *Kensho* lacks as an artificial reef, she more than makes up for as an excellent and easy wreck to explore. Starting on the bow is a good place to begin a tour of the wreck. The small deck gun installed in 1942 during her refit is still there, covered in marine growth. Behind the bow in the area of the first cargo hold the damage from the torpedo that broke her back is very evident. The way the ship is deformed and bent in this area is a sight to behold and stark evidence of the violence of the blast. Heading towards the superstructure there really isn't much to see as the holds are badly damaged and they were empty at the time of sinking.

The superstructure and amidships area is where the *Kensho Maru* really shines as a wreck. There is very little damage in this area and the wreck sits upright which makes navigating the dark interior much easier. Entering the bridge is best done from either the port or starboard passageways, as the portholes in front make for a very tight squeeze. The entire area of the bridge and the decks above and below are dimly lit by light filtering in through the various openings. In this area can be found many interesting artifacts, including plates and various dishes plus a large radio rack that looks an awful lot like a refrigerator. It is a pleasant area to look around as there are plenty of visible exits and the shallow depth makes for more bottom time.

Heading behind the bridge the skylights to the engine room can be found. The *Kensho Maru* has an amazing engine room. The shallow depth allows for plenty of light to spill in from the skylights and the room is big. The catwalks and ladders are all intact and gently hovering in here is almost like meditating in a cathedral, except one dedicated to machinery and engineering. Spending time in this engine room is a must, even for those who may be hesitant about penetrating deep into wrecks.

The exit from the engine room is easy through the skylights and the area around the skylights has several boat davits with an incredible bloom of soft coral growing on them. This is easily the most colorful area of the ship and the colors found in this area rival those found on any other wreck.

The stern provides some more interesting penetrations even for those who aren't into that activity. Inside the cargo holds can be found a mess of welding and equipment associated with the repairs being conducted on the ship. It appears the areas that formerly held wounded soldiers and even pigs was converted into a workshop of sorts. Astern of the holds is the poop which is an interesting area to enter. In this area there is a large steering mechanism and ample evidence of the first bomb to strike the ship on February 17, 1944. The torn plates from the explosion make it possible to exit at the extreme stern with ease. This provides an excellent view of the big four bladed propeller and rudder below. The *Kensho Maru* led a generally peaceful existence in the war without much of the drama of her compatriots on the bottom of Truk Lagoon. The wreck is a reflection of this; it is a peaceful wreck and very easy to explore without a whole lot of drama.

Opposite: The Kensho is always surrounded by big schools of fish.

The propeller on the Kensho is aligned perfectly with the rudder.

70   COMBINED FLEET AND REPAIR ANCHORAGES

The Kiyosumi Maru in her civilian colors. She was a wolf in sheep's clothing. (Yamashita)

A lantern on the hull of Kiyosumi today.

The top of Kiyosumi hosts amazing scenery.

KIYOSUMI MARU

The *Kiyosumi Maru* was laid down in the Kawasaki dockyards in Kobe, Japan in May of 1933 and at 450 feet long and 6,991 tons she was a big ship. Although the *Kiyosumi* was built in a more peaceful time, the Japanese military was actively involved in expanding the empire and had much bigger plans. Towards this end the government would subsidize the construction of many merchant vessels, with the understanding that when war came they would be taken into service. So the *Kiyosumi* was built as a state of the art passenger and cargo ship, but also with a far different use in mind should war erupt in the oceans.

The *Kiyosumi* was launched and completed in October 1934 and joined the Kokusai Kisen line as a cargo and passenger liner. Passengers on the *Kiyosumi* would travel in comfort with the ship tastefully decorated in Japanese style, but with certain English features. For seven years the *Kiyosumi* travelled the prestigious Yokohama to New York route under charter to the NYK line. Three times a year she departed Japan and travelled through the Panama Canal enroute to New York loaded with the exotic cargoes of the Far East. In New York she would take on new passengers and return with American raw materials and industrial goods, in addition to vast quantities of mail. During these happy years the *Kiyosumi* also stopped at Singapore, Manila, Penang, Los Angeles, Baltimore, New Orleans and Galveston. She was truly a world traveler and she did so in comfort and style. The end of this era ended in the late summer of 1941 as she left New York for the last time. As the American dockworkers waved goodbye to her they had no idea that the next time she would be seen by American eyes she would be a heavily armed warship.

The *Kiyosumi* had been wearing a disguise for all those years visiting the United States. To everyone, including her passengers, she appeared to be the stylish liner of a peaceful Japan. In reality she was built with another purpose in mind and upon her return to Japan the time had come to drop this charade. It only took two weeks to convert the *Kiyosumi Maru* into an armed merchant cruiser, or XCL in naval terms. She went from 6,991 tons to 8,613 tons in displacement and now the Imperial Navy ensign replaced the flag of the NYK line. Across her decks gun platforms were added to the hidden supports already in place and eight 5.9-inch guns were put in place on them. To give the ship a heavy punch when attacking ships, two 21-inch torpedo tubes were also added, which could carry the excellent Long Lance torpedo that was far and away the best in the world. Finally the *Kiyosumi* was modified to carry a single E7K2 Alf reconnaissance floatplane to search out targets to hunt beyond the horizon.

She was placed under the command of Captain Kita Shoichiro and joined the sister merchant raiders *Aikoku Maru* and *Hokoku Maru* in Cruiser Squadron No. 24; their mission to roam the seas hunting unsuspecting merchant vessels. The *Kiyosumi* and *Aikoku Marus* would begin the war together and it would end together years later on the bottom of Truk Lagoon. To the naked eye from afar they appeared to be simple merchant ships, but they were wolves in sheep's clothing.

As the war began the *Kiyosumi* could only watch as her sister ships in the Imperial Navy went from one amazing victory to another. The crew grew impatient, ready to have their chance to earn glory but for the first five months of the war they only carried out mundane troop transport operations in friendly waters.

The boilers inside the engine room are imposing.

Visiting the newly conquered territories like Guam was interesting and provided a small diversion, but this was a heavily armed ship and she longed to be on the front lines doing the job she was built for. Finally her time came and she was ordered to join the vast invasion force assembling for the invasion of tiny Midway Island; it appeared she would be a part of the final decisive battle after all!

On May 28, 1942, the *Kiyosumi Maru* finally steamed towards battle as part of Vice Admiral Kondo's Midway Invasion Force. She joined 12 other transports: an oiler, three patrol boats (one of which would rest near hear on the bottom of Truk Lagoon), a dozen destroyers and a light cruiser. The force carried the troops who would storm ashore on the island and seize it for the Empire. These men were from Kure Special Naval Landing Force, an airfield construction unit and the Army's Ichiki detachment which would later famously battle the US Marine Corps on Guadalcanal. On the *Kiyosumi* were the naval soldiers of the Kure SNLF who could only marvel at the former passenger areas of the ship. Steaming towards Midway full of elite soldiers, the *Kiyosumi* was a long way from the many years on the New York run.

On June 3 the convoy bored down on Midway Island, confident in the coming victory. Unknown to the men aboard, the Americans already knew they were coming and search planes fanned out from Midway to locate them. The *Kiyosumi Maru* had the unusual honor to be one of the first ships sighted by either side during the Battle of Midway. Ensign Jack Reid was flying a US Navy PBY Patrol plane that sighted the taskforce, but his crew misidentified this invasion force as the main fleet and at 12:30 pm bombers departed Midway to attack it. At 3:30 pm the crew on *Kiyosumi* was startled by a sudden barrage of fire as the escorting destroyers began hammering away at something flying high overhead. Straining their eyes to see, the men soon made out the shapes of nine US Army B-17 Flying Fortresses flying in formation towards their convoy. The big four engine bombers ploughed through the puffs of black anti-aircraft fire and dropped their bombs. The men on *Kiyosumi* were briefly nervous as they saw the bombs release, but they quickly realized they would miss and fall harmlessly in the ocean. The *Kiyosumi Maru* had been part of the very first shots fired during the Battle of Midway.

Darkness fell and across the Invasion Force everyone knew that the battle had begun and tomorrow would likely bring more attacks as the fleet pressed towards Midway with the actual invasion set to take place the following day. Just as the crew and soldiers aboard were finally able to relax and drift off to sleep they were jolted awake by a loud blast clearly audible above the regular sounds of wind, waves and machinery. Men across the ship ran to the railings to see the explosion from a torpedo flare up from the stern of the nearby *Akebono Maru*. They barely had enough time to wonder where the torpedo came from before the awkward shape of an American PBY Catalina floatplane came roaring out of the darkness. The shocked men were quickly sent diving for cover as the gunners on board the plane hosed down the decks of the *Kiyosumi* as the plane roared overhead. The bullets zipped and pinged off the metal decks and as the plane disappeared into the night the cries of eight wounded men of the SNLF could be heard. Now the men on *Kiyosumi Maru* had also been a part of the first blood to be drawn in the Battle of Midway.

Dawn found the crew still on alert after the successful night attack. The wounded had been cared for and no damage had been done to the ship. Confidence was high as the crew ate breakfast at their stations and guns were cleared and ready for action. As the day began to drag on the crew grew weary from the tension of waiting for the battle to resume. Those in the radio room could hear unusual reports and updates coming across the airwaves in English and Japanese. It was obvious that a great battle was underway, but the Invasion Force was not part of it yet. As the long day ended the force continued steaming towards Midway, so it was simply assumed that victory had been achieved and now it would be soon be their turn to put the men ashore. Then something happened in the pre-dawn hours of June 5; the ships began a long turn back to the west away from Midway. Admiral Yamamoto had cancelled Operation MI and the invasion was off. The men aboard had little idea of the scope of the beating the Japanese Navy had taken on that day and the time of endless victories was over.

A week after they had planned on storming ashore at Midway the men of the Invasion Force instead calmly disembarked on Guam and the force of ships was disbanded to go their separate ways. The mood on the ship was somber and confused as they set sail for Manila to join a convoy heading back to Japan. Upon arrival in Japan the men welcomed aboard a new captain, Captain Kurosaki Rinzo, and awaited their next assignment. The ship had seen battle, but never victory and the men longed to correct that. Finally a promising new assignment came In July 1942 and the *Kiyosumi* departed Japan for her new base in Singapore. She would be part of operations in Sumatra and the Indian Ocean where she could assume her role as a merchant raider. Spirits picked up at the thought of what the future now held, but an American landing on the island of Guadalcanal would change everything.

In Singapore the *Kiyosumi* was assigned the duty of transporting troops from the Army's 58th Division from Sumatra to the Solomon Islands where these men were desperately needed if the islands were going to be defended. To facilitate large numbers of men aboard the ship spent several days undergoing repairs in Singapore before heading for Sumatra to pick up their cargo. This was not the glamorous work of raiding merchants on the high seas, but it was critical to the war effort so the men buckled down to make it happen. In Sumatra they joined a convoy of ships and loaded an amazing 2,931 Army soldiers aboard; which was far more then she had ever had aboard before in her prior life as a passenger liner.

For the next three months the *Kiyosumi* spent her time moving men to the new main theatre of battle in the war in the area of New Guinea and the Solomon Islands.

Soft coral and sponges adorn the masts.

She even rejoined her former partner *Aikoku Maru* in these ferry operations during Operation HEI-GO in December of 1942 and HINOE-GO during January 1943. The operations would become a blur of open blue water and dense green tropical jungle as the ship constantly brought more troops to New Guinea, with the occasional trip home to Japan to get fresh troops from there and bring them south. These operations would continue through September 1943 and at one point she even carried a number of Army Type 99 "Lilly" bombers to Wewak as part of their relocation from Manchuria.

In September 1943 the *Kiyosumi* found herself in Shanghai as part of Operation Tei No.2 which would place her in a large convoy, including the *Heian Maru*, charged with transporting the Army's 17th Division to Rabaul via Truk. The *Kiyosumi* boarded 1,300 men and a large number of vehicles and the convoy set sail. The trip to Rabaul was anxious after the convoy was sighted by an American patrol plane, and the men aboard were made ready to disembark in a hurry. The ships pulled into Simpson Harbor and successfully unloaded in under 24 hours and were heading back to Truk before any attacks could be mounted.

China was the main battle ground for the Japanese Army and this also made it an excellent source of units to reinforce the southern islands. For this reason *Kiyosumi* returned to Shanghai and picked up another 1,342 men and joined a convoy headed back to Rabaul via Truk, retracing her route of the previous month. The ships left Shanghai on October 21, 1943, and the men aboard all the ships were given a huge scare when ten torpedoes raced through their formation during the night of the 23rd. They had been fired by the submarine *USS Shad* directed by radar, who beat a hasty retreat following a nasty depth charging by the escorts. Amazingly no ships were hit and the convoy steamed on. What the crews of the ships didn't know is that this attack was no chance encounter, US codebreakers knew that this major convoy was underway and where it was going.

Somehow the ships made it all the way to Truk without further incident, even though they were being hunted by three submarines. Once again the stay in Truk was brief and the convoy turned south for Rabaul where American planes were ready and waiting for them. Not far north of Kavieng a squadron of American B-24 Liberators found the convoy and began the onslaught. The large planes lined up on the ships below which were all jammed full of thousands of troops. The bombs fell out of the bombers and hit the water in lines sending concussion waves ripping across the waves. One stick of bombs straddled the *Kiyosumi Maru* and the troops braced themselves for what they must have thought was their end. The big ship rocked heavily from the force of the blast in the water and the shock wave was strong enough to buckle the hull near the engine room and water began to pour into the engineering spaces. As the attacking bombers departed the *Kiyosumi Maru* drifted to a stop, dead in the water.

Even in the dark of the engine room there is life.

As shouts and reports raced around the ship it became obvious to the Captain that his ship was unable to navigate. Being full of over a thousand men plus their munitions and dead in the water, all while within range of American bombers was not a good place to be. The Captain requested help and the light cruiser *Isuzu* passed over lines and quickly took the *Kiyosumi* under tow as the rest of the convoy continued on. Besides the *Isuzu*, the light cruiser *Yubari* plus the destroyers *Isokaze* and *Minazuki* remained to help the stricken *Kiyosumi*. The group kept a close watch for submarines and more air attacks as they slowly covered the last miles of the journey and into the protected waters at Kavieng. Once in the anchorage the priority was to get the *Kiyosumi* seaworthy again, but first the soldiers aboard and their artillery pieces needed to be off-loaded as there was no way the *Kiyosumi* would be headed for Rabaul. The warships took turns coming alongside and offloading the men, artillery and ordinance; placing it on their decks to be taken on to Rabaul. Following the successful operation to unload the ship the crew frantically began work on getting the engines functional so they could return to Truk for more substantial repairs as Kavieng did not have adequate repair facilities. On Christmas Day 1943 the crew found themselves still at Kavieng along with the several other ships when, in a preview of what was to come less than two months later in Truk, American planes roared in with the dawn.

The crew manned the guns and made ready to defend themselves as the American fighters made short work of the defenders overhead. With control of the air the dive and torpedo bombers appeared and began their deadly work. The attackers swooped in and promptly blasted the transport *Tenryu Maru*, setting her afire and soon thereafter to the bottom. The gunners on *Kiyosumi* blazed away with their machine guns at the low flying attackers as they shifted attention to their ship. Bombs began to rain down on the other ships and a near miss started several minor fires in the superstructure, while nearby a pair of minesweepers were also burning. As the smoke began to clear it became apparent the raiders were gone and the guns went silent. The planes that day came from the *USS Bunker Hill* and *USS Monterey* and the *Kiyosumi Maru* would see them again in two months during Operation Hailstone.

Kiyosumi spent Christmas Day putting out fires aboard their ship and in the engineering spaces below efforts were redoubled to get the engines functioning in any way. She needed to leave Kavieng very soon. For five days the men worked with sweat and welding torches and finally the *Kiyosumi* was able to get up enough steam to get underway with the destroyer *Yukaze* as escort along with the damaged minesweeper *W-22*. Slowly the convoy crawled north towards Truk, the lookout's eyes peeled for submarine periscopes and patrol planes overhead.

Sink found inside the Kiyosumi Maru.

It did not take long for them to be spotted. On New Year's Eve the *USS Balao* began to stalk the convoy. After the sighting the submarine easily raced ahead of the slow movers and submerged to wait for them. The *Balao* was patient and at almost midnight on New Year's Day the big and slow *Kiyosumi* filled the sights in her periscope. Six torpedoes hissed out of the bow tubes and sped towards the *Kiyosumi* as the submarine made its escape. The crew of the submarine were rewarded for their efforts when three loud rumbling explosions were heard.

On board the *Kiyosumi* the darkness turned to day as three rapid explosions almost knocked the ship over. The force of the impacts sent men flying from their bunks and slammed others on watch against the metal decks. The ship quickly began to go down by the bow, the forward holds devastated by the explosions. Water began to roar into these compartments as the crew fought valiantly to seal them off. In the engine room the force of the blasts was so severe that the repairs to the engine simply fell apart and the ship began to drift. Luckily the ship was empty of cargo at the time and riding high in the water; this allowed her to somehow stay afloat. It is simply amazing that a ship like *Kiyosumi Maru* could take three torpedo hits, after already being damaged, and survive. Hits like that were often enough to sink an aircraft carrier!

The crew radioed for help as they began to drift in the dark, all the while fighting for their lives. The ship was severely damaged and without help she would likely sink. The Navy at Truk heard her distress calls and dispatched a small flotilla of ships to assist. The mixed force of light cruisers and destroyers arrived and took the wallowing ship under tow. It took the group an entire week to make the trip back to Truk, a voyage that normally would only require a day or two. Entering the lagoon under tow the *Kiyosumi* was quite a sight to behold as she rode low in the water, the torn metal near the bow visible along with black scorch marks. The tow came to an end as the ship dropped anchor for the last time on January 8, 1944, in the Repair Anchorage.

The crew was dead tired from the battle to save their ship, which was in very bad shape and in no condition to go anywhere. Priority was given to keeping her afloat and to lighten her the deck guns the crew had hoped to use battling the enemy were removed. In the bow the first hold was basically welded shut to contain the damage and like the other ships in the repair anchorage her cargo holds began to fill up with torches and metal working gear as they become workshops. Hammers echoed and sparks flew as men swarmed over the ship to get her ready to resume her role in the war. They didn't know that she would never see the open sea again and would never get her guns back. The once well-armed raider would end her life as a helpless invalid tied up at anchor.

The *Kiyosumi* was a sitting duck when Operation Hailstone began. There was still a lot of damage in the forward areas from the three torpedo hits and the ship was immobile.

This lantern from the wreck cleaned up well.

As the American planes filled the sky the men knew they were in the fight of their lives as it became quickly apparent that this was a much bigger attack then the one they had been part of several months before in Kavieng. The first to find the *Kiyosumi* was an SBD-5 Dauntless dive bomber from the *USS Yorktown* who lined up and an executed a perfect attack on the stricken vessel. The pilot guided his plane down through the scattered anti-aircraft fire and planted his 1,000-pound bomb straight in the number two cargo hold. The explosion blasted yet another gaping hole in the bow and killed a number of the men working in that damaged part of the ship. All the repair work of the prior month was ruined as water again began to flood the forward cargo holds and the ship began to go down by the bow. Captain Maki pushed his crew hard to contain the damage and keep the ship afloat.

The Captain's efforts paid off for a little while as the ship remained afloat by the middle of the day. The scene nearby was total devastation as ships burned and sank everywhere when the next wave of attackers arrived. More SBD-5s, this time from the *USS Enterprise*, were next to hit the Repair Anchorage. With a number of his crew already dead and his ship going down by the bow the Captain watched as the planes plunged down towards him, bombs falling clear as the planes pulled up and roared away over the waves. Two 1,000-pound bombs hit both sides of the bridge almost simultaneously killing him instantly as the whole area disappeared in a fireball and pieces of metal tore away becoming deadly shrapnel that struck down and killed even more. The force of the impacts was too much for the former raider to bear and flames spread out of control. In the bow the repairs gave way and she began to go down quickly even as the superstructure burned. The surviving crew leaped into the water to escape the rapidly sinking inferno as the ship rolled on to her port side and sank by the bow. She took 43 men with her to their graves.

Today the wreck of the *Kiyosumi Maru* is famous for one thing, and that is leaking oil. Many of the ships in the lagoon are still leaking oil, but the *Kiyosumi* is especially notable for this. The oil slowly drips out of her fractured bunkers and rises to the surface creating a rainbow-like slick on the surface with a strong petroleum smell. There are not many shipwrecks that you can actually smell, and it is as if the ship is still weeping for the many men killed on her so many years ago. The ship itself is laying on her port side in about 120 feet of water and the violence of her last month's afloat are evident everywhere. The length of the 450 foot *Kiyosumi Maru* bears many scars. Starting at the bow the ship is still intact and the area under the deck gun mounting is interesting to look around in, but the forward cargo holds are a mess due to the damage caused by the fatal bomb and the three torpedoes before that. Even today the torn and missing metal from those long-ago attacks is obvious.

Air compressor in the inky blackness.

The bridge is almost totally gone and the damage in this area is massive. The final grave of the bridge crew is best left alone as it is a dangerous mass of twisted metal. On the topside of the bridge area is an awesome amount of colorful marine life that decorates the wreck in a profusion of color, almost as if they were flowers decorating a grave. It is the stern area that is the most interesting and unique area on the *Kiyosumi Maru* and where she truly shows her colors as a former merchant raider. Near the opening of the fifth hold there are a pair of torpedo launchers on either side. These were the most deadly weapons on the ship, yet, despite the aspirations of her crew, they were never fired in anger. In the same area there is a long narrow opening which was specially designed to bring the torpedoes up from their storage area below. Around the opening there are what appears to be railroad tracks, which were actually used for trolleys to move the torpedoes to the launchers for reloading. In the final cargo hold there are a number of oil barrels and a large number of small fish that live among them.

The *Kiyosumi Maru* had an amazing career filled with long voyages and plenty of drama. It is easy to picture the ship proudly steaming into New York harbor or through the Panama Canal in her civilian colors. Yet she was also a warrior, who took part in some of the most dramatic early moments of the great battle at Midway. Later she would take an incredible punishment while hauling thousands of soldiers to the battles of the South Pacific. In the end though there is something unfulfilled about her story. Despite all her achievements she never once was able to fulfill her ultimate mission and that was to find and sink enemy merchant ships on the high seas. It feels empty, much like the torpedo launchers still waiting on deck to be fired for the first time at the enemy.

Porthole with glass still inside.

Ladders and railings disappear into the darkness of the lower engineering spaces.

Patrol Boat 34

PB 34 isn't really a name, it is more a designation and it takes away some of the sense of life and history from this very interesting ship. This ship was not always just a designation, she began her service as the destroyer *Susuki* and at one point was one of the fastest warships in the world. The *Susuki* was part of the *Momi* class of destroyers. Launched in 1921 she was 770 tons and could make an incredible 36 knots at top speed. *Susuki* had ten years of peace during which her only action was training and short patrols in the 1920's and into the 1930's. She had a succession of captains who came and went, several whom went on to have prominent careers during the war. In 1932 *Susuki* went to war, but not against the US Navy in the Pacific as there were nine more years before that war would start. Susuki went to Shanghai and joined the squadron of Japanese ships operating against the Chinese along the Yangtze River. She spent almost eight years on the China Station, sailing up and down the broad Yangtze and supporting Japanese Army operations as they constantly pushed into China gobbling up territory.

The *Susuki* operated in hostile waters for eight years before she finally returned home in 1940, her time as a first line destroyer was over. She was nearly 20 years old when she became a patrol boat and lost her name and much of equipment that had made her a deadly adversary. Along with the name *Susuki*, the ship lost her torpedo tubes, aft main gun and all her minesweeping gear. Additionally a boiler was removed and the once fast ship was reduced to a mere 18 knot top speed. To compensate a number of 25-millimeter machine guns, depth charge racks, throwers and depth charges were added. The decision was made midway through the refit to give her the ability to function as a fast troop transport and the entire stern was cut down to form a ramp from which a 46 foot landing craft could be launched. Internally changes were made so that 150 soldiers could squeeze in. After nearly a year in the yard the newly renamed *Patrol Boat 34* returned to sea and began seven months of training exercises designed to acclimate the ship and crew to their new role as a patrol boat and fast troop transport.

In late November 1941 *PB 34* joined Patrol Boat Squadron 1, which was assigned to support the landings at Legaspi in the Philippines. Her first taste of action as a patrol boat came in the early morning hours of December 12, when she was detached to depth charge a suspected submarine near the invasion force. Whether there was actually submarine is highly suspect, but the crew had fired their first shots in anger at the Americans or at least whales with American sympathies. The pace of operations for the next two months was furious as *PB 34* acted as an escort for the invasions of Bangka, Kendari, Ambon, Makassar, Timor, Surabaya and finally Christmas Island before heading to Singapore on April 10, 1942. During these operations *PB 34* was often operating closely with *Kiyosumi Maru*, and the two of them shared many early victories together and even to this day they are very close to each other. *PB 34* also worked with the destroyer *Fumizuki*, another future permanent resident of Truk Lagoon, performing escort duties. Despite her age the former destroyer held up well in these operations and in May 1942 she was again joined with *Kiyosumi Maru* and ordered to proceed to Saipan to load troops for the forthcoming invasion of Midway.

The unassuming old destroyer and heavily armed transport joined a much bigger number of ships to create the Midway Invasion Force Transport Group. On May 28, 1942, they set sail from Saipan and by June 3rd they were bearing down on Midway. Their arrival was expected and the sneak attack on the American island was in fact an ambush.

Opposite: Inside the cramped engine room.

Momi class destroyer at the end of the war. This is a sister ship of PB-34. (US Navy)

PB 34 and *Kiyosumi* had the unusual honor of being some of the first Japanese ships spotted and attacked during the battle of Midway when a group of nine B-17's appeared high in the air over the invasion force on June 3. The gunners on *PB 34* couldn't reach the planes overhead as they dropped their bombs, but high level bombing of moving ships was a nearly impossible task and the bombs exploded harmlessly in impressive strings of huge waterspouts. That night the Americans returned at low level and torpedoed the oiler *Akebono Maru* and strafed the decks of the *Kiyosumi*. First blood had been drawn.

With the initial burst of action finished the transport group pushed on during an entirely uneventful June 4; but to their north the pride of the Imperial Navy had been destroyed and the war had forever changed. The Battle of Midway ended quietly for *PB 34* as she and her group turned about in the early morning hours of June 5 and returned to Guam and ultimately back to Japan. The war would change again on August 7, 1942, when the US Marines landed on Guadalcanal in the Solomon Islands. This would initiate an 18 month war of attrition far to the south in which the Japanese Navy would be slowly ground down. *PB 34* was one of the first ships sent into the meat grinder.

The Japanese response to the American landings on August 7 was to embark what was essentially two regiments of soldiers to land and counter attack the American positions. These were the same troops that had been tasked to invade Midway and they set sail from Truk heading towards Guadalcanal in three waves on August 16. *PB 34* was in the second wave with *PB 35* and the light cruiser *Jintsu* escorting two transports carrying over 1,000 men of the Ichiki Regiment. As the last two waves came south more slowly, the initial wave raced forward on destroyers carrying almost 1,000 men crammed on their decks. This first wave was meant to establish a foothold on the island and await the follow-on waves for a single decisive attack. They made landfall on August 19 and their commander, Col. Ichiki, decided not to wait and immediately led his small force in a frontal attack on the American positions the next night. They were slaughtered almost to a man by well-dug-in Marines and Ichiki committed suicide shortly after.

This sudden reversal and loss of command caused chaos and it was decided that the following waves would be supported by a substantial force of warships and carriers. As *PB 34* closed with Guadalcanal on August 24 the carriers clashed in the Battle of the Eastern Solomons and the Americans retired south, leaving Guadalcanal undefended except for a small force of Marine dive bombers and fighters on the island. In the early light of day on August 25 this small force of Marines found *PB 34* and her convoy. Six SBD Dauntless dive bombers rolled into their dives as the men on *PB 34* opened fire with their 25-millimeter guns.

Things began to go wrong almost immediately. Despite a constant barrage from the escorting ships one of the bombers planted a bomb squarely into the *Kinryu Maru* and she began to sink, while a second bomb hit just off the *Boston Maru* causing flooding and structural damage. As other escorts moved to get the troops off the doomed *Kinryu*, *PB 34* and *Jintsu* moved to assist the *Boston Maru*. On board *Jintsu* Admiral Tanaka moved to rally his battered ships when a bomb struck just forward of the bridge, the explosion sent shrapnel flying through the bridge and caused flooding in the forward areas. The gunners on *PB 34* flailed away with everything they had as ships were seemingly blowing up all around them. Just as the *Jintsu* slowed to a halt nearby the men of *PB 34* spotted a new threat heading their way; American B-17 heavy bombers. The big bombers would have a hard time hitting moving warships, but many of the ships in the area were damaged and unable to maneuver. The bombs fell and a tremendous explosion erupted as bombs rained down on the destroyer *Mutsuki* which was unloading men from the rapidly sinking *Kinryu*. Finally the signal was received on the bridge to turn around. There was a sense of relief mixed with frustration as the battered survivors turned back to the north and returned to Bougainville. They left hundreds of their comrades dead on the sunken ships left behind.

PB 34 returned to Truk for minor repairs and refit. The battles in the Solomons were no place for the old ship, but there was still a role for her. From November 1942 until March 1943 *PB 34* performed anti-submarine patrols in the areas between Bougainville, Rabaul and Kavieng; occasionally taking a break to escort cargo ships in this same area. Her missions were almost nonstop and the fatigue on the crew was intense, but she was not directly in the line of fire anymore. Despite this she could see the evidence of the fierce battles just to the south in the parade of battle scarred ships limping back into port, or never returning at all.

The propellers of PB-34 still are an impressive sight.

On the night of March 6, 1943, the ship was on yet another patrol mission, this time in the area around Kavieng. Whether due to crew fatigue, bad weather or simple dumb luck it is unclear what the cause was for what happened next. On board *PB 34* the crew was passing an uneventful night when the men were suddenly thrown to the deck and slammed into bulkheads by a tremendous grinding crash. The men in the bow section of the ship were not so lucky and for many of them they would just simply never wake up as they were almost instantly killed when the bow of *PB 34* crashed into the port side of another old China veteran, the destroyer *Yakaze*. On the *Yakaze*, which would finish the war with a number of severe collisions, there was massive flooding in the boiler and engine rooms. For *PB 34* the damage was even more catastrophic with the entire bow section crushed and torn off and the area around the bridge hopelessly mangled. It is a testament to the skill of the crew and strength of her design that the old patrol boat didn't sink immediately.

Onboard the remaining amidships and stern areas the men scrambled to their feet and somehow managed to secure all the watertight doors before the rest of the ship flooded. Sitting dead in the water with almost half the ship missing it seemed that *PB 34* would soon be headed towards the bottom, but the doors held and she remained afloat. As daylight came it was decided that the ship could be salvaged and she was taken under tow, at low speed and stern first. Somehow *PB 34* made it to Truk and was brought alongside the repair ship *Akashi*. First priority was given to lightening the ship and to make this happen the remaining guns were stripped off. With this complete the remains of the ship were put into the floating dry-dock and the tangled remains of the bow were cut off. This left nothing forward of the stack; basically *PB 34* had lost the forward 1/3 of the ship.

To get the truncated vessel back in the water a new bow was welded on. Truk lacked serious manufacturing capabilities so the new bow was essentially just two big sheets of steel welded into a triangle and stuck on the front. A new smaller bridge area was built in this area and the ship was finally refloated. The odd looking patrol boat was certainly unique and was not operational when the attacks of February 17 began. Without guns, or really even a true crew, *PB 34* quietly rode out the attack at anchor. It is amazing that with all the destruction around her somehow the broken former destroyer came through the

Three toilets sit inside the head on PB-34. No privacy here.

attacks unscathed. Perhaps the American pilots assumed the ship had already been severely damaged and assumed she would soon sink!

The amazing luck of *PB 34* would carry on through the second major carrier raid in April 1944. During this attack there were no big ships to attack and the pickings were slim for the bomber pilots amongst smaller support vessels yet, once again, the mystery half patrol boat made it through without a scratch. Ultimately though she was a doomed vessel as she had no mission and was still not operational. As the calm summer days came to the lagoon the tranquility was regularly shattered by American raids of heavy bombers, usually B-24 Liberators coming from the south. On July 3, 1944, one of these raids finally found the old destroyer still in the Repair Anchorage on the west side of Dublon. It appears from the wreck that a bomb struck the bridge area and

Colorful soft coral bathed in the afternoon sun.

destroyed that temporary structure. There is also evidence of a fire that burned amidships. The location of the damage suggests that there was also damage to the new bow structure which would have allowed water into the ship. At this point in the war Truk was isolated and the men stationed there were in a desperate situation in which simple survival was their priority. With no facilities, ships or equipment to fight the fires and flooding *PB 34* settled gracefully upright on the shallow bottom. Her long career was finally over 23 years and two wars after it began.

The wreck of *PB 34* is easy to find and she is easily seen from the surface. Diving the wreck the unusual bow is very prominent and the location where the original construction begins is very obvious. There is some structure left in the amidships area and it is heavily covered in both hard and soft corals. When the sun is shining through the shallow water the colors on the ship simply explode and are best appreciated from the deck looking up. Moving towards the stern the conversion that allowed her to carry a landing craft is very obvious, as is the very old whaleback design of the hull. This is typical of World War 1 era torpedo boats. There is a head with several toilets still visible and the engine room can still be entered. The engine room is a tight squeeze, but it also houses the best view of what the old ship used to look like when she was in service. Numerous pipes, gauges and much machinery is still inside and in good condition. Heading towards the stern there are two depth charges in their launchers immediately above the propellers. Descending to the bottom both propellers are clearly visible and are very impressive with an orange colored sponge coating them that really makes them stand out. It is easy to image these props churning the waters of the Yangtze River at high speed back in the 1930's. *PB 34* is not one of the more popular wrecks in the lagoon but she is a unique wreck, with a very long history.

The Sapporo Maru's bell.

The bow emerges from the silty water.

A light illuminates the ghostly bridge.

COMBINED FLEET AND REPAIR ANCHORAGES

Sapporo Maru

The *Sapporo Maru* is by far the smallest and least glamorous of any of the wrecks in Truk Lagoon that actually appear on any map. At only 145 feet long and 361 tons, she is very small by lagoon standards. Officially a Special Deep-Sea Fishing Trawler, she was basically like literally hundreds of other Japanese fishing boats built during the 1930's. The *Sapporo* was completed in Hiroshima in 1930 and went to work for the Japanese Marine Products Company.

For ten years the *Sapporo* was just a basic deep sea fishing vessel, her biggest battles being with tuna and snagged nets. There was a notable Japanese fishing fleet based out of Truk and it is likely that is how she came to be in the lagoon. When the war began to go badly for the Japanese it required many garrison islands to fend for themselves, as American submarines sent millions of tons their food to the bottom. The *Sapporo* was probably taken into Navy service while at Truk and she began to catch fish for the Imperial Japanese Navy. After the attacks of Operation Hailstone, the *Sapporo* was still in Truk and in operation. She either was not present or was simply ignored during the two days of attacks. In the two months after the devastation the *Sapporo* was vital in trying to keep the men on the islands fed. Starvation was beginning to take a serious toll and the fish brought in by the fishing fleet was critical.

On April 5, 1944, yet another wave of heavy four-engine B-24 Liberator bombers came to blast the wreckage of Truk. That day 20 of the big bombers dropped their bombs over the islands causing numerous fires; this was nothing new and most men hid in caves during the attack. A ship the size of *Sapporo* was also safe, it being highly unlikely that a high level bombing attack could hit her. Then much to the surprise of the men on board two B-24's came roaring in from the northeast at low level. The huge planes coming in low and fast were an awesome sight as they came straight for the *Sapporo*, which they had mistaken for a small cargo ship. The bombs fell and straddled the boat as the planes roared overhead, their prop wash sweeping the deck. Explosions and shrapnel flew in all directions punching many holes into the ship. Several areas were torn open as if hit by a rocket and water began to fill the engine room. At first the ship seemed as if she might survive, but several days later the damage was too much and she sank.

The *Sapporo Maru* today is just north of Fefan Island in about 80 feet of water. The water in this area is heavy with silt caused by rain runoff from the nearby island. This is probably the siltiest wreck in the lagoon and visibility is usually poor. Exploring the wreck is still interesting as she sits almost perfectly upright and is small enough to completely cover in a single dive. The midships area has interesting features on deck from her fishing days and it is possible to very carefully enter her engine room. Heading forward, the bridge is easily accessible and is almost perfectly intact. The bow has a small forecastle that is interesting to slowly swim around in. For a great story on the *Sapporo* find a documentary made on her discovery by an Australian TV station in 2002.

Shinkoku Maru

The story of *Shinkoku Maru* begins in February 1940 in Kobe, Japan where she was built and first took to the sea. At 500 feet long and just over 10,000 tons the *Shinkoku* was simply massive. Oil was perhaps the most critical resource for Imperial Japan as her big and modern fleet of warships consumed huge amounts of this black gold which Japan had almost no ability to produce on her own. Japan was completely reliant on oil from the United States and the Dutch East Indies and *Shinkoku* was built to bring oil from these distant ports back to home waters. This made her one of the most strategically valuable ships in the Japanese inventory the moment she entered service.

Throughout 1940 and the first half of 1941 *Shinkoku Maru* spent her time in the rough seas of the North Pacific Ocean. She would leave her home in Japan and head to Los Angeles where she would bask in the California sun and take on American crude oil, so desperately needed by the empire gearing up for war on the other side of the ocean. For a time she was a regular sight to the citizens of Los Angeles, her huge size making her stand out to observers on shore. *Shinkoku Maru* had a secret, though. She had been built using designs and funds provided by the Imperial Navy, which had every intention of turning her into a key cog in the attack on Pearl Harbor.

As the summer of 1941 drew to a close *Shinkoku Maru* left the California sunshine for the last time loaded with one last load of oil. After unloading this cargo she entered the shipyard in Osaka for her long planned conversion to a fleet oiler. There was no need for a disguise anymore and heavy guns were mounted on her bow and stern, along with some structural changes to allow her to support heavy fueling lines. The work was quickly accomplished as *Shinkoku* had been built with these changes in mind from the beginning and training of the crew was begun. Time was critical as the countdown to December 7th was rapidly progressing.

Shinkoku Maru off the coast of California. (US National Archives)

Opposite: The engine room of Shinkoku is an enormous space.

The Japanese Navy had been designed to fight within the waters of the western Pacific; however the plan to attack the US Navy at anchor in Pearl Harbor required an entirely new type of operation to be perfected. This was the art of underway replenishment. If the carriers of the Kido Butai wanted to get within range to strike Hawaii then they would need to be refueled while sailing at high speed. *Shinkoku Maru* was built with the speed to keep up and the ability to carry large amounts of fuel, but there was no experience with this type of refueling operation anywhere in the entire Imperial Navy. To remedy this the officers and men of *Shinkoku* set about training and preparing with urgency.

The crew worked long hours during the early fall of 1941 to be ready for when they would be called to action. By the end of October the crew was ready to begin training with their primary customers, the big fleet carriers. *Shinkoku* put to sea and headed south for Kyushu to conduct underway refueling exercises, even as her crew continued to reconfigure their ship to adapt to lessons learned along the way. Finally the moment of truth arrived and the long flat topped shapes of the carriers appeared and came alongside. The crew of *Shinkoku Maru* knew the entire operation depended on the ability of the oilers to refuel the big ships and the eyes of the fleet were upon them. One after another the carriers *Shokaku, Zuikaku, Akagi, Hiryu* and *Soryu* came alongside to refuel. It was a success but the crew had little time to savor it, as the fleet received the signal to commence Operation Z. The date which would live in infamy was almost upon them.

The huge fleet weighed anchor and headed to the far north of the Japanese home islands, where they would essentially "disappear" to assure surprise for the coming attack. The time spent heading north was not to be wasted though and frantic training continued on the seven oilers supporting the attack. The crew of *Shinkoku* fought exhaustion and the force of the ocean waves to refuel all the ships of the fleet an amazing ten times enroute to Etorofu Island. Finally they felt confident that they could do their part in the coming operation. In a short two months' time the crew of *Shinkoku Maru* had perfected the extremely difficult art of refueling two ships simultaneously while underway. The carriers would now have the "legs" to make it all the way to Hawaii and back.

The engines still look like they could start today.

The air was damp and cold, with low overhanging clouds as the fleet left home waters on November 26, 1941 with bows pointed to the east. Poor weather was welcomed as it would mask the movements of the fleet as it secretly headed east across the North Pacific, back across the same waters that *Shinkoku Maru* had once used to haul oil from California. The fleet silently moved east until reaching a point roughly a thousand miles north of Midway Island, pretty much the loneliest part of the North Pacific. In this lonely and cold place the fleet received the signal, "Climb Mount Niitaka". The attack on Pearl Harbor was a go!

Immediately preparations for refueling operations began, with literally nothing for a thousand miles in every direction.

Opposite: Profusion of aquatic life on the bridge.

Decorative vase that survived the sinking.

Any problems with refueling in this place in the middle of nowhere would lead to complete disaster as the fleet lacked fuel for many of the vessels to make the return trip to Japan. There were problems as the weather worsened on the 4th of December causing the ships to roll almost 45 degrees side to side throwing the crews inside about like toys. The situation was critical as the fleet needed to refuel for the run in to make the attack and any delays added to the likelihood of discovery by American patrol planes. The *Shinkoku Maru* gave her all, but operations were cancelled for 24 hours. The clock was ticking even louder now.

The fleet pressed on towards Hawaii and their rendezvous with destiny without regard of the weather. On December 5 refueling operations were finally conducted and half the tankers turned away to the north, but *Shinkoku* was not one of them. The huge ship continued south with the carrier strike force, and finally on December 6 signal flags and blinker lights ordered the final refueling prior to the attack. Under complete radio silence the *Shinkoku Maru* pulled alongside the pride of the Imperial Navy and transferred fuel into the hungry bunkers of the fleet carriers. The tension was high and the crew congratulated each other as they finally turned north and watched the big flat tops accelerate away into the night to launch their attacks early the next morning on Sunday, December 7, 1941.

Following the attack on Pearl Harbor the strike group returned to Japan in preparation for the next phase of operations. The men of *Shinkoku Maru* stowed away their cold weather gear; the ship would be heading south to the tropics. Morale was high following their return from the successful Pearl Harbor attack and the men were happy to again join Admiral Nagumo's carrier striking force as it moved to support the invasions of Rabaul, New Britain and New Ireland. For nearly two weeks the *Shinkoku* pulled alongside the heavy fleet units and refueled them as they launched airstrikes against Australian positions in the lightly defended islands. With operations winding down in the area the *Shinkoku* returned to Japan.

In the pleasant early spring weather of March 1942, *Shinkoku Maru* left Japan just as the cherry blossoms were beginning to bloom. She was headed south again to join with her old comrades of the *Kido Butai* on an audacious operation that would take them into another ocean. In the sultry heat of newly conquered Singapore the *Shinkoku* joined the task force and they headed west. For the first time the Imperial Navy would conduct carrier operations in the Indian Ocean where the mission was to attack British ships and bases around Ceylon. The mission was called Operation C and continued for two weeks. *Shinkoku Maru* carried out her regular refueling duties and watched as the Navy dive and torpedo bombers launched off the decks to rain death and destruction on the Royal Navy. The operations were by this time routine for the officers and crew: refuel the big ships and cheer the victories. The Imperial Navy seemed unstoppable and the good times would seemingly never end. As the fleet left the Indian Ocean they headed home as an even more ambitious operation was underway, one that the admirals believed would end the war.

Shinkoku Maru returned to home waters almost a month to the day after departing Singapore and was assigned to Supply Group No. 1, which was to support Operation MI. This group of tankers was to again support the big flat tops in an attack that was designed to bring out the American aircraft carriers at long last and sink them in a decisive battle near the island of Midway. The supply group weighed anchor on May 26, 1942, and two days later joined the carriers *Hiryu*, *Soryu*, *Kaga* and *Akagi*. The combined force headed east across the Pacific at 14 knots towards their rendezvous with destiny near Midway.

In the early dawn hours of June 3 the carriers pulled alongside *Shinkoku Maru* to refuel again. The crew were old hands at this by now and completed their mission efficiently, detaching from the big carriers certain they would soon be celebrating the successes of their comrades. Confident in the outcome the supply group turned west and waited to refuel the victors in the battle sure to erupt as the fleet attacked Midway. This was the moment the Combined Fleet had longed for, the decisive battle and once again the *Shinkoku Maru* was to be part of the victory. It never happened, and the carriers the crew had so confidently waved off were completely smashed in an ambush by the US Navy in one of the most one sided naval battles in history. As the *Shinkoku Maru* made her way home in defeat, the fortunes of war had forever changed.

The Imperial Navy still had a very strong surface fleet and they were soon called upon to defend the Solomon Islands when the US Marines landed on Guadalcanal in August 1942. This fleet could still deliver victory, but to do so it needed oil. Towards this end *Shinkoku Maru* left Hiroshima Bay and headed south with a convoy destined for the bastion at Truk. The trip was routine for the first week out of the home islands, but sitting in their path just northwest of Truk was the submarine *USS Gudgeon*. At noon on August 17 the calm tropical seas were shattered by the sound of a loud clang against the hull of *Shinkoku Maru*.

The decks of Shinkoku today are one of the greatest displays of soft coral on the planet.

The crew barely had time to register their luck in being hit by a dud torpedo when a much louder and violent explosion rocked the ship. Alarms sounded as the crew rushed to contain the damage from the torpedo. The bridge was tense as the reports of damage came in and the escorts hunted the submarine seeking revenge. Finally it was reported that *Shinkoku Maru* had suffered only minor damage and she would be able to continue on to Truk for repairs. The remainder of the voyage was tense up until the moment the *Shinkoku Maru* pulled alongside the repair ship *Akashi* in the shelter of the lagoon.

The good news for the *Shinkoku* was that she had survived her first wounds and was still in condition to sail, but the bad news for the fleet was that she would require repairs back in Japan. With the temporary repairs in place on August 28, 1942, the *Shinkoku Maru* steamed through the North Pass in Truk Lagoon and back to Japan. It would be several months before the *Shinkoku* was back in action and it wasn't until after the new year that she was able to fully resume duties as a tanker. For the first six months of 1943 her duties carried her across the Empire hauling oil from the East Indies to where it was needed, both in the home islands and the fleet bases far to the south. Meanwhile the front lines were creeping steadily north and desperate operations were underway in the Solomon Islands and New Guinea.

Engine telegraph on the bridge of Shinkoku Maru.

In the first week of July the *Shinkoku Maru* was hauling a cargo of oil from the East Indies enroute to Truk when she was diverted south to the base at Rabaul. Her cargo of heavy oil was needed there to fuel the near nightly runs of warships down into the Solomon Islands, unfortunately the area around Rabaul was no longer the safe bastion it had once been. On the evening of July 7, 1943, *Shinkoku Maru* was nearing Rabaul, when the submarine *USS Peto* welcomed her to the neighborhood with a salvo of torpedoes. The first notice the crew had of the presence of the *Peto* was the shuddering of the hull and a massive spout of water flying skyward from the bow. The high explosives of the torpedo ripped into the first hold and caused thousands of gallons of oil to spill out into the sea. The massive ship barely slowed. Designed to carry liquid in separate holds, she was hard to sink when a single hold was ruptured and the *Shinkoku* soon arrived safely in Rabaul.

A sink from the wreck of Shinkoku Maru.

In Rabaul the desperately needed oil was unloaded and repairs were undertaken. For nearly a week she sweated out the threat of air attacks in Simpson Harbor, but luck was with her this time. Finally, with a temporary patch in place, she departed Rabaul on August 15, 1943. She would leave the tropics for a short time and return to Japan where her repairs were completed. Twice the *Shinkoku Maru* had been torpedoed and both times she had escaped relatively unscathed.

The remainder of 1943 saw *Shinkoku Maru* plying her intended routes hauling oil from Balikpapan to places such as Palau, Truk and Ulithi. During these trips she was often in the company of fellow Truk Lagoon wreck *Fujisan Maru,* as they were both big fast tankers. Overall it was routine duty, nothing like the thrill of the early operations in support of the long sunk big carriers. The glory days were over and the only action was scanning the sea in search of periscopes and torpedoes from the ever present submarines. At one point while in the company of the *Fujisan* one of the other tankers in the convoy was badly damaged by the submarine *USS Raton* but would survive. Everything was routine when *Shinkoku Maru* entered Truk Lagoon on February 14, 1944, and pulled alongside the *Tonan Maru* to offload oil onto her.

The gradually increasing drone of engines and the clanging of alarms ended the routine permanently on February 17. As the huge fighter battle raged overhead in the early morning light the crew of *Shinkoku Maru* shook off their sleep and scrambled to action stations on the big guns on the bow and stern; which were of little use. Sitting anchored and exposed in the Combined Fleet anchorage the *Shinkoku Maru* made a perfect target and it wasn't long until she first attracted dive bombers off the *USS Yorktown*. The pilots guided their planes down as the crew below were only spectators while the bombs fell as if in slow motion. Thunderous blasts showered the ship with water and noise as the bombs hit all around the middle of the ship. Yet somehow they had missed the massive tanker sitting stationary at anchor.

Incredible collection of bottles and glass items like those found in the infirmary.

Next came the boxy shapes of TBF Avenger torpedo bombers spotted coming in from the north. The planes came in low with plenty of time to concentrate on the largely defenseless tanker. Six planes took their aim and dropped their lethal cargo into the water. The crew knew their time had come and could only watch in fascination as the wakes of the six torpedoes sped towards their huge motionless ship. Perhaps they believed it was divine intervention, but whatever the reason somehow all six torpedoes missed. As the sun set on the first day of the attack the crew could only think that maybe the "Divine Country" really did have the protection of the gods. Somehow one of the most prized targets in the lagoon, riding at anchor had come through the day unscathed.

Dawn on the 18th brought the US Navy pilots set to finish the job of the previous day. The crew held on to the thought that their ship was divinely protected as anti-aircraft fire from the island batteries ripped through the morning calm. Across the ship the men stood at their stations ready for whatever the day would bring. They did not have long to wait as more TBF's from the *USS Bunker Hill* came in first thing to avenge their poor shooting from the day before. Whatever tongue lashing the pilots received from their commanding officer seemed to have worked as the very first torpedo of the day streaked just beneath the waves and slammed into the *Shinkoku* near the engine room on the port side. For the third time in her career the ship shuddered from the shock of a torpedo impact; but unlike the submarine torpedoes that had hit the oil tanks this one hit the engine room which was not designed to carry liquid.

The blast ripped open a jagged gash, exposing the lower engineering spaces and unleashed an explosion that tore through the entire stern area of the ship. The explosion killed many of the engineering crew at their stations and then flashed through the remaining stern structure literally cooking men where they stood. There was little time for the surviving men to assist before sea water began to pour into the wide open spaces in a raging torrent. The *Shinkoku Maru* was built for speed and her wide open engine room near the stern was built to facilitate this. It was not built to be blasted open and quickly filled with sea water. On the bridge it was amazing to the officers how quickly the big ship began to go down by the stern. There was little need to order "Abandon Ship" as she was going down already, heading to her final grave in shallow gently current-swept water. The veteran of Pearl Harbor, the Indian Ocean raids and Midway came to rest upright in 125 feet of water. She took 86 men with her to their graves, most of them killed in the engine room blast.

Today the *Shinkoku Maru* is one of the most amazing places on earth. She is an almost perfect mix of perfectly preserved historic wreck and impossibly magical reef. That such a lush and colorful reef has sprung up on this scene of intense violence and tragedy is something that will leave the diver almost speechless at the end of the day. Having been in the Combined Fleet anchorage placed the wreck in an area where gentle currents move nutrients through and generally keep visibility good. When entering the water *Shinkoku Maru* is almost instantly visible and beckons the diver with the promise of a once in a lifetime dive; but better plan on at least two as the ship is too big to be explored on a single tank.

Heading to the stern and the location of the fatal blow to *Shinkoku* is the perfect place to begin a tour of the wreck. Resting upright on the bottom the jagged hole in the port side is easy to spot and swim through. This takes the diver through a dark maze in the lower engineering spaces full of fascinating objects which finally ends in the large, dimly-lit engine room.

Operating table covered with bottles and bones in the Shinkoku Maru.

Many larger animals make the Shinkoku Maru their home, like this Star Puffer.

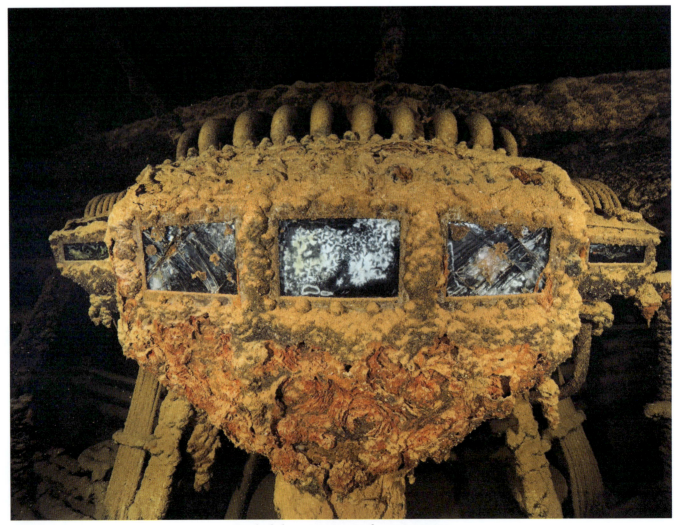

Cracked glass on gauges in the engine room.

This space is an amazing sight and the big engines that drove the *Shinkoku* while refueling the big carriers look like they are ready to come to life again at any time. There are some other interesting areas in the stern, including the big deck gun, and the evidence of the flash explosion that killed so many is visible everywhere.

Moving forward it is a long swim to the bridge superstructure in the middle of the wreck. Here the dark and dramatic mazes of the interior give way to an explosion of marine life. Clouds of bright fish drift everywhere, joined by resting turtles and big puffer fish getting cleaned by small wrasse. The colors of the soft corals and sea fans are almost beyond description, waving gently in the nutrient rich waters. Entering the superstructure is a shock after the bright sun and colors outside, but the mood changes on this wreck are what make it so special. Inside there is a large open space, which would once have had wooden walls that are long since rotted away. On one side there is a head with toilets, baths and urinals all still intact and seemingly ready for use. The highlight though is the former infirmary and the operating table still clearly visible in it. The table is home to a collection of artifacts, bottles and even the occasional bone. The bones are human remains of the crew, so they should also be shown respect and not handled. An excellent way to leave this area is to head up through the corroded floor and into the bridge areas. The bridge area is half collapsed and is home to an incredible collection of marine life. Where the captain once stood the engine telegraphs are still standing at attention, but the windows are now full of soft corals and not the long lost view of the *Kido Butai* sailing towards victory in the early war years.

There is another long, and incredibly beautiful, swim to reach the bow area. The sun is often shining down and the light playing across the wreck in this area is magical. On the bow is the second big deck gun, now home to a huge assortment of corals and small fish. Below there are some interesting artifacts in the deckhouse, including lanterns used to signal other ships long ago. There are no other ships nearby to signal anymore, but there are the occasional sharks patrolling off beyond the anchor chain. The anchor is still set and even all these many decades later the *Shinkoku Maru* is still anchored, upright and seemingly ready for action.

Massive schools of fish inhabit this amazing wreck.

Urinal inside a head within the superstructure.

Yamagiri Maru

Almost four years to the day before the attack on Pearl Harbor the keel of a big 6,400 ton 439 foot-long ship was laid in the shipyards in Yokohama. She was being built for the Yamashita Steamship company to carry passengers and cargo on the South America routes, a long haul that required a big ship with plenty of range. In six months' time she was launched and finally finished in July 1938. The *Yamagiri Maru* began her service that summer of 1938 and set sail for New York by way of South America. She would begin her service with the longest voyage of her career. Far away from her home port of Kobe for many months she transited the Cape of Good Hope and visited the exotic ports of South America and finally all the way up to New York. Not many vessels in New York flew the flag of Japan and her crew enjoyed a taste of the Big Apple. When the time came *Yamagiri* bid adieu to Lady Liberty and retraced her steps on the long journey back to the land of the rising sun. In February 1941 she would depart Kobe one more time on the journey across the Pacific to South America, but her civilian service was cut short by the coming war.

In September 1941 the *Yamagiri* joined the Japanese Navy and the following month was refitted to perform the role of an Auxiliary Transport. The outbreak of war saw the *Yamagiri* at sea and after a simple supply run to the Marshall Islands the big ship returned to Japan to prepare for more dangerous missions. In the last few weeks of January 1942 *Yamagiri* bid goodbye to Japan and headed to Bangka Island just off the port of Manado where she was to take part in the invasion of Dutch East Indies. *Yamagiri Maru* joined nine other transports in transporting the men of the 1st Kure and Sasebo Special Naval Landing Forces and army troops of the 228th Infantry Regiment. They were escorted by 12 destroyers, five minesweepers, two subchasers, two seaplane tenders, one patrol boat and finally the flagship *Jintsu*.

First Aid kits like this were common on Yamagiri.

Massive 14 inch shells for battleships.

Opposite: The masts of Yamagiri have a shocking variety of colors.

The Yamagiri Maru in the paint scheme of the Yamashita Line. (Yamashita)

In the darkness on the last day of January 1942 the invasion force put their small boats overboard loaded with men and sent them into the darkness. The crew on deck of *Yamagiri Maru* was tense with anticipation as they watched their passengers head towards the beach as they stood to offshore. The Dutch were quickly scattered and the advance pushed towards the goal of Ambon and the anchorage there. Early in the morning of February 3 the *Yamagiri* got underway again and travelled the short distance from the invasion beaches to drop anchor in their prize; Ambon Bay. Her part in the invasion of the East Indies completed, the *Yamagiri* returned to Japan.

The ship would spend the next three months delivering cargo back in the Marshall Islands. Her route took her to islands such as Wotje, Tarawa, Mili, Eniwetok and even the recently captured American island of Wake; now renamed Otori Jima in honor of the new ownership. This was routine cargo duty and this early in the war the crew wasn't yet wary of submarines or American air attacks. In May, 1942 the *Yamagiri* left the tropical islands of the Empires far eastern perimeter for the exotic Oriental ports of Japan, China and Vietnam. She crisscrossed these routes bringing much needed raw materials to the industry in Japan and returning with the supplies needed by the rapidly expanding empire. These were peaceful times and they lasted another five months until the increasing fighting in the Solomon Islands drew the *Yamagiri Maru* back to the southern seas.

These early visits to the southern seas continued the comfortable and peaceful career of the *Yamagiri Maru*. She saw no attacks and the only thing to impede her passage was the occasional rain squall and rough weather. As the fall wore on she carried cargo to Rabaul from the major bases in Truk and Palau, returning occasionally to cold and wintry Japan to load up her holds with more cargo for the southern operations. The *Yamagiri Maru* and her crew were well travelled and happy in their peaceful service to the Emperor. Finally on the last day of July 1943 the submarine *USS Pogy* served notice that the happy days were over.

The *Yamagiri* was sailing in a small convoy numbered 3724 out of Yokosuka bound for Truk, riding low in the water with her holds full of goods. In the middle of the night the sleepy watch was startled awake by a bright flash followed by a deep boom. Scanning quickly with binoculars they saw a big auxiliary aircraft transport dead in the water with fires spreading on her decks. In horror they watched as hundreds of army soldiers poured from their quarters in the cargo areas and jumped in the water to avoid certain death as the ship sank. The soldiers were strongly motivated to get off the ship as they were sharing the cargo holds with a huge supply of torpedoes bound for submarines in Truk! The *Yamagiri Maru* could only wish the men the best as they increased speed and fled the scene into the dark, hopefully getting away from the unseen submarine.

Four days after arriving in Truk with the ill-fated convoy 3724, the *Yamagiri Maru* departed on a cargo run to Rabaul. The run was uneventful and, after quickly unloading under the ever present threat of American bombers, the ship joined the convoy O-605 heading back north. They were being watched as they steamed out of port. The submarine *USS Drum* was hunting and the big silhouette of the *Yamagiri Maru* made a fine target. Aboard the *Yamagiri Maru* the crew was just feeling the relief of putting war torn Rabaul behind them as four torpedoes were screaming just beneath the waves towards them. A massive explosion served notice that the peaceful days for the fine ship were over once and for all.

The torpedo tore into the starboard side of the ship right between the number 2 and 3 cargo holds ripping open a giant hole to the sea and shattering the hull. In almost the blink of an eye the *Yamagiri Maru* was in mortal peril. The crew raced to fix the damage as best they could and hoped that the hole was not torn open further by the roll of the ship. Meanwhile the escorts reacted in anger, churning up the ocean and dropping depth charges in an effort to sink the unseen enemy. The only hope for the crew and ship was to limp back into Rabaul as the rest of the convoy sailed on.

Yamagiri returned to Rabaul roughly a day after she left, immediately entering dry dock for emergency repairs. While in dry dock she was soon noticed by American recon planes and she joined the target list for upcoming bombing missions. The crew and shore parties worked around the clock in the sweltering heat to get the *Yamagiri* seaworthy again. As the bombing raids continued and repairs dragged on it was decided to tow the *Yamagiri* back to Truk for extensive repairs.

The USS Drum nearly sank the Yamagiri Maru. (US National Archives)

Her cargo holds were now empty except for massive battleship shells in the fifth hold in the stern, which along with some heavy construction equipment likely served as ballast to offset flooding in the bow to keep her level. On a more even keel the *Yamagiri* slowly left Rabaul and limped back to Truk. During this long slow trip the crew's nerves were driven to the breaking point between wondering if the temporary patch in the bow would hold and if another submarine would find the sitting duck and just finish the job.

The men could finally relax as the ship entered the south passage and the safety of Truk Lagoon. She immediately made her way to the repair anchorage and dropped anchor. Little did anyone know that this would be the last time she would ever drop anchor. During the remaining months of 1943 the time was spent performing massive repairs to the hull in very primitive and hot conditions. Truk may have been a major base, but it was no Pearl Harbor. The crew worked in sweltering heat day after day with the most basic of tools hammering and welding new metal work into place. Her hull had been badly shattered and it would need to be reinforced in places throughout the ship, not just in the immediate are of damage. This was a time-consuming task, but finally as February 1944 came the ship was beginning to come to life again and was almost ready to leave the repair anchorage and resume her duties.

On the morning of February 17th she was still at anchor just north of Fefan Island as the battle began to rage in the skies. Thousands of men were locked in mortal combat and many of them died that day or the next. However, despite all those eyes on the battle there is much mystery as to what transpired with the *Yamagiri Maru* that first day of Operation Hailstone. The cluster of ships in this area were the targets for dive bombers flying off the *USS Enterprise* and *Yorktown* and they roared in the vengeance in the early afternoon.

Lanterns like this were in constant use on the ships.

One of several skulls inside the engine room, where most of the fatalities occured.

The first to lay claim to an attack on the *Yamagiri Maru* were pilots from the *Yorktown*, who rocked the ship with a pair of near misses. The crew scrambled to make sure the newly repaired hull had held as more bombers came into view. These attackers were from the *Enterprise* and they planted two more bombs in the water close alongside the *Yamagiri*. Once again the ship shook and the metal strained and twisted; but it held. The ship likely began to take on a little water as the repaired area must have been weakened but at the end of the day she was proudly riding at anchor. It is likely the fury of the attack had damaged her to some extent, but when dawn came on the 18th she was still afloat and her crew prepared to meet the new dawn.

The *Yamagiri Maru* did not have long to wait. On the morning of February 18 the first waves of US Navy aircraft roared over the lagoon looking for anything that had survived the first day. At around 8 o'clock in the morning the big SB2C Helldivers off the *USS Bunker Hill* came over the north side of Fefan Island and began their attack runs. The gun batteries ashore and on the other ships nearby threw their weight at the attackers as they fell all the way to 500 hundred feet before releasing the bombs out of their internal bomb bays. The pilots were not about to miss again as they had done so often on the first day. Six 500-pound general-purpose bombs and one big 1000-pound were dropped on the *Yamagiri* from almost point blank range and one 500 and the 1000 pounder hit.

The hits were likely simultaneous and the location where the smaller 500 pound bomb hit would have to have been around the third cargo hold. The bigger bomb was the doom of *Yamagiri*. It actually plunged into the water just off the starboard side outside of the third hold and detonated beneath the ship. The explosion caused a huge shockwave that crumpled the repaired area of the hull for the last time, this time the metal blew inward and twisted back like a crushed aluminum can. The blast was so strong, and the hull in the area so weak already, that almost the entire starboard side and bottom of the third cargo hold were totally annihilated.

The bombs set off a substantial secondary explosion, likely highly flammable repair material in the third hold. As the metal twisted and curled back in the blast flames roared and shot out of the top of the hold like a giant flare. The fireball sent a huge cloud of black smoke roiling skyward for thousands of feet into the air; which served as the tombstone for the *Yamagiri Maru* and 11 of her crew. Water and flames quickly consumed the ship and the crew followed the lead of Captain Matsukawa and scrambled into the safety of the water. They had to move quickly as it took only two minutes for the vessel to roll over and settle on the shallow bottom only a hundred feet below.

Today she is one of the prettier wrecks in the lagoon laying on her port side with her shallow starboard side completely covered in hard corals, while soft corals in the colors of the rainbow festoon her kingposts and masts. Diving on the *Yamagiri Maru* usually begins on this side and divers follow the curve of the hull down and towards the bow. This is where they come face to face with a massive fifty foot gaping hole that acts as a giant window which allows divers to look straight through the ship. It is very obvious that this is the fatal wound, now dripping with whip coral and sea fans.

Fuel drums inside the Yamagiri still leak oil.

A light on the Yamagiri illuminated with a diver's torch.

YAMAGIRI MARU

The *Yamagiri* had been under extensive repairs for many months, so she lacks much of the interesting cargo found in other wrecks. Divers enter the massive hole, which is actually in the bottom of the hull, and exit out the top of the cargo hold on the other side. The damage inside the hold is overwhelming and it is interesting to try and put the jigsaw puzzle of pieces back together. This is the area of the ship that took two torpedo hits from submarines before the fatal blow, and if you look carefully evidence of the extensive repairs underway can be seen. From the cargo hold divers usually head towards the superstructure and enter the bridge through the now empty windows. The bridge is fairly spacious now that all the wooden floors and ceilings have rotted away. This area is now home to schools of small baitfish and the overgrown portholes glow like stained glass windows, creating an eerie and beautiful area.

Exiting the bridge and staying near the superstructure one quickly comes upon the big funnel of the *Yamagiri Maru* with a giant metal "Y" inside a circle clearly visible. This is not a reflection of the ship's name, but of the original owner: the Yamashita Line. From this area it is not far to the engine skylights and entry into the engine room. Inside the engine room everything is sideways but by slowly playing lights around everything falls into place. Overall the area is in good shape and the big engines that carried the *Yamagiri* all the way to New York are plainly visible. The engine room is also famous for more solemn reasons, as the human remains of the engineers are still here.

The Yamagiri Maru as she sits today viewed from the stern.

The most famous of the skulls in the engine room.

Most famous is the red skull that that has fused with the hull and stares back at divers with vacant black eyes. Near the skull are often other bones and proper respect should be shown to these sailors who died on February 18th, 1944. They likely were trapped in here and drowned when the ship quickly rolled over and sank.

Heading towards the stern and cargo hold number five divers come across the most famous, and only, cargo on the wreck. Strewn about the hold are the massive 14-inch shells for the main guns of the battleships of the *Nihon Kaigun*. These are not the even bigger 18-inch shells for the *Yamato* and *Musashi* often reported, but they are very impressive none the less. Looking around in this area will also reveal steam roller and some other random pieces of machinery. Why this cargo was left in this hold for so long is a mystery. A possible explanation is that this was ballast that offset the flooding and damage caused by the torpedoes to the bow holds. Whatever the reason the big shells are very unique and worth exploring. This is usually the end of the dive, although the stern and propeller area are also worth a visit if time and air are available. The *Yamagiri* did not have a long and illustrious history, but her highlights are memorable. Whether it was the first voyage all the way to New York, the early invasion of Ambon, the huge blast that sank her or the unique skull and battleship shells, she is a ship whose highlights continue to impress many decades after she sank.

The ships in the 4th Fleet Anchorage under attack on February 17, 1944. (US National Archives)

112   FOURTH FLEET ANCHORAGE

Fourth Fleet Anchorage

The Fourth Fleet was part of the Central Pacific Forces and had its headquarters in Truk. From a strategic point of view, their mission was to man, defend and supply the Japanese bases and islands of the central Pacific. These were bases like Kwajalein, Eniwetok, Roi, Ponape and Palau; basically the old Mandated Islands seized from the Germans in World War One. Many ships were required to keep these garrisons supplied and these generally fell under the jurisdiction of the Fourth Fleet. The nature of this command is reflected in the ships that are found in the Fourth Fleet Anchorage.

Ships at anchor in this area tend to be medium sized basic cargo ships that were ideal for transporting the essentials of war to more remote forward islands. Ships like the *Hoki*, *San Francisco* and *Nippo* are all perfect examples of what type of ship the Fourth Fleet operated. The nature of the cargo carried on these ships is exactly what one would expect from a fleet servicing forward islands in danger of imminent invasion. There is a large amount of construction materials and equipment which was needed to build fortifications. In addition vast quantities of anti-personnel and anti-tank mines compete for space with all the parts of shore based anti-ship gun batteries. Then there is the mundane cargo of water, food, ammunition and sake; always in short supply. The Fourth Fleet was focused on logistics and the ships and cargo here largely fall into this category.

There are a few exceptions though and they are largely due to the fact that this anchorage also encompasses the primary airfield on Eten Island. This means that there are auxiliary aircraft transports, like the *Fujikawa Maru*, and even nonspecific cargo ships in this area carry a huge amount of aircraft parts and supplies. Ships like the *Momokawa* and *Kikukawa* are full of engines, propellers, cowlings and even disassembled aircraft. The big tanker *Fujisan Maru* is also in this area, but that is due to the tides of battle and not any specific organizational reason.

Being the headquarters and primary base of operations for the Fourth Fleet meant that there were always a lot of ships in port either coming or going. This creates a very high density of wrecks today, with many of them concentrated in one very small area just north of Fanamu Island. Unfortunately the underwater terrain here is mostly a slope that leads into deeper water. Often called the "Deepwater Anchorage", this area certainly lives up to its name. Some of the most famous wrecks in the world lie in this area and divers will typically spend many of their days in these waters.

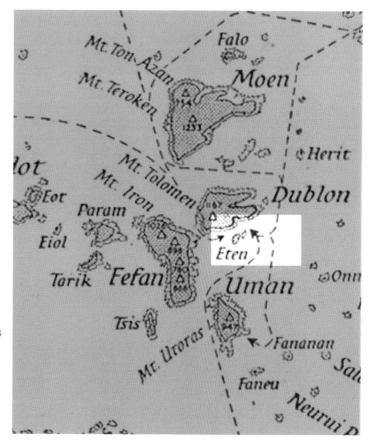

The bell of the Aikoku Maru.

114 FOURTH FLEET ANCHORAGE

Aikoku Maru

The *Aikoku Maru* represents the pinnacle of prewar Japanese civilian ship building. She was laid down and built right before the outbreak of the war and was designed for fast high capacity passenger service. The *Aikoku* had a pair of powerful diesel engines that turned two big propellers that could push the ship at over 20 knots through the waves. Even her cruise speed was 17 knots, which made her and her two sister ships faster than almost all merchant ships in the world. Not only was she a fast and sleek vessel, but she had tremendous range being designed for around the world service. When she left the yards on August 31, 1941, she was almost 500 feet long and weighed over 10,000 tons.

With her huge size, big and fast engines and great range the *Aikoku Maru* sounded more like a warship than a luxurious passenger liner. This is because secretly she was. Like many other merchant ships built in Japan during the 1930's, the *Aikoku Maru* was financed and built using secret directives from the Imperial Navy. In exchange for financing, these ships had certain design features that were useless for their intended civilian service but once taken into naval service these features helped the ship rapidly transform into a new military role. *Aikoku Maru* was the last of these special ships with the hidden secret mission. She was completed on August 31, 1941, and taken into the Imperial Japanese Navy the next day.

There were to be no around the world cruises or fashionable passengers for this ultra-modern ship, she reentered the shipyards five days later with her civilian paint job barely dry. It was left on as a disguise to allow her to get close and ambush unsuspecting ships. At the same time the welders came out and furious activity exploded across her decks. Four big 152-millimeter guns were installed along with two 533-millimeter torpedo tubes; all of this was intended to sink ships. For protection against aircraft two 76-millimeter anti-aircraft guns plus a host of smaller 13.2-millimeter machine guns were bolted to their hidden mountings. Finally a heavy duty boom was installed to accommodate a pair of Type 94 "Alf" floatplanes. The round the world passenger liner was simply a ruse, in reality the *Aikoku Maru* was always intended to be the heavily armed auxiliary cruiser that came out of the docks on October 15.

The big and deadly *Aikoku* and her sister ship *Hokoku* joined fellow Truk Lagoon wreck *Kiyosumi Maru* as the members of Cruiser Division 24, their mission to raid enemy merchant shipping deep behind the front lines using their appearance as merchant vessels as a disguise.

Aikoku Maru upon completion, but before conversion. (OSK)

Imperial headquarters authorized Operation Z, the attack on Pearl Harbor, and the raider vessels headed to their forward base in the Marshall Islands. With the beginning of the war on December 8, 1941, (they were on the other side of the international dateline from Pearl Harbor) the fast raiders were turned loose to hunt American shipping between Australia and the American west coast. The seemingly innocent looking ships swept across the seas for five days before the lookouts spied smoke on the horizon. As alarm bells rang on the ships the crews eagerly manned their guns, ready to make their own mark on the constantly unfolding roll of victories by the Japanese Navy. Their victim was the American ship *SS Vincent*, which had the misfortune to be at sea hauling rice from Australia to Panama when the war began. On the *Vincent* it was unclear who the approaching ships were, but at least they were not warships.

Or so the men thought until the 152-millimeter guns on the Hokoku blasted two broadsides at the *Vincent*. The guns boomed in the fading light of the setting sun, and on board the *Vincent* an explosion lit up the sky as one of the shells struck home. Before *Aikoku* could open fire her men were told to stand down as the fire on board the *Vincent* began to spread and she came to a stop. The American flag was run down and the crew abandoned ship entering the lifeboats. The Japanese raiders came to a halt and the *Hokoku* picked up the officers and crew, sending them to a long a brutal captivity in Japan. While this was going on the *Aikoku* fired a single torpedo into the *Vincent* and with a single great blast in the tropical twilight the 6,000 ton freighter rolled over and went to the bottom.

Two more weeks would pass in the warm tropical waters before another victim was found. Onboard the men were growing anxious that the war would be over before they could even fire their main guns. It was New Year's Eve 1941 when the Alf floatplane sighted the 3,275 ton American freighter *Malama* which was heading to Manila from Hawaii. The floatplane found the ship and circled it while radioing the position back to the nearby *Aikoku*. As the day wore on the plane failed to return and it did not respond on the radio. Concerned that the plane may be floating helpless on the waves a concerted search was launched with the *Aikoku* and *Hokoku* plus their search planes. After hunting for all of January 1, 1942, the search was called off and the crew held a ceremony to commemorate the lost aircrew. Thoughts then returned to the *Malama*.

In the morning hours of January 2 the second Alf off the *Aikoku* returned to the *Malama* and the radio operator began to signal the ship in Morse code to halt. When no reply was received and the ship continued on the pilot brought the biplane in low and the rear gunner swept the ship with a long burst from his 7.7-millimeter machine gun. This made men on the *Malama* duck for cover, but this small gun could never make the ship change her intended course. The pilot opened his throttle and returned to the *Aikoku* landing in the gentle ocean swells alongside her before being brought back aboard by the big aircraft crane. Back on board the pilot asked that two 60-kilogram bombs be mounted on their racks.

When the Alf returned to the *Malama* she again came in low and slow and buzzed the ship. The captain on board could clearly see the two black bombs on the bottom of the biplane and he decided to spare his men by ordering the ship to a halt. As the plane continued to circle the crew abandoned ship and entered their lifeboats. The *Aikoku* would get the kill but not a capture as the crew had quietly scuttled the ship on their way off. In the heat of late afternoon the

Canteens belonging to soldiers killed on Aikoku.

116 FOURTH FLEET ANCHORAGE

two big raiders appeared and took the men off the boats and into captivity while their former home slipped beneath the waves and plunged into the depths. After over a month at sea orders were received to return to Japan and deliver the prisoners.

The two warships turned north for the cold winter waters of Hashirajima and the false merchant paint schemes were removed while at sea. There would be no more old fashioned false flag operations; this was a total war and all ships were fair targets. Back in Japan the 76 POWs were taken into custody and shortly after the *Aikoku* went back into the shipyards to replace her four old 152-millimeter guns with eight new 140-millimeter guns. She had almost doubled her firepower and she even had her holds converted to carry submarine torpedoes which would expand her potential missions.

Following the victories in the South Pacific the merchant raiders would now join the big fleet operations designed to disrupt and damage the British in the Indian Ocean. In the vast Indian Ocean the *Aikoku* and *Hokoku* would continue to act as raiders, but they would also carry fuel and torpedoes for submarines operating in the area. The force departed Hiroshima on April 16, 1942, and entered the Indian Ocean on May 6. The two sister ships had come to know each other well and had tasted victory together. The men on board toasted each other as they set out for promising prospects deep in the trackless emptiness off the east coast of Africa.

Even at this depth life still flourishes.

On May 9, 1942, the hunters found their first victim, the 8,000 ton Royal Dutch Shell tanker *Genota* two weeks out of Abadan, Iran. The tanker had no chance and as the two big fast ships bore down on her the captain did the only thing he could and struck his colors and hoisted the white flag. As the guns crews on both ships kept their weapons trained on the tanker a message was sent ordering the ship to stop and make no radio signals. Any violation of this would result in the quick destruction of the *Genota*. The three ships rolled gently in the mid ocean swells as a prize crew and 30 armed Special Naval Landing Force (marines) troops made their way across the water to take possession of the tanker. The Japanese came aboard with guns ready in a scene reminiscent of the days of piracy, but the crew put up no resistance. The *Genota* was a prize capture as tankers were always in critically short supply and it left the two hunters and returned to Singapore. Within two months she would be converted to a fleet oiler and renamed the *Ose* and begin two years of service in the Imperial Japanese Navy before being sunk in Palau in March 1944.

With spirits high the next two weeks were spent searching out new targets and resupplying submarines operating in the same waters. On June 5, 1942, the *Aikoku* and *Hokoku* were operating several hundred miles off the coast of South Africa when they sighted the 7,000 ton *SS Elysia* carrying supplies and some troops from England to India. The older steam powered ship immediately turned away and smoke poured from her stack as she brought her engines up to full speed.

The Royal Dutch Shell Tanker Genota, Aikoku's first victim. (Royal Dutch Shell)

The captain also dropped some smoke floats to try and mask her escape, but he had no idea of knowing how fast the two Japanese raiders really were. The *Aikoku* signaled for her to stop, but the ship continued to try and escape. On the sister ships the big engines churned and they quickly began to box in the *Elysia*. With a touch of frustration the captain ordered the *Aikoku* to open fire on the fleeing ship. The eight big 140-millimeter guns rocked the ship as they all opened fire together sending shells ripping through the air with the sound of a tearing sheet. One of the big 52-kilogram projectiles tore into the aft areas of the *Elysia* sending debris, smoke and flame flying high into the air. To prevent a serious loss of life the captain of *Elysia* ordered her stopped and the crew and passengers entered the lifeboats.

On the *Aikoku* the men watched as the burning *Elysia* was abandoned by her crew; little thought was given to capturing the ship as she was old, slow and already damaged. The captain did give in to the request of one of the Alf floatplane crews to use the ship as bombing practice. With a quick "banzai" the three man crew climbed into their biplane and took to the sky, joining another plane from the *Hokoku* for some easy bombing practice. Each plane made a pass dropping two small 60-kilogram bombs, three of which embarrassingly missed the stationary target. One of the bombs did manage to hit the ship and the explosion set off some small fires, but the damage was not severe. The pilots would not get another chance as the raiders did not have the time to simply sit in place, the Royal Navy would come looking for the missing ship soon. The *Aikoku* fired a single torpedo into the empty *Elysia*, hitting her in the stern. The resulting explosion ripped open the hull like a tin can and the old ship quickly sank by the stern.

Aikoku in her wartime colors. (Japanese Navy)

June 1942 was mostly spent refueling and resupplying submarines, which left the men on board chomping at the bit to get back in action. The twin raiders had been very successful and the men wanted more, even as they began to work their way back towards Singapore for resupply. The hunters were allowed to sweep the seas around Ceylon (Sri Lanka) before returning home and on July 12 they struck gold when they sighted a big cargo ship heading west.

118   FOURTH FLEET ANCHORAGE

This was the 7,113 ton New Zealand Union *SS Hauraki* out of Australia bound for Egypt carrying supplies for the Australian and New Zealand soldiers battling Rommel in the deserts of North Africa.

Special Naval Landing Force troops on deck. (Asahi Shinbum)

The *Hauraki* was no match for the armed raiders and the captain followed the orders of the *Aikoku* to immediately stop and cease all radio communications. Again just like the pirates of old, a prize crew and SNLF troops came across in small boats and boarded the big freighter under the watchful guns of the cruisers. The ship was quickly secured and joined the two raiders as they returned to Singapore. The *Hauraki* was refit and renamed the *Hoki Maru*. She served the Imperial Navy until she was sunk less than half a mile from the ship that captured her and on the same day. The two ships are forever linked almost in sight of one another on the bottom of Truk Lagoon.

Back in Singapore the sister ships went into the yards for some modifications. The ships had tremendous success in their dual role as raider and sub tender, so even more room was made for submarine torpedoes. This would have devastating consequences for one of the raiders. On top of the superstructure two twin 25-millimeter anti-aircraft guns were installed and the entire ship was repainted in a radical three color dazzle scheme. Finally the old Alf floatplanes were replaced by the bigger, longer ranged and sturdier E13A Jake seaplanes. August 1942 saw the raiders ready for more action, but to the dismay of the crew an unheard of island called Guadalcanal had been invaded by the US Marines and Japanese soldiers were desperately needed in that theatre. So for nearly ten weeks the *Aikoku* left her sister and was attached to the Southwest Area Fleet with the job of hauling soldiers to Rabaul where they would be forwarded to Guadalcanal. This was necessary but mundane duty for the victorious warrior and everyone on board was thrilled when they were reunited with their old comrades on *Hokoku* to resume raiding operations in November.

There was not long to wait before their first quarry was located. Far ahead on the horizon the lookouts sighted another tanker of the Royal Dutch Shell Company, this one being the 6,341 *Ondina*. Another worthy prize indeed! The two raiders picked up speed as the chase began with the *Hokoku* well in the lead when a second column of smoke in front of the *Ondina* was sighted. This belonged to a ship much smaller than the tanker and this one was painted in a striking camouflage scheme with a prominent deck gun on the bow. This was the new corvette *HMIS Bengal* and she quickly turned to engage the raiders. For the first time the *Aikoku* and *Hokoku* had a real battle on their hands and all hands raced to their stations and braced for action. The three warships all steamed towards each other at top speed while the slow tanker tried to get away, the fight was on!

Nambu pistol like those used by the SNLF troops on Aikoku.

AIKOKU MARU   119

With *Hokoku* in the lead the gunfight began at high noon with her 14-centimeter guns targeting the smaller *Bengal* racing towards her. As the shells began to splash around the charging corvette, Captain Horsman sent one last SOS signal before ordering his small 12-pound bow gun into action. Meanwhile on the *Ondina* the captain realized he could never outrun the fast Japanese ships and ordered the crew on the stern deck gun to open fire in support of the *Bengal*. Five minutes into the battle the first hit was achieved when a 14-centimeter shell splintered the mast on the *Ondina*; this caused no real damage but served notice to the gun crew that they were in a fight for their lives. This gun on the tanker was the biggest gun the Allied ships had, being 10.2-centimeter, and it would be critical if they were to survive. The Japanese ships mounted a combined 16 14-centimeter guns, plus torpedoes and heavy machine guns. The Allied ships were massively outgunned, but incredibly brave.

The *Aikoku* was still not in range and the crew could only watch as their friends on *Hokoku* blasted away with all guns at the two enemy vessels. On the *Ondina* the stern gun opened fire using only their eyes and the gun barrel to aim the gun; there was no fire control gear at all. The first shot went wide, but the crew corrected their aim and the second sent up a geyser of water just off the bow. They knew they were close and the aim was slightly corrected before the gun fired again. This time the 10.2-centimeter shell struck the *Hokoku* in the deckhouse, but the big raider kept coming. As the gun crew adjusted their aim yet again the *Hokoku* and *Bengal* continued to hammer away at each other, but neither side was hitting anything as the ships twisted and turned. The *Ondina* continued to fire but her shots were now missing off the stern, but this was soon fixed. The *Ondina* fired off her sixth shot of the battle; which turned out to be one of the luckiest shots of the war.

The Ondina before the war. (Royal Dutch Shell)

The Japanese auxiliary cruisers were well armed and fast, but they were not well armored nor did they have the internal structure and damage control of a true warship. In addition they carried a supply of 70 torpedoes in the stern cargo holds for use in resupplying submarines; this was literally tons of high explosives. The shot from the *Ondina* easily punched through the thin skin of the *Hokoku* and detonated in the torpedo storage area. From the decks of the *Aikoku* the men watched in horror as a huge column of yellow fire shot skyward out of the rear hold followed a second later by a massive explosion that literally blew the stern section of the ship off. The men were literally in shock as they watched the detached stern section sink as the burned and broken remains of the planes fell off the deck into the water. The remainder of the ship was still afloat but fires were burning and she was beginning to settle in the water. While the men on the *Ondina* went wild in celebration at their incredible fortune, the men on *Aikoku* grimly vowed to avenge their stricken sister ship.

Just as the gun crews on *Aikoku* prepared to open fire the *Hokoku* began to list slightly. This list caused ammunition and other torpedoes to break free and roll about and on the burning ship it wasn't long before the ordinance met with the raging flames. This set off another string of explosions that literally blew the side off the ship. With a roar of defiance the captain on *Aikoku* ordered his crews to open fire, and his guns began to blast away with a vengeance. Half the guns on *Aikoku* took aim at the tanker, while the other half targeted the corvette and soon hits were seen blossoming on both. Several rounds hit the *Bengal* in quick succession and her gun ceased firing, seemingly knocked out of action but actually just out of ammunition.

Twin barreled 25-millimeter anti-aircraft gun still pointed towards long gone planes.

The *Bengal* was now left with only a pair of 20-millimeter cannons and depth charges for weapons, but these were useless in this battle. The only thing the ship could do was throw up a smokescreen to try and allow the ships to escape. During this time the *Aikoku's* guns were repeatedly finding their mark and both the corvette and tanker were burning. One shot smashed into the bridge of the *Ondina* at which point the *Bengal* gave her up for lost and made a run for the horizon. Unable to catch the speedy little corvette, the *Aikoku* turned her full furry on the *Ondina* closing to under two miles. With the last of her 10.2-centimeter shells expended the *Ondina* was helpless and the second in command ordered the white flag run up in surrender. Captain Horsman had been killed in the hit on the bridge.

Almost at the same time the *Ondina* surrendered a last explosion shook the *Hokoku* and the surviving crew abandoned ship leaving 76 of their shipmates dead including the captain. The sister ship and longtime partner of the *Aikoku* quickly slipped beneath the waves only an hour after the battle had begun. The officers and men on the *Aikoku* seethed with rage as they closed to 400 yards of the *Ondina* and came to a stop. The crew of the *Ondina* had abandoned ship and were in their lifeboats when the *Aikoku* launched a pair of torpedoes into her, hitting the number 1 and 2 fuel holds. The explosions shrouded the ship in smoke and she began to seriously list to starboard, quickly nearing 30 degrees. With the *Ondina* seemingly finished the *Aikoku* moved to rescue the crew of the *Hokoku*, but before they did the rage at seeing their friends and comrades die was too much. As the *Aikoku* moved past the bow of the *Ondina* her anti-aircraft machine guns opened up on the lifeboats.

Hokoku Maru, sister ship to the Aikoku. (OSK)

Japanese were taught never to surrender and the men in the rafts had killed their friends before giving up. No quarter was given as the heavy bullets turned several of the lifeboats into splinters, leaving the water red with the blood of bodies torn to pieces. *Aikoku* moved away from the carnage and rescued 278 of their comrades from the water before leaving the scene. What they would never know is that there were many survivors still alive on the lifeboats and the *Ondina* did not sink. Tankers are hard to sink, especially when empty and hit in the fuel holds. The surviving crew of the *Ondina* climbed back on board and eventually managed to nurse the ship back to Australia!

This was to be the last hurrah of the merchant raiders. Losses, changes in the war and the desperate need for big fast transports spelled the end of an era. The *Aikoku Maru* returned to Singapore and was reunited with her last surviving sister ship, the *Gokoku Maru*, and another former heavily armed raider the *Kiyosumi Maru*. The ships were stripped of their aircraft and the torpedo storage was converted to troop quarters and bulk cargo space. *Aikoku*, *Gokoku* and *Kiyosumi* would now become fast heavily armed transports and assigned to help rush reinforcements to the main area of battle around Rabaul and New Guinea. The three ships would spend the next three months ferrying thousands of troops and tons of equipment from Korea, China and Japan south into the meat grinder.

The first of these big operations was called Hinoe-Go and involved moving two complete infantry divisions, the 20th and 41st, from North China and South Korea to New Guinea. This was a massive undertaking and it involved twelve ships fully loaded with men and equipment. The *Aikoku* would operate with her last sister ship the *Gokoku* and would be carrying the staff and maintenance soldiers for an Army air unit plus anti-aircraft guns and provisions. The second part of this operation took part during the first two weeks of February 1943 and was even bigger than the first. *Aikoku* again operated with *Gokoku* plus the *Kiyosumi*. During this run the three ships would be attacked by the submarine *USS Runner*. All the torpedoes missed the fast transports and the submarine was finally damaged and driven away by a "Rufe" floatplane from nearby Palau. All told this operation brought 11,825 soldiers, 94 heavy vehicles and 85,643 cases of ammunition to New Guinea, a truly amazing achievement!

Spring and early summer 1943 saw the three ships often separated, but each continued performing the mundane duties of bringing troops to the front. *Aikoku* had her routine violently broken on July 10, 1943, just north of Truk when she was hit by a torpedo fired by the *USS Halibut*.

The corvette HMIS Bengal (Royal Navy)

The torpedo hit the ship like a haymaker punch to the jaw, the big ship rocked wildly on her keel and everyone onboard was stunned. The torpedo had hit the number 6 hold and there was flooding that was spreading through the stern areas. The location of the hit was very similar to the lucky shot that had spelled doom for the *Hokoku* and the men could only offer thanks that they were carrying dry cargo and not a hold full of high explosives. Crewmen sealed off the hold and kept the engines going, all while treating 21 of their shipmates who had been wounded in the blast. Being close to Truk the *Aikoku Maru* was able to limp into port for repairs.

Over the course of the next several weeks the *Aikoku* was patched up in Truk Lagoon, but she would need to return to Japan for more substantial work. On August 22, 1943, she rejoined the *Gokoku* and several others ships and returned to the wonderful cool fall weather of Japan. *Aikoku* entered the shipyard on October 6 where she was repaired, given four new twin 25-millimeter anti-aircraft guns and also two 152-millimeter main guns. She was formidably armed, but she would never return to the golden days in the Indian Ocean as she was officially rerated a special transport. Her work was finished on New Year's Eve 1943 and she returned to service.

Her timing seemed fortuitous as the Japanese Navy was planning a major effort to reinforce the Marshall Islands in anticipation of American landings. *Aikoku* embarked the 66th Naval Guard Unit of 629 men along with dynamite, artillery shells, rice and over 1,000 anti-tank mines. She joined the big sub tender *Yasukuni Maru*, fellow former raider *Akagi Maru*, two destroyers and the minelayer *Nasami* in a convoy and left for the Marshalls with a stop in Truk to refuel. The *Aikoku* left Japan for the last time on January 25, 1944.

Engine telegraph.

January 31 would completely change the fate of the convoy. It all started at 2 am when the *USS Trigger* fired six torpedoes into the convoy while on the surface. All missed their intended targets, but one of the misfires went on and hit the minelayer *Nasami* which completely obliterated the small escort vessel. Amidst the chaos and confusion that followed the two destroyers raced to the scene and began depth charging the area, not realizing the submarine was on the surface and making her escape in the darkness. While the convoy steamed on, the *Trigger* raced at high speed on the surface to get ahead of them. At 5 am five more torpedoes were launched at the biggest target on radar, the *Yasukuni Maru*. Two of the torpedoes hit and it was not long before the big ship slipped beneath the waves. She was carrying over 1,200 men; only 43 survived.

The second major event of the day was of much more consequence to the fate of the *Aikoku*. On that day the US Navy launched Operation Flintlock which was the invasion of Kwajalein, Roi-Namur and Majuro in the Marshall Islands. Upon arriving in Truk the *Aikoku* was to await further developments; it was late in the day on February 16, 1944. The crew and soldiers onboard passed a hot night aboard in the balmy equatorial air and were relived in the morning when the rising sun brought a breeze from the east. It also brought hundreds of American planes.

The *Aikoku Maru* was in the 4th Fleet Anchorage when the first waves of planes appeared overhead and she made a very attractive target with her imposing size. The pilots could see the crew scrambling over the decks to man their guns and it wasn't long before long strings of tracer bullets began to crisscross the sky searching for targets.

The shallowest point on Aikoku Maru; the top of the stern mast.

Inside the holds of the *Aikoku* the hundreds of soldiers could only hunker down and nervously await their fate. The first planes to come after the former raider were TBF Avengers armed with 500-pound bombs off the carriers *Intrepid* and *Essex*. These torpedo bombers came in on steep glide attacks and released their bombs at the big stationary target. At about 8:30 am the first bomb struck the *Aikoku* near the officer's galley, but damage seemed minimal. On the decks and superstructure the twin-barreled anti-aircraft guns swung about and took aim at the next plane powering towards them.

This was an Avenger piloted by Lt. J.E. Bridges flying off the *USS Intrepid* with two other crew members on board. The Avenger's aim was true as her bombs hit just forward of the bridge even as the guns on board the *Aikoku* began to find their mark. The bombs penetrated inside the cargo hold full of over a thousand mines and detonated. The first blast was so titanic that is simply vaporized J.E. Bridges's Avenger. A flash of flames shot forward into the first cargo hold and a second later the cargo of dynamite and artillery shells detonated. The near simultaneous twin explosions created an explosion that completely blew the entire front of the *Aikoku Maru* off, the pieces of jagged metal flying high in the air and creating a rain of steel that fell on anything within almost a quarter mile. All this was accompanied by a shockwave that ripped across the entire lagoon and blew out windows and eardrums for over a mile in all directions. Within a minute a huge mushroom cloud was rising over the lagoon and the *Aikoku Maru* was gone. In an instant over 600 men had been killed and within two minutes the remaining stern half of the mighty ship was on the bottom.

The stern half of the *Aikoku Maru* plunged into the depths and came to rest at 240 feet. At this depth the water is a deep cerulean blue that only adds to the sense of darkness and drama that hovers over this wreck. Although *Aikoku* is rarely dived upon as she far beyond recreational limits, there are some parts of the wreck that are worth visiting by the experienced diver. The descent into the deep blue is a long one before divers finally reach the stack and the top of the superstructure at over 140 feet. This is a fascinating area to explore on a short dive. The highlight is the memorial to those who died and the Buddha statue. Around the memorial are a collection of artifacts from inside the wreck including human remains. The other highlight of this area are the two twin anti-aircraft guns that are still pointing in the direction of the attacking planes that sunk the ship so long ago.

Elsewhere on the wreck things get very deep very fast. For experienced divers, exploring the stern is very worthwhile as the big deck gun is still there and almost totally clear of marine life. It still presents a formidable sight that is only enhanced by the darkness and deep blue that surrounds divers. Inside the holds and superstructure is the realm of only the most well-trained and experienced technical divers. The *Aikoku Maru* is a war grave and there are still the remains of many of her crew and passengers entombed within; respect should always be given. This is a very dramatic wreck with an incredible history that if shallower would be perhaps the greatest dive in the lagoon.

The memorial on the superstructure of Aikoku Maru is surrounded by the remains of those who died on her.

Fujikawa Maru

Perhaps the most dived, and certainly the most famous, shipwreck in Truk Lagoon is the *Fujikawa Maru*. At 433 feet long and almost 7,000 tons she is a big ship, but not even close to the largest; yet still she has seen thousands of divers and almost uncountable articles in dive and travel magazines. Her popularity can be attributed to several things: she is upright, shallow, covered in incredible reef life and has cargo holds full of amazing discoveries. In this case the story of the ship while she was in service is far surpassed with the amazing shipwreck she has become today.

The *Fujikawa* was built in Nagasaki by Mitsubishi Heavy Industries and was completed on July 1, 1938. She was designed for the long haul Japan to the United States run and had ample cargo space in addition to stylish accommodations for passengers on the long journeys. Despite all this she never served the route across the North Pacific; instead she sailed between Japan and India with the job of bringing raw Indian silk back to Japan for use in more advanced manufacturing. There was not much time to complete many of these trips as she was taken into naval service an entire year before the war broke out.

On December 9, 1940, the *Fujikawa Maru* was taken into the Imperial Japanese Navy for use as an armed auxiliary aircraft transport. No longer carrying silk, she instead would be full of another very precious cargo: aircraft and all the supplies they would require. In the vast expanses of the Pacific this was a critical function and ten ships were eventually converted to this role. At the time of her conversion two big British-made 5.9-inch guns were installed on deck. These were huge guns for a ship like *Fujikawa* and they dated all the way back to the Russo-Japanese war in 1905. The manufacturers stamp is still visible to this day!

Fujikawa began active service transporting aircraft, spare parts and fuel between Japan and the Japanese bases along the central Chinese coast. These planes would find their way into battle against the American supplied Chinese and the famed Flying Tigers. The start of the bigger war with the United States and Great Britain brought the *Fujikawa Maru* to Malaya, Indochina and Siam.

The Fujikawa Maru while in the service of the Toyo Kauin. (TK Line)

Opposite: *The bow of the Fujikawa Maru viewed from the bottom.*

A6M Zeroes in flight over the Solomon Islands. (Japanese Navy)

She operated behind the invasion forces, bringing planes and parts to newly captured bases spread all across Southeast Asia. The early war months for the *Fujikawa* were a peaceful time and the crew was well satisfied in knowing that they were transporting the finest fighter aircraft in the world for immediate use in combat.

In April 1942 the operations to seize the Dutch East Indies and Malaya were winding down and the focus of the Japanese offensives was shifting towards New Guinea and Australia. To support these operations the *Fujikawa* began operating between the Home Islands and the rapidly expanding bases in the Marianas, Rabaul and the fleet bastion at Truk. Many more peaceful and productive months went by as she transported many badly needed A6M Zero fighters and their parts to the raging cauldron of battle that had engulfed New Guinea and the Solomon Islands. Concern about a US attack into the Marshall and Gilbert Islands saw the *Fujikawa* begin to also service such islands as Tarawa, Kwajalein and Roi-Namur.

The remainder of 1942 and the first five months of 1943 were spent shuttling as many fighters as possible to the forward bases in the Marshalls. It was finally on May 14, 1943, that the *Fujikawa Maru* had her first brush with the Americans, which in this case was an unsuccessful torpedo attack on her convoy by an American submarine near Truk. Most other ships in naval service had become battered and scarred veterans of many battles by this point, but the *Fujikawa Maru* was too valuable to risk in forward operations. She suffered another submarine attack in June while in the company of fellow Truk Lagoon wreck *Amagisan Maru* but this too was unsuccessful.

USS Permit (US Navy)

The *USS Permit* would bring an end to the *Fujikawa's* charmed war on September 12, 1943, while in a convoy near Kwajalein. The submarine sighted the *Fujikawa* and fired three torpedoes at her. One hit near the stern on the port side, ripping open the fifth cargo hold. The peaceful war had ended in a thunderous blast and a torrent of sea water. Upon regaining their bearings, the crew worked desperately to shore up the hole in their ship as the navigator set a course back to Kwajalein for emergency repairs. The *Fujikawa* limped back into the lagoon and the men did what they could in the shelter of the anchorage; but she was in bad shape and not able to get underway. It seems that the old light cruiser *Naka* was dispatched from Truk as a tow, a role she would perform for several of the future wrecks of the Truk Lagoon. It would take several weeks, but the *Fujikawa Maru* was able to return to Japan for major repairs late in the fall of 1943. By the end of the year the *Fujikawa* returned to service and she was promptly loaded with more planes and parts. These were intended to reinforce the now very threatened base at Kwajalein. Arriving back at the site of her near sinking at Kwajalein, the *Fujikawa* began to unload her cargo.

Once again this was not a good place for the *Fujikawa*. The powerful US Navy Taskforce 50 had just finished supporting the invasion of Tarawa and the Gilbert Islands to the south and it was decided that they would strike Japanese forces in the Marshalls on their way back to Pearl Harbor. *Fujikawa Maru* had just pulled into the lagoon when the Task Force passed by and launched their attacks. Planes from the *USS Yorktown*, *Lexington* and the light carrier *Independence* pounced on the shipping gathered inside the atoll. This was a harrowing experience for the men on the *Fujikawa* as they had never been under any type of air attack.

Onboard all they could do was try and get their big unwieldy deck guns in action against the planes zipping across the sky. Mostly all that could be accomplished was to watch the shore-based anti-aircraft guns and the few smaller caliber machine guns on the anchored ships open fire as dozens of dive bombers, torpedo bombers and fighters attacked. Explosions echoed across the anchorage and total chaos reigned as ships began to be torn apart and sunk. In the end it was only a small preview of what was to come in Truk Lagoon two months later.

Cockpit of an A6M inside the Fujikawa Maru.

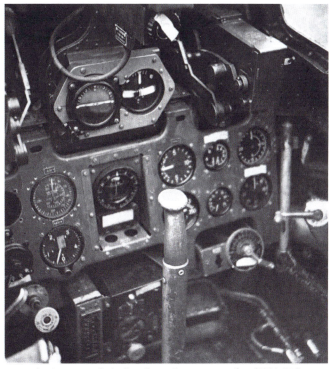

An intact cockpit shot from the same angle. (USAAF)

FUJIKAWA MARU

The *Fujikawa* drew the attention of TBF Avenger torpedo bombers armed with big 1,000-pound bombs. Two of the big bombs hit just off the stern and the underwater shockwave blasted into the hull and knocked loose hull plates and heavy machinery in the engineering areas. The leaks were easily patched and the ship appeared to not be in any danger of sinking but she could not operate under her own power.

The crew knew they had been very lucky as the attackers disappeared over the horizon back to their carriers. Looking across the lagoon they were treated to the sight of six other ships torn, blackened and burning but still afloat. Four other ships were nowhere in sight, the only evidence of them being debris and oil slicks intermixed with bodies floating in the fouled water. Kwajalein was no longer a safe harbor and the surviving ships hastened to escape. The convoy limped away to the west with *Fujikawa* having to be towed by other vessels. Once again *Fujikawa* would be towed from Kwajalein back to Truk and then ultimately back to Japan for further repairs.

By the beginning of February 1944 the *Fujikawa Maru* was again fit for service and she was loaded with a big shipment of B6N Jill torpedo bombers plus several A6M Zero fighters and oddly some old and obsolete A5M Claude fighters. With this deadly cargo stowed, along with a variety of engines and spare parts, the ship departed in a massive convoy of 16 ships bound for Formosa and then she would proceed on to Truk. This convoy was only lightly escorted and they were pounced on by the submarine *USS Snook*. It is noteworthy because the single ship sunk was the massive transport *Lima Maru* carrying 3,241 men. Of these 2,765 would die in the frigid winter waters. It was one of the most deadly single ship loses for Japan, almost equal to the number who died on the *Titanic* and *Lusitania* combined.

The *Fujikawa* completed her voyage without incident, but somewhat shaken by the experience. Upon arrival the ship anchored very close to the primary airfield on Eten Island and the long process of unloading the aircraft began.

The magnificent binnacle recovered from the Fujikawa Maru.

130   FOURTH FLEET ANCHORAGE   *Opposite: The lifeboat davits are not to be missed.*

Cockpit of A6M Zero inside hold. (top) *The Fujikawa is a spectacular reef today. (bottom)*

A5M Claude, there is at least one of these obsolete planes in the hold with the Zeroes. (Japanese Navy)

First off were the 30 Jill bombers in the stern cargo holds which were offloaded and lined up on the tarmac awaiting final assembly. Aircraft were not shipped in a condition where they could be immediately flown; they usually had their engines and wings removed for ease of transport and to save space. Attention turned towards the forward holds containing the Zeros and Claudes on the morning of February 17, 1944.

The fighters would never get off the ship. Just after dawn the air filled with American aircraft and the crew just beginning work on the *Fujikawa Maru* was filled with a terrible sense of déjà vu. This time though there were hundreds of planes attacking and the volume of noise and destruction was many magnitudes greater than it had been in Kwajalein. Over the course of the morning the battle raged all around the *Fujikawa* but she did not come under direct attack until 1:24 in the afternoon when the third wave of American planes arrived and commenced their attack. Torpedo bombers from the *USS Bunker Hill* and *Monterey* took aim on the aircraft transport anchored close in to the airfield on Eten Island while the men on board swung the two big 5.9-inch guns into action.

The big old guns were swiveled to starboard and pointed in the direction of the incoming planes. When the guns opened fire they rocked the ship to port with their recoil. The crews were frantic and new shells where slammed into the breech, while the spent casings fell into the cargo hold. Wham! The guns fired again and again, but to no avail as these guns were designed to hit slow moving targets and had been made long before when the Wright brothers were still making bicycles. Two of the big Avengers roared towards them and dropped their torpedoes, one malfunctioned and ran wild striking the reef near Eten. The second seemed to also malfunction when it stopped running short of the target, but it had enough momentum to hit the starboard side of the *Fujikawa* almost dead center. The torpedo may have been travelling slowly, but the explosive force was enough to punch a triangular hole in the ship that caused the steel hull to twist like melted plastic. Onboard the ship rolled to port and then settled again as water began to pour through the relatively small gash.

Fujikawa Maru slowly sinking at left. (US Navy)

Shell casings from the big 5.9-inch deck guns.

What the exact sequence of events that led to the eventual sinking of the *Fujikawa Maru* are remains a mystery. The most common story is that the torpedo hole caused the ship to slowly flood and sink, while other sources say the ship was attacked several more times and then sunk. Damage on the ship points to the single torpedo being the likely culprit, but there is the potential for other hits to have occurred in the superstructure area which has collapsed over time. What is known is that the crew of *Fujikawa Maru* abandoned the ship; which then slowly settled in the water and came to rest on the relatively shallow bottom almost perfectly upright. The ship sank in a slow dignified manner taking none of her crew down with her.

The wreck of the *Fujikawa Maru* is first and foremost an amazing reef. The entire outside of the ship is covered in marine life and often large schools of jacks and barracudas can be seen circling in the open blue off the stern, while the areas on top of the collapsing superstructure are draped with some of the most amazing colored soft corals anywhere on Earth. Overall the ship is intact from the deck down, but the superstructure is in the process of collapsing. The *Fujikawa* is fairly shallow and this means that when storms have passed through over the years they have hit her harder than the deeper wrecks.

The wreck is shallow by Truk Lagoon standards with the deck being at 60 feet and this makes her accessible to all divers of every skill level. Starting at the stern the deck house provides in interesting small penetration being full of interesting artifacts while the outer hull area is peppered with holes that create fantastic patterns of light. On top of this area is one of the huge 5.9-inch deck guns, still pointing to starboard and forward which is very likely the direction the torpedo planes that sunk her were coming from. Heading into the stern cargo holds there is a very interesting air compressor in the tween decks area. Historically speaking the fourth hold, which is the furthest forward, is the most interesting as it has the torpedo hole and a lot of visible damage. The bent and twisted metal is fascinating and the opening itself is big enough to swim through, but just barely and it is very sandy so care should be exercised.

The midships area is badly decayed, but it is very open with some very interesting swim-through opportunities. In this area there is a small memorial to the ship and to Kimiuo Aisek that is surrounded by interesting artifacts brought up from deeper within the ship. The topside of the superstructure has some of the most spectacular soft corals in the world on the life boat davits, these are not to be missed. Heading forward to the front half of the ship is where the show really starts.

The third hold, which is closest to the bridge area, is not easily accessible and the cargo consists mainly of fuel barrels. It is the second hold that is the star of the show as it had not been unloaded yet when she was sunk. This hold is full of A5M and A6M fighters in various stages of disassembly. These are amazing and unique aircraft to see in a museum and to see them inside a shipwreck is a sight that will remain frozen in any divers mind for the rest of his or her life. The fact that there are A5M Claude fighters in here presents an interesting mystery as these planes had been obsolete even before the war started, so what were they doing being sent to the front lines towards the end of the war? Theories from training aircraft to simple clerical errors are common, but it is also possible that these were to be used as the first kamikazes. Whatever the reason for their being there they are an incredible and unique aircraft to see.

Continuing forward into the first hold the almost surreal display of cargo continues. With careful exploration of this area divers can find aircraft wings, fuel drums, heavy machine guns, gas masks and vast variety of other miscellaneous cargo. The many spent shell casing for the 5.9-inch deck gun above tell a vivid story of the battle and are a moment frozen in time. Heading up to the gun it is also still pointed towards the incoming planes from long ago, forever locked in the moment when the attack occurred. What is most incredible is the manufacturers mark showing the guns serial number, size, foundry and date of manufacture. This gun was made in England in 1899, but ended up on a Japanese ship sunk in the central Pacific almost 50 years later. Simply incredible. At the end of dives the masts and kingposts are well worth exploring during a safety stop as the number of colorful fish on them will put any aquarium to shame. Despite slowly crumbling, the *Fujikawa Maru* is still one of the top ten wreck dives in the world for the recreational diver.

Looking down the barrel of the bow deck gun.

Fujisan Maru

At almost 10,000 tons and 490 feet long the *Fujisan Maru* was a big tanker, but also something of an anomaly. She only had a single propeller, which would normally indicate a much slower speed more in line with the *Hoyo Maru*, but she was fast with a cruise speed of 16 knots. Not quite fast enough to make her a good candidate for an underway replenishment ship like the *Shinkoku*, but she still had the speed and size to operate on the front lines. Her story begins on May 31, 1931, when she was launched and named the *Fujisan Maru* in honor of the legendary Mount Fuji that looms over Tokyo.

In 1931 the *Fujisan Maru* began a long stretch of years where she joined most of the Japanese tanker fleet in hauling oil from the California coast across the North Pacific Ocean and back to Japan. With her speed it would only take the *Fujisan* two weeks to make the crossing each way, which made her a very familiar sight to those in the Los Angeles area. In the ten years between 1931 and 1941 the *Fujisan* made 100 round trips between the two future enemies! What people in California did not realize is that the vast majority of the oil that was pumped and loaded was shipped back to Japan for use by the Imperial Japanese Navy. The ships that attacked Pearl Harbor would be running on fuel supplied by the United States.

While most of the Japanese merchant fleet suddenly stopped appearing in August 1941, the tankers like the *Fujisan* kept operating until the very last minute as every last drop of oil was going to be crucial. It wasn't until late November 1941 that the *Fujisan* departed the West Coast for the last time and returned to Japan to be taken into Navy service. She began her conversion to a Converted Merchant Transport on December 2, 1941, and the war would be two weeks old before she was finished and ready for service. Gone was the civilian paint scheme of the Iino Shoji's tanker fleet, replaced by Navy gray with two menacing 12-centimeter guns and two 25-millimeter anti-aircraft guns added for good measure.

The first five months of her service were spent supporting the operations to seize the critical oil fields in the Dutch East Indies. She spent most of her time refueling submarines that were hunting American, Dutch and Australian warships. With operations in that theatre winding down her ability to haul oil a long way at high speed was going to be needed in some very familiar waters. It felt like returning home to the crew when the *Fujisan* returned to the frigid waters of the North Pacific in June 1942.

Operation AL was the seizure of the islands of Kiska and Attu in the Aleutian Island chain of Alaska. While the operation was designed as a diversion for the invasion of Midway, it would still draw both sides into battles in some of the most forbidding terrain in the world. On June 7, 1942, both Kiska and Attu were secured and the *Fujisan* moved into position to refuel the invasion fleet.

Fujisan Maru before the war. (Iino Kaiun)

Opposite: Looking up from the bridge towards the sun far above.

The bane of the Fujisan, American B-24 Liberators. (US Army Airforce)

For two weeks the *Fujisan* moved between different groups of Japanese ships to refuel them in anticipation of imminent battle against American forces. The Americans that first appeared were not the Navy, but long range four-engine bombers of the 11th Air Force. The planes that began to appear whenever there was a gap in the weather were a mix of LB-30 and B-24 Liberators plus early model B-17 Flying Fortresses.

At first light on July 3 the Fujisan was conducting refueling operations for a flotilla of six destroyers in the MacDonald Bay anchorage along with two other support ships. The three big ships stood out as prime targets for a flight of seven B-24's tasked with bombing the anchorage. Action stations was called on all the ships in the bay and the guns were cleared for battle. On the *Fujisan* the big 12-centimeter guns were all that could reach the high flying bombers and they had almost no chance of actually hitting one. This turned gunners into spectators as seven strings of bombs grew bigger and bigger before finally churning the cold ocean into a raging storm. Geysers of water erupted into the air and completely soaked the men on deck. Shrapnel rattled off seemingly every surface. Damage was minor and nobody was killed but the message was firmly received. It was time to get such a valuable ship out of range of land-based bombers, so the *Fujisan* returned to Japan.

August 1942 was the great turning point in the war where Japan was finally placed firmly on the defensive with the invasion of Guadalcanal. This invasion would impact the future of almost every ship in the Japanese arsenal. For the *Fujisan* it would pull her from the familiar North Pacific and bring her to new places in the hot steaming jungles with names like Rabaul and Shortlands. In her new operational area *Fujisan* was assigned as a forward refueling vessel at the closest substantial Japanese anchorage to Guadalcanal, which was the Shortlands. This placed her at the top of the legendary channel that ran straight through the Solomon Islands known as "The Slot", at the other end was the new American airfield at Guadalcanal. This stretch of azure water and gleaming chain of emerald islands was an illusion that masked a savage battlefield in the air, sea and in the dank jungles that would decide the fate of the war.

Simple glasses provide a glimpse of daily life.

Over the course of the next several months the *Fujisan* would bear witness to a constant parade of Japanese warships coming and going from the battle area known as "Ironbottom Sound". As the months wore on these ships would become ever more battered when they returned often full of starved walking skeletons they had saved from what they now called Starvation Island. Many ships never returned at all. What did come were American heavy bombers escorted by twin engine P-38 Lightning fighters flying from the ever improving airfields on Guadalcanal. On December 10, 1942, eleven B-17's escorted by eight P-38's of the 339th Fighter Squadron arrived to attack shipping in the anchorage areas. A fierce aerial battle ensued and a number of Japanese fighters rode a streak of flame and smoke as they fell from the sky. On the *Fujisan* men gripped the railings and watched in fear and fascination as all the bombers seemed to line up on them, which they likely did as she was a huge and valuable target. Nearly a hundred 500-pound bombs fell from the bomb bays in neat lines; this was just like the attack in Attu all over again. This time though there was more than some bent railings and shrapnel damage.

One of the sticks of bombs came straight down and straddled the stern of the *Fujisan* and with a giant flash and steel-shattering bang one of the bombs plunged into the stern structure and exploded in her engine room. In a single horrible instant of incredible heat and bone crushing force thirty of the crew were killed and the diesel engines were wrecked. As the bombers turned a lazy "U" in the sky and flew home they left the *Fujisan* with her stern burning ferociously. It would take all the efforts of the remaining crew, plus those of the minelayer *Tsugaru*, to extinguish the raging flames. In a way the *Fujisan* was lucky as she was full of oil at the time and if this cargo had started to burn she almost surely would have gone down. For days afterwards the survivors pumped the fuel into another tanker while engineers made her seaworthy for the short trip back to Rabaul.

The *Fujisan* would survive those perilous days in the Shortlands and return to Rabaul for more emergency repairs on December 22, 1942. Once there all efforts would be made to get the priceless tanker ready to return to Japan for permanent repairs and overhaul. She would finally limp into the dry dock at Yokohama on January 19, 1943. The exhausted crew and battered ship got a well-deserved break. It would take almost four months to repair the damage to the engines and to fill out the crew, but in the end the *Fujisan* put to sea again and returned to the southern seas on May 10. At this point in the war the surviving fast tankers were too valuable to risk in forward bases so they were put to use bringing oil from the

Sake serving sets.

FUJISAN MARU 139

Fujisan desperately pulling away from the dock during the attacks of February 17, 1944. (US Navy)

Dutch East Indies to the major fleet bases like Palau, Truk and occasionally a fast run into Rabaul.

For nine months the *Fujisan* would work these routes hauling the lifeblood of the Imperial Navy, usually under heavy escort and often in the company of fellow Truk Lagoon wreck *Shinkoku Maru*. The speed of ships like *Fujisan* and *Shinkoku* allowed them to move huge amounts of fuel quickly and it also made them more difficult targets for submarines. The crew was happy to perform these duties far from American bombers as the memories of the past two bombings and the many fallen friends was still fresh in their minds. They were also very lucky never to feel the sting of a torpedo, which made them part of a very small number of Japanese ships in this club. The long months of fuel convoys came to an end when *Fujisan* entered Truk Lagoon for the last time on February 14, 1944, in the company of the *Shinkoku Maru*.

The *Fujisan* arrived in Truk and soon pulled alongside the fuel dock on Dublon Island where the long process of pumping out her holds into the big storage tanks onshore began. She was still at the fueling dock on the morning of February 17 when all hell exploded over the tranquil lagoon. As the attacks began the men on board opened fire with their 25-millimeter guns when planes got too close in a desperate attempt to buy their comrades time to shut off the valves and get away from the dock.

Lantern with intact glass.

140   FOURTH FLEET ANCHORAGE

Captain Watanbe's men succeeded in getting the nearly empty tanker free from the dock and underway as planes roared overhead and ships began to explode and burn all around him. The plan was that the *Fujisan* was fast and nearly empty so she should take her chances in trying to escape. Full speed was ordered and the *Fujisan* raced towards the North Pass and safety.

Outside the North Pass safety was an illusion as a strong American surface force lurked. This was a massively powerful collection of ships called Taskforce 50.9 that included two new battleships, four heavy cruisers and four destroyers. Two things stopped her from proceeding and attempting her escape. First was the sound and smoke of a sharp surface battle raging to the north, the second was SBD Dauntless dive bombers off the *USS Bunker Hill*. The dive bombers pounced on this incredible target and soon 1,000-pound bombs began to throw huge columns of water into the air around the ship. The *Fujisan* tried vainly to throw off their aim by desperate maneuvers and fire from the few guns onboard. None of this was enough to stop one of the big bombs from striking the ship and igniting a large fire. In defeat the big tanker turned about and headed back towards the raging battle in the center of the lagoon. Her only hope lay in the protection offered by land based anti-aircraft guns.

The *Fujisan* survived the first day and either stopped or slowly made her way back to the south. That night priority was given to getting the fire onboard under control, and by dawn the fire was out and the ship underway between Moen and Dublon islands. More SBD's from the *USS Enterprise* found her there just as the sun was coming over the horizon.

The skeletal remains of the bridge area.

FUJISAN MARU

Once more she was subjected to a torrent of 1,000-pound bombs. Two huge explosions hit just off the stern of the ship and literally lifted the back half of the ship out of the water they were so strong. With a huge lurch the massive ship lifted up and then slammed back down, the bow got pushed down far enough that there was actually flooding forward. Men on board were thrown violently into the bulkheads and power flickered in the dark engineering spaces. Just as the ship settled a third bomb smashed into the storage area for depth charges on the stern. This had the dual effect of killing four men on deck and setting off a massive fire in the stern structure. For the survivors of the attack in the Shortlands this was like living that horrible day all over again.

The *Fujisan* began to burn furiously at the stern and she ground to a halt. Men scrambled to fight the fire only to realize that the ship was taking on water from damage to the hull caused by the near misses. It was a hopeless situation as the great tanker foundered and burned. Finally Captain Watanabe ordered "abandon ship" and the men reluctantly scrambled into the lifeboats. The stern of the massive ship went down first and struck the bottom, while the bow still stuck up from the surface like a giant tombstone. It would take some time for the bow section to lose buoyancy and sink to the bottom at 200 feet with a severe 45 degree list to port.

Today the *Fujisan Maru* is one of the deeper wrecks in Truk Lagoon and she sits off by herself away from the other wrecks in the 4th Fleet Anchorage. With the depth of the bottom at 200 feet this places her deck at 150 feet, beyond the range of most divers. Luckily the most interesting part of the wreck is her bridge and central superstructure, which is around 130 feet. The entire area is intact and the view of the ship heading into the darkness towards the bow and stern is both eerie and amazing.

The bridge area is very skeletal as the wood decking has long since rotted away, but what remains begs to be explored. Inside there are many fascinating things to find including sinks, toilets and engine telegraphs. The area has a number of colorful sponges, but overall she is not heavily encrusted with marine life. This gives the whole wreck a very clean look as opposed to some of the shallower wrecks. This deep the light is darker and a deep blue color that just accentuates the mystery and drama of the ship. Exploration of the bow and stern areas is very deep and there is little to see, especially towards the stern where the bomb and fire damage is very severe. The *Fujisan Maru* is still a big and intimidating wreck and her location gives the diver a very isolated and lonely feeling while ascending from her rusting decks.

Sinks inside the superstructure.

142   FOURTH FLEET ANCHORAGE

A lifeboat davit makes for a perfect deep reef.

HOKI MARU

The story of the *Hoki Maru* is not a Japanese story, or at least not until the very end. The *Hoki Maru* served most of her time and had her most famous moments as the *MV Hauraki* while serving with the Union Steamship Company of New Zealand. The *Hauraki* was built in Scotland in 1922 for use on the Trans-Pacific route from Sydney, Australia, to Vancouver, Canada. She was the first diesel powered vessel in service for the company and she would primarily haul cargo, but she could carry a dozen passengers. At 450 feet long and 7,113 tons she was a big ship with two strong engines. During the 1920's and 1930's the *Hauraki* worked this route constantly at her cruising speed of 12 knots.

Her most famous voyage came in 1936 when she loaded the first Douglas DC2 passenger plane on her decks. This plane was very similar in appearance to the famous DC3 that would become probably the greatest passenger/cargo plane of all time. This first DC2 was bought by Holman Airways for use carrying passengers and mail across the vast distances of the continent. For Australia this was a proud moment in their civil aviation growth and it reflected well on the *Hauraki* that she was chosen to carry this first aircraft to her new home. Things almost went badly when the ship encountered strong storms in the South Pacific and the crew thought for a while that they were going to have to cut their deck cargo loose. In the end the ship and plane made it safely to Australia and into the history books.

The *Hauraki* spent the next several years on her regular runs, but the beginning of the war in Europe in September 1939 would end these forever. Great Britain had declared war on Germany and this would draw in all her colonial possessions which included Australia and New Zealand. There was now a great need to get ANZAC soldiers across the Indian Ocean and into the fight against the Germans and then to keep them supplied. Towards this end the *Hauraki* was requisitioned by the British War Ministry in 1940, just as Italy entered the war and the fighting spread to North Africa. The *Hauraki* began making regular runs from Fremantle across the Indian Ocean to Egypt and Palestine bringing troops and their supplies to fight the Axis powers as they attempted to seize the Suez Canal.

Hauraki would make many trips across the Indian Ocean carrying thousands of tons of war supplies to the men fighting Rommel and by July 1942 the tide in North Africa had turned. *Hauraki* had been a cog in the great machine that had brought about impending Allied triumph in North Africa. On July 4, 1942, she left Fremantle on yet another cargo mission, but things had changed in the Indian Ocean. The Imperial Japanese Navy had joined the war and they were going hunting.

Before she was the Hoki; the MV Hauraki. (Union Steamship Co.)

Opposite: The towering stern mast of the Hoki Maru.

Two of these hunters were the *Aikoku* and *Hokoku Maru* and they would find the *Hauraki* eight days out of Fremantle headed for Colombo. At 10pm on the night of July 12 a sudden commotion broke out on the ship and men who looked outside noticed that the ship was brilliantly lit up by searchlights from big ships off either quarter. Two loud booms echoed across the waves followed by a sound that was reminiscent of ripping canvas as two warning shots flew across the bow. These were followed by a message via signal lamp ordering the ship to stop and cease all radio traffic.

Being unarmed the Captain ordered the ship to follow the orders and the big ship slowly ground to a halt. In the engine rooms the crew waited nervously for orders or any news of what was going on topside and finally one of the junior ratings went to see what was afoot. He returned minutes later with Japanese marines behind him with pistols ready and festooned with grenades. It was like something out of a Blackbeard story as the men were rounded up and brought on deck. Everything remained calm and orderly as the Japanese secured the ship and then ordered the crew to return to their stations and get the ship underway for Penang.

At around midnight the ship was in Japanese control, but still crewed by the Australians and New Zealanders. The change of ownership was driven home when the ship's clock was reset from Greenwich Time to Tokyo Standard Time.

Trucks in the cargo hold lit up from within.

Ashrtrays of various types.

Hoki Maru in wartime service. (Australian War Memorial)

Knife, bayonet and sword; boarding weapons of the SNLF.

It would take an amazing nine days to reach nearby Penang, during which the *Hauraki* had to stop ten times. The crew was deliberately dragging their feet and causing minor mechanical issues to give their Navy a chance to find them. At night men would drop lifejackets and notes inside bottles over the side with the ships heading and destination in the hopes one of these would be found. In addition the 2nd Officer pretended to get very drunk and was promptly ignored by the Japanese marines, after which he snuck into the second hold and retrieved twelve bags of secret mail. He then hid the mail and slowly dropped it over the side piece by piece for two days to dispose of it.

The crew did an outstanding job of passively resisting and giving the Royal Navy a chance to find them, but they never found the messages strewn across the Indian Ocean. Finally they arrived in Penang on July 22 and the officers were taken ashore and questioned before returning to the ship. In Singapore the crew of the *Hauraki* was broken up with only the engineering crewman remaining aboard, while the rest went into the infamous prison camps at Changi. Overall the Japanese Marines and their officers from the *Aikoku* had treated the crew very well, but unfortunately things would begin to change when an Army police unit took over in Singapore prior to an ultimate journey to Japan.

The men remaining onboard began to do everything in their power to sabotage the operation of the ship. They covertly dumped spare parts over the side and leaked oil whenever possible. They appeared to be a very sloppy and disorganized mess, but in reality is was a systemic and methodical job of trying to ruin their own engines.

Despite increasing frustration on the part of the Japanese, which lead to increasing harsh treatment, the men continued their work. Amazingly the men were so successful that the *Hauraki* wouldn't arrive in Japan until Christmas 1942. Their arrival in Japan meant the game was up and the men were taken into frigid prison camps in Japan where they would endure the rest of the war in brutal misery.

The *Hauraki* was taken into the Mitsubishi Dockyard in Yokohama where she had the damage done to her engines repaired as well as other modifications made. The crew had been incredibly successful sabotaging the engines as it would take all of 1943 to get the ship seaworthy again. When she emerged from the yards in early 1944 she was no longer the *MV Hauraki*, she was now the *Hoki Maru* in service of the Imperial Japanese Navy. After over twenty years serving the union jack flag the *Hoki* would spend little more than two months serving the rising sun.

The *Hoki Maru* had a much less interesting story than the *Hauraki*. During her short service she hauled mostly construction materials and equipment to the Japanese bases in the Caroline Islands. These bases, like Truk, were all desperately in need of things like cement, steel rebar and trucks so that they could construct bunkers and other defensive positions from which to fight the imminent American invasions. It is not clear if she ever made more than one trip in Japanese service and there are no records of her ever being attacked or damaged by US aircraft or submarines. Ironically it was only the Japanese themselves who had fired on her.

The *Hoki Maru* entered Truk Lagoon in the second week of February 1944 with a cargo full of construction materials, equipment and fuel. On the morning of February 17, 1944, she was still fully loaded and awaiting her turn to unload when the US Navy swept across the sky. The first wave of the fighter sweep had barely finished when the hordes of bombers showed up and a number of bomb-armed TBF Avengers from the *USS Essex* struck first. At least one 500-pound bomb struck her amidships and fires broke out in this area. On board damage control parties battled the flames just as another group of Avengers came in at mast top height armed with bombs. These were from the *USS Yorktown*, while another group armed with torpedoes came from the *USS Bunker Hill*. It is not entirely clear whether it was a torpedo, bombs or both that tore apart the *Hoki Maru* in these afternoon attacks.

Whichever planes it was, the *Hoki Maru* was an inferno as flames got into the gasoline storage drums in the forward cargo holds. The damage from the fire twisted and blackened the metal of the ship, yet she still managed to stay afloat.

Sea fan on the aft kingpost.

148   FOURTH FLEET ANCHORAGE

Ship's bell for the MV Hauraki.

Simple pottery dishes.

HOKI MARU

Inside one of the trucks in the hold.

The next morning during the second strike of the day SB2C Helldivers from the *Bunker Hill* attacked the severely damaged, but still floating *Hoki*. Three of the big "Beasts" winged over on the ship and dropped their big 1,000-pound bombs, two of which struck her amidships and forward. These heavy bombs were too much for the battered ship and a tremendous explosion enveloped the entire front half of the ship as the fuel there finally exploded. Before the smoke cloud cleared away the former pride of New Zealand had disappeared beneath the waves taking with her a treasure of amazing cargo.

The first views divers get of the *Hoki Maru* don't appear to be all that great as the ship suffered massive damage. Except for the bow and forecastle the entire forward and midships areas is a total mess of utter destruction and does not really present anything of interest to the diver. Even the stern area is badly damaged, which leaves only two stern cargo holds and a single mast as her main features, but these remaining areas deliver some of the most unique cargo and sights in the lagoon. Divers usually head straight for the aft cargo holds and these begin at just over 100 feet deep, with depths deeper in the holds being between 140 and 145 feet.

An inventory of the cargo in these holds would take many pages and something would still surely be left out. The most famous cargo are the three trucks tucked away in the blackness. These trucks are unique in the lagoon as they are still intact, most other trucks have the body rotted away. These trucks are covered in rust and silt, but they still look like they could be made to run with a little work. In this same area there is a huge bulldozer that has crashed down off the steel beams that were supporting it. Before leaving this area be sure to check out what appears to be a John Deere tractor tucked over towards the starboard side.

Elsewhere in the holds there are tons of miscellaneous machinery. Everything from air compressors, to more tractors and trucks to radial aircraft engines are strewn about. Also be sure to see the still neatly stacked fuel drums, as these are what ultimately caused her to explode and sink. Leaving the cargo holds divers often face a long ascent to the surface and the *Hoki Maru* provides some excellent entertainment for the journey back up. The stern mast is still sticking straight up almost 70 feet above the deck. The mast is home to a massive amount of marine life and swarms with big schools of fish of all sizes. All this turns what is normally the most tedious and boring part of a dive into an experience to be remembered. The *Hoki Maru* is not a common dive, but it is well worth exploring the amazing story of this vessel and the cargo in her holds given the chance.

Divers explore the reef growing on the incredibly tall mast.

Engine cowling and propeller spinner for an A6M Zero.

Airplane propellers and beer bottles in the hold.

KIKUKAWA MARU

The *Kikukawa Maru* bears the distinction of being the first of the famous wrecks in Truk Lagoon to sink, but her sinking had nothing to do with Operation Hailstone nor was she ever even damaged in combat. Other than her unique place in Truk Lagoon history she is the epitome of the generic cargo ship. At 384 feet long and 3,833 tons she was a completely average sized mixed-use cargo ship. She was built in 1936 for the Kawasaki Kisen K.K. for service on the Japan to East Africa route. Like many of the K line routes this was a combined cargo and passenger service, but she only serviced this route for a single year.

Kikukawa Maru prewar. (Kawasaki Kisen)

The *Kikukawa* was taken into Imperial Japanese Army service in August of 1937 and given the designation Number 188. The *Kikukawa* joined a number of other ships taken into service that year supporting the Imperial Army's war in China as that conflict began to rage out of control. Her most noteworthy contribution was to carry a company of the 5th Tank Battalion and to land them during invasion of Shanghai. This was one of the very first Japanese amphibious operations and it is noteworthy that *Kikukawa* took an active role.

Following the Shanghai operation the *Kikukawa* was released back to her civilian owners. Despite being in her civilian colors, the *Kikukawa* would remain in China the next three years hauling military cargo to support the war raging there. This was easy duty and the ship never faced any real threats. In March of 1941 she would return to military service, this time with the Imperial Japanese Navy. During the months leading up to the start of the Pacific War the *Kikukawa* would shuttle almost nonstop between Japan and bases around Formosa that were being used as spring boards for the coming attacks to the south.

With the outbreak of the war and the rapid expansion of the Japanese empire most ships followed the front lines as they pushed outwards, but not the *Kikukawa*. She would continue to haul basic war supplies between Japan and China well out of any danger. Her routes were so far away from immediate danger that it wasn't until mid-1942 that she was even armed. There was a growing menace from submarines by that point so it was necessary to put a small 8-centimeter deck gun and a single light machine gun on her. At least submarines would think twice about surface attacks now.

The *Kikukawa* finally got orders to take part in operations in a combat zone in July 1942 and when the men received cold weather gear they knew they were heading to the Aleutians Islands. The *Kikukawa* made a single trip carrying troops and supplies to the newly captured island of Kiska. The trip took several weeks and she wouldn't set out for home until August 6 in wet and soupy weather conditions. As the ship made way through the big swells a loud metallic clang caused everyone onboard to freeze and look about with wide eyes. It took several minutes to figure out they had been torpedoed, but the hit was a dud! The thought of sinking in these frigid waters sharpened the eyes of the lookouts and the *Kikukawa* made it back to Japan without further incident.

Japanese ships unloading while under attack in Simpson Harbor, Rabaul. (US Army Air Corps)

After the Aleutian operation the ship went into port for maintenance and repairs that lasted until the end of September. With the American invasion of Guadalcanal the war had shifted and like so many other ships the *Kikukawa* was drawn towards this battlefield. The constant combat operations in this theatre required vast quantities of ammunition and the *Kikukawa* was tasked with hauling the dangerous cargo. The crew was under no illusions about what would happen to her now if she were torpedoed and strict restrictions were put on any type of open flame.

These ammunition runs to Rabaul went on without letup. In mid-April 1943 the *Kikukawa* was unloading mountains of bullets while American heavy bombers rained bombs around Simpson for two days. They were lucky though and they finished unloading and made their way back to the safety of Truk. These hair-raising ammunition hauling missions took a pause in May and June when the ship went back into port for more repairs. After these pleasant two months *Kikukawa* resumed hauling ammunition and also gasoline. Now though she would be headed to the Marshall Islands to bring supplies for the outposts there that were in imminent danger of invasion.

On her second run to Kwajalein the ship got another scare when the submarine *USS Snapper* attacked north of Truk. Luckily for *Kikukawa* the submarine hit the escort *Mutsure* and sunk her along with 46 of her crew. Upon returning to Japan the *Kikukawa* loaded a full cargo of ammunition, aircraft parts and fuel and on September 21, 1943, she departed Tokyo Bay for the last time. The *Kikukawa* left in Convoy Number 3921 with five other Marus and two costal defense ships as escort. The *USS Gudgeon* knew they were coming and promptly attacked when they came in sight.

Glass lights that somehow survived the explosion.

A decorative metal lamp.

Two torpedoes tore into the port side of the *Taian Maru* and she slowly ground to a halt even as the two escorts tore up the water where the attack had come from with depth charges. The *Gudgeon* did not try to escape by running away, instead she submerged and went under the convoy, firing her two stern tubes at the ships as she made her final escape. Both of these shots hit the unlucky *Taian* from the opposite side as the prior hits; the damage was fatal. There was nothing the men on *Kikukawa* could do as the Taian rolled over and sank taking 60 men, 2867 tons of cargo and 1,400 packages of mail to the bottom.

It was an amazing fact that the *Kikukawa* had never been damaged in any way up to that point in the war. She had endured only two air attacks, one dud torpedo and seen another ship in her convoy sunk only twice. This was incredibly uneventful duty by the standards of the time and the *Kikukawa* seemed a safe ship to serve on. On October 1 she entered Truk Lagoon and anchored just east of Eten Island. Unloading began soon thereafter in the forward holds and continued for the next several days. By the evening of October 7 the forward cargo holds were almost empty and attention was beginning to focus on the fuel in the aft holds.

At some point somebody got careless in the gathering darkness and a small fire started in the forward areas and quickly grew. The alarm was raised in the harbor and a call went out for help as the crew on board was having trouble containing the blaze. The salvage and repair tug *Ojima* responded and tied up alongside the *Kikukawa* to help fight the flames. Due to even more carelessness in how hazardous materials were stowed and transported the fire continued to grow and finally flames flicked into the fourth hold that was full of fuel. In seconds the fuel in both aft holds went up in a single roaring blast that lit up the entire lagoon and blew out windows on shore. The explosion was so strong that it even tore the leaves off trees on Eten and Dublon Islands. The poor *Ojima* was simply obliterated and almost her entire crew was killed instantly in the fireball while several other small craft assisting also simply vanished. On the *Kikukawa* 44 men were killed in the blast, most in the aft half of the ship which had simply ceased to exist. The remaining bow section broke in two just forward of the tangled remains of the bridge and quickly sank. Of the three ships that violently exploded in Truk Lagoon (*Aikoku*, *Kikukawa* and *Sankisan*) the evidence points to this being the biggest and most violent blast.

The remaining bow section of the *Kikukawa* came to rest on a mixed sandy and rock bottom at 110 feet. Only the forward holds remain, there is very little left after the break in the hull. This remaining section is almost completely capsized and it is only being held up by the forward mast which acts like a crutch. Diving the *Kikukawa* is VERY rarely done, but it can be a real treat. It also takes some serious imagination to see through the damage to visualize the ship. It is more like cave diving than wreck diving.

Deep inside the holds of the Kikukawa Maru.

Inside things are very dark with only dim blue light coming from the gap along the bottom/port side that is being held open by the mast. The inner cargo holds are an amazing cavern of twisted and torn metal with incredible artifacts just littered everywhere. No attempt has been made to clean up or create little selections of things for divers to see, everything you see here is as it was in 1943. Looking around reveals everything from engine cowls for A6M Zero fighters to propeller blades to sake bottles and even what appears to be a motorcycle, but is more likely a landing gear assembly for a twin engine aircraft. Poking around the ruins easily occupies an entire dive in the dark, cave-like surroundings.

Exiting the wreck is done by swimming down and out the gap along the port side railing. From the outside the missing stern section is very apparent. Swimming back up along the hull many more objects can be found that spilled out into the sand. Also from here it is clear how the ship is being propped up by the mast. There is some marine life and growth, but this is a dive all about exploring the dark and cavernous interior spaces. Given the chance it is a highly recommended experience.

The mast acting as a crutch preventing the ship from completely rolling over.

A ladder to nowhere in the darkness of the holds.

What appears to be a motorcycle, but is more likely a landing gear assembly. (below)

Pretty reef on the starboard railing with the shadow of the bridge in the background.

Two heavy truck chasis inside the cargo hold.

158   FOURTH FLEET ANCHORAGE

Momokawa Maru

The *Momokawa Maru* was never intended for use in tropical seas and when she was launched in July of 1940 it would have surprised many on hand that she would end her career on the bottom of Truk Lagoon. At 352 feet long and 3,829 tons she was a standard sized medium freighter and of very similar design to *Kikukawa* and *Nippo Maru*. It is interesting that all three of these near identical ships would end up together in a very small area on the bottom of Truk Lagoon. What set *Momokawa* apart from her sisters was that she was designed for use in arctic waters.

Momokawa and her very heavy mast. (Kawasaki Kisen)

While many Japanese ships of this era were built for long range voyages carrying passengers in style, the *Momokawa* was specially built for the far more mundane chore of hauling timber from Siberia back to Japan. To accomplish these voyages the *Momokawa* had to be able to handle water choked with ice for almost half the year and her hull was substantially reinforced accordingly. In addition her cargo of long timber could not fit through the hatches on normal cargo holds, so hers were lengthened and much stronger cranes and handling gear were installed. With these changes the *Momokawa* entered service on the frigid Siberian route for her owners the Kawasaki Kisen K.K. Line.

The timber from Siberia was a critical war material for Japan and the decision was made to leave her in civilian service. In the cold northern waters she was largely safe from American submarines and her only dangerous enemy was the constantly shifting ice floes. She stayed in these waters for almost two years before shipping losses to American submarines required her to enter Navy service. Big cargo ships were desperately needed and in June 1943 the *Momokawa* entered military service with the Imperial Japanese Navy.

The heavy cranes on board were put to immediate use in her first mission that same month. *Momokawa* joined a convoy carrying supplies and equipment for use in the construction of heavy fortifications on Tarawa in the Marshall Islands. *Momokawa* was loaded full of cement and sent into the tropics for the first time. The cement and machinery carried in that convoy was used to make the heavy bunkers and pillboxes that would be responsible for 3,166 casualties amongst the US Marines who attacked the atoll. It is likely the ship made this run hauling cement to the Marshall Islands numerous times between June and November.

In November 1943 the *Momokawa* joined a convoy returning to Japan from Kwajalein that included two other cargo ships, the fleet tanker *Shiretoko* and three light escorts. The addition of the *Shiretoko* was very unusual though as she had been torpedoed in the atoll back in September in the same attack that had badly damaged the *Fujikawa Maru*. A fleet tanker was a prize asset at this point in the war and she needed to be saved, staying in harm's way at Kwajalein was no longer an option. To get this tanker back to Japan the *Momokawa* was ordered to take her under tow.

The tanker Shiretoko; rescued by the Momokawa Maru. (Japanese Navy)

Just after dawn on November 13 the convoy was slowly making their way north when it was sighted by the submarine *USS Scorpion*. This big slow-moving convoy was just the kind of target the submarine was hunting and the prize was the big tanker in the middle. Four torpedoes hissed out of their tubes and streaked through the startled ships, one hitting the *Shiretoko* in the stern on the port side. As the escorts charged towards the scene of the attack and began dropping depth charges, the crew on the *Momokawa* began to frantically signal the *Shiretoko* for a damage report. In this case the reply was good, damage was not severe. This shows once again how incredibly difficult tankers are to sink if they are not hit in the engine room. The crew on the *Shiretoko* simply allowed the empty oil tank to fill and then trimmed the ship slightly to account for slightly increased drag. It meant the *Momokawa* would have to pull a little harder and go a little slower, but the ships could continue on. The convoy dodged the submarine for the next six days before finally arriving in Japan on November 23. The men of the *Momokawa* were given a hero's welcome and given special commendations.

Following her heroic actions in saving the *Shiretoko* the *Momokawa* went back to her regular duties hauling supplies to Kwajalein. She carried everything from basic military stores to coal to sampans to aviation fuel and even secret documents! The trips to Kwajalein were mostly uneventful, which was surprising as the American submarine menace was rapidly growing. On her final voyage she was loaded with airplane parts, trucks, machinery and even a disassembled DC3 transport plane. The DC3 was very interesting cargo as she was one of the Japanese versions of the classic American plane built under license. The Japanese version was code named "Tabby" by the Americans. It speaks well to the utility of the DC3 that it was used by both sides in the Pacific War.

Soft coral growing on the line.

160   FOURTH FLEET ANCHORAGE

The *Momokawa Maru* entered Truk Lagoon with her cargo holds loaded during the second week of February 1944 with the *Kensho Maru* in tow. The convoy had already dropped off cargo in Kwajalein before heading to Truk and it was decided to try and save the *Kensho* by towing her back to Truk for repairs. After dropping off the *Kensho* in the Repair Anchorage, *Momokawa* was sent to the 4th Fleet Anchorage as her cargo of aircraft and aircraft parts was to be unloaded on nearby Eten Island. The ship was still waiting to unload when all hell broke loose on the morning of February 17.

For an entire day planes from the *USS Bunker Hill*, *Essex* and *Yorktown* savaged the ships in the area of the *Momokawa Maru*. The *Momokawa* fought back with everything she had, which mainly consisted of two improvised deck guns on the stern. At some point the *Momokawa* had been fitted with a pair of old Army howitzers (likely French designed 75-millimeter) with their wheels removed and these two guns kept up an almost constant barrage of fire. It is unlikely they hit anything with these old guns designed for use by infantry in a close support role, but the large number of spent shell casings in the stern testify that the crew did put up a heroic fight.

At some point during the chaotic first day two 500-pound bombs hit the *Momokawa*. One appears to have hit near the port side near the deck gun in that area and a second bomb may have hit near the funnel. No specifics are known for sure, but reports are that the *Momokawa* was damaged and had smoke coming out of her at the end of the first day. Over that hellish night the fires were put out and the *Momokawa* prepared to meet the coming day with only a slight list to starboard and largely superficial damage. The morning brought SB2C Helldivers from the *Bunker Hill* looking to finish off any ships in the area off Eten that had survived the night. The *Momokawa* stood out as a perfect target given that she had suffered only minor damage the first day. The big dive bombers went to work on her with their 1,000-pound bombs.

SB2C Helldiver (US National Archives)

An American plane in Japanese colors; the "Tabby"   (Japanese Army)

One of the first bombs hit in the area of the aft cargo holds, likely penetrating into the hold and detonating with massive force. The blast tore apart the bulkheads in the area and the shockwave heavily damaged the hull as secondary explosions began to go off. Seconds later a devastating flash fire gutted the aft cargo holds and smoke boiled into the sky as massive torrents of sea water began to pour in through the shattered hull. The fire and explosion destroyed whatever cargo was in the holds, but the flames never spread as they were quickly doused by the flood of water rushing in. By the time the Helldivers pulled out of their dives the *Momokawa* was finished with her stern resting on the bottom and only her bow poking above the water. It did not take long for the last of the trapped air in the bow to hiss and blow out of her, then she settled on the bottom with a severe list to port. Amazingly only one of her crew was killed in the violent attacks.

The *Momokawa* came to rest almost completely on her port side on a slight slope. The depth of the bottom at the bow is 130 feet and 145 feet at the stern, while the starboard railing is between 80 and 90 feet. This makes the *Momokawa* a candidate for almost any experienced diver to explore, especially given her interesting cargo and fairly minimal damage. Most of the damage on the *Momokawa* is at the stern and the explosion and fire destroyed any interesting cargo in the aft cargo holds. Given this, plus the fact that the stern is a little deeper, means that most exploration of the ship is focused on the superstructure and forward cargo holds. The entire midships area is open to exploration and the bridge area is very interesting.

Exploration of the forward holds reveals some amazing cargo. Most obvious are a couple of trucks that are laying up against the hatches, their bodies have decomposed but the chassis and wheels are all still in place. There is also a huge amount of aviation machinery and even parts of disassembled aircraft. The most impressive of the aircraft is the DC3 "Tabby". Seeing a famous American aircraft in the service of her enemy is very unique, even if piecing her together requires a little bit of imagination. This plane is big even when in pieces. In the other holds there are more aircraft pieces and a number of radial engines. On the outside the *Momokawa* has less marine growth compared to some other wrecks, but this area still teems with big schools of fish of all sorts. Diving the *Momokawa* provides unique opportunities to see a famous aircraft and even the former timber hauler is a sight to see in her own right.

Looking into the engine nacelle and landing gear area of the Tabby.

A glass vase or paper holder.

A ship's lamp with part of the glass remaining.

Nippo Maru

Perhaps the cleanest wreck in Truk Lagoon, the *Nippo Maru* is often vastly underrated and really should rank as one of the top five wreck dives in Chuuk. She sits mostly upright, with only a slight list to port, and her clean modern lines are easily apparent as visibility is usually very good at the site. She is almost identical to the nearby *Kikukawa* and *Momokawa* both in construction and size; being 354 feet long and 3,764 tons. Aside from the amazing intact structure of the ship she is also full of amazing cargo that rightfully draws comparisons to that found on the nearby *San Francisco*. On the other hand the *Nippo Maru* may have had the least glamorous wartime job of any ship, she was a water tanker.

The Nippo Maru   (Okazaki Honten Co.)

Launched in 1936 for the Okazaki Honten Steamship Company and like every other ship of the line she was given a name that started with the letter "N". The *Nippo* was a modern 5 hold cargo ship that also had space to carry passengers in comfort. She is a perfect example of the "normal" Japanese cargo ship that would have been built in the late 1930's leading up to the war. By December 1936 she was finished and ready for civilian service.

Her first year was spent on fairly short haul routes between Japan and Formosa. She made the trip routinely and was a regular visitor to Takao and Kirun out of her home port of Kobe. In 1938 the Imperial Japanese Army required transports to move troops and supplies for the war raging in China, and the *Nippo Maru* fit their needs perfectly. For all of 1938 and into 1939 the *Nippo* carried men and supplies through familiar waters and into battle as Army Transport Number 612. By the time the *Nippo Maru* was released back to her owners she had brought thousands of soldiers to China where over a million Japanese soldiers now fought.

An even bigger war was looming in the Pacific and now it was the Imperial Japanese Navy that needed ships. So after spending 18 months back on her old Japan to Formosa route, the *Nippo Maru* was taken into naval service like so many other ships in August 1941. In her case she was registered as an Auxiliary Water Tanker and several large fresh water tanks were installed in the bottom level of her cargo holds. The ocean is like a giant desert where fresh water is concerned and the *Nippo Maru* would be vital to keeping men and machine alive and running.

The *Nippo* officially began her Navy career in October 1941 right back on the same routes she had always serviced. The next several months would be spent bringing soldiers from Japan to Formosa for use in the invasions of the Philippines and the Dutch East Indies. It was not until May 1942 that the *Nippo Maru* finally left the familiar waters between Japan and Formosa for the central Pacific. Like her sister ships, she received a single light machine gun and a small deck gun at this time. She would spend the rest of 1942 hauling water, men, supplies and armaments to the key bases at Rabaul and Truk.

Opposite: The bridge of the Nippo is perhaps the most photogenic.

A fascinating interlude to these mundane voyages took place in late December 1942 when the *Nippo* would take part in a unique operation while in Truk Lagoon. In September of that year the submarine *I-33* was at anchor off the submarine base on Dublon, in roughly the same spot that the *Heian Maru* is today. While half the crew was ashore on liberty the remaining crew was doing repair work on one of the torpedo tubes when some very poor decisions by the officer in charge (the navigator!) would lead to the submarine rapidly flooding and sinking in under two minutes. The story is very similar to that of the *I-169*. Efforts were made to rescue the trapped crew, but these failed and all aboard eventually suffocated. For two months various efforts were made to raise the submarine but these all failed. On December 19, 1942, the *Nippo Maru* joined the salvage vessel *Mie Maru* in yet another attempt to raise the submarine.

The first attempt was made and the crew gathered on the deck of the *Nippo* watched anxiously as the compressors roared to life and air was pumped into the sunken sub. In a torrent of boiling bubbles the bow of the *I-33* suddenly broke the surface and saw daylight for the first time in three months. The cheers had barely begun when the compressed air blew open the bow hatch with a loud bang and water flooded back in. With a groan the men watched as the submarine again slipped beneath the waves. On December 29 the hatch was resealed and another attempt was made. Again the compressors roared to life, but this time much slower. Finally after many agonizing minutes the bow of the submarine again surfaced, followed soon thereafter by the rest of the ship.

The *Nippo Maru* remained with the stricken submarine as the remains of the crew were removed and during three months of repairs. The *Nippo* hovered watchfully over the submarine she had helped raise and she was finally given the honor of towing the *I-33* back to Japan on March 2, 1943. The journey was slow but uneventful and the ships arrived in Kure on March 16, where the crew of the *Nippo* were given hearty congratulations and commendations. The lowly water tanker had saved a valuable warship!

The massive brass range finder from the Nippo Maru in the Kimiuo Aisek Memorial Museum.

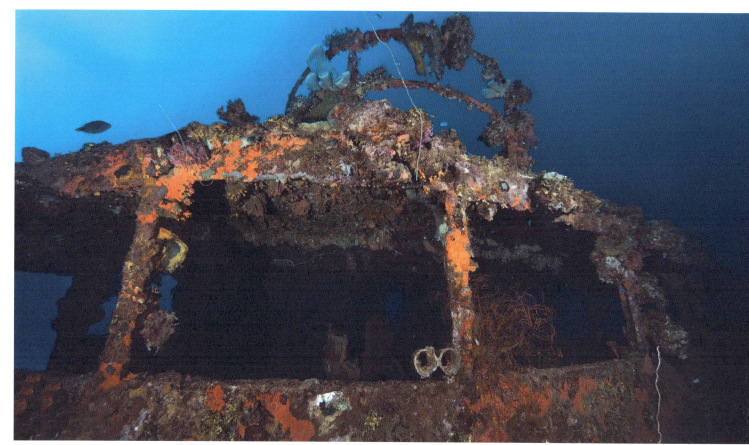
Looking into the bridge of the Nippo as a pair of binoculars stare back.

Following this amazing episode the *Nippo Maru* resumed her routine duties moving men, supplies and water between the various bases in the central Pacific. This duty was not glamorous, but is was critical to the war effort. The Americans were closing in on these bases by late 1943 and every man, bullet and gallon of water supplied could mean the difference between victory and defeat. It was during one of these missions near Ponape that the *Nippo* finally encountered the enemy for the first time while in a small convoy.

At just after midnight on January 26, 1944, the submarine *USS Skipjack* attacked the convoy firing four torpedoes at the ships passing in the night. The night watch on *Nippo* was jolted awake by two towering explosions, but not from their own ship. As they quickly scanned the waters for the submarine they noticed that their primary escort, the destroyer *Susukaze*, had simply vanished taking most of her crew with her. The *Nippo* and the other auxiliary transport *Okitsu Maru* were ordered to make flank speed away from the scene while the small subchaser *CH-33* depth charged the area where the submarine had been.

The *Skipjack* wasn't done. In the darkness she took off on the surface after the fleeing cargo ships, while their escort remained behind in the darkness. Just as the sky began to turn gray with the coming dawn she fired a full spread of torpedoes at the fleeing ships before submerging to make her escape. One of the torpedoes smashed into the *Okitsu Maru* and within 25 minutes she would sink. The crew of the *Nippo* was ordered to continue fleeing at maximum speed and the men could only watch in horror as their 176 comrades were left to drown or perish on the surface.

The *Nippo* would make one more island hopping trip during the first week of February 1944, this time in the company of fellow Truk Lagoon wreck *Yubae Maru*. On February 10 they returned to Truk and they were still there on the morning of February 17, 1944.

Bomb and artillery shell fuses found on the Nippo Maru.

The light tank sitting on the forward deck. Oddly it is missing the main gun.

168   FOURTH FLEET ANCHORAGE

Small wheeled artillery piece on the deck; either an anti-tank gun or howitzer.

It appears that the *Nippo Maru* was preparing to leave Truk with another convoy to supply the more forward islands as she was fully loaded with critical supplies the morning of the attack, yet she had been in port for a week. In the early morning light American fighters streaked overhead and the fierce aerial battle began as they tore into the Japanese defenders who got aloft. The gun crew on *Nippo* barely had a chance to get their twin-barreled gun loaded before the next wave hit.

At just after 8 am bomb-armed TBF Avengers from the *USS Essex* began to attack the shipping lined up in the 4th Fleet Anchorage. The *Nippo Maru* was one of the first ships struck in the attacks of Operation Hailstone, in her case it was a trio of bombs that were very near misses just off the port side. Although these bombs did not directly strike the ship they almost acted as torpedoes as they hit the water and waited a split second before detonating. These subsurface explosions below the waterline caused a massive pressure wave to strike the hull which blew it in, causing the metal to bend inward just like in a torpedo explosion. These impacts violently knocked the ship on her side, which broke loose a lot of the cargo stowed on deck. Water rushed in and the *Nippo* quickly sank. She sank so quickly and so early in the battle that few people even noticed; it was as if she were never there. The nature of the damage and the rapid but orderly sinking meant that no crewman died on her that day. In fact it seems that no crew were ever killed while serving on the ship during the entire war.

The *Nippo* came to rest on the bottom at 170 feet with a slight list to port. Her depth is not so deep that recreational divers cannot reach her, but to really explore her requires experienced deep divers. The *Nippo* is in a position where she can be subjected to occasional currents, which is rare in the lagoon. This means that visibility is also usually very good on the site and the water is often a deep blue. It takes several dives to fully explore this incredible wreck and all the treasures she took with her to the bottom.

For more casual divers the bow section makes for a memorable dive. Descending on the forward deck, divers can quickly make out the sight of a tank sitting just in front of the number 3 hold. Also in this area is a twin barreled anti-aircraft gun that has fallen against the superstructure. Just forward of the tank is a truck partially hanging over the rail, the body has rotted away but the truck is still clearly recognizable. The time on deck will be limited, as the depth is 130 feet but this just means going shallower and exploring the bridge. The bridge of the *Nippo* is perhaps the most lifelike of any wreck in the lagoon with both the helm and engine telegraph still standing ready. Hovering in the bridge just behind the helm, divers can look out over the entire bow area and easily place themselves in the captain's shoes and see what he saw so long ago.

For more technical and experienced divers the cargo holds and engineering spaces are full of fascinating objects to see. Starting in the deepest hold (No. 5) divers can find all the pieces for a shore based anti-ship gun battery. Everything from big 12-centimeter gun barrels to powder and gun bases. Moving into the No. 4 hold there are literally tons of smaller objects to observe such as: radios, medical supplies, china dishware, tires and electrical components. Forward of this hold on deck are three artillery pieces. They have been described as howitzers, but they appear to be 45-millimeter anti-tank guns with splinter shields and wheels. The wheels are in pristine condition and the writing on them is still clearly legible. Heading back down into the ship the engine room and galley are both well worth visiting and divers will pass a constant stream of interesting objects as they move through the darkness.

The first hold forward (No. 3) is basically empty and it appears to have held water tanks that floated away when she sank or have come loose and floated to the surface since then. The No.2 hold has some of these big water tanks still inside on the bottom. Elsewhere in the area are many artillery shells and piles of warheads and bottles. This looks like ammunition for the battery stored in the No. 5 hold. Finally in the No. 1 hold are a large number of detonators for land mines, but most of the mines have been taken for use in dynamite fishing. There is still a very nice assortment of bottles, barrels and even small arms and ammunition. Overall the *Nippo Maru* is an amazing wreck to explore on repeated dives, but she does not have the notoriety of the nearby *San Francisco*. Have no doubt though that this is one of the best wrecks in Truk Lagoon.

Spent shell casings from the Nippo.

The bridge of the Nippo as seen from the forward deck area.

A second anti-tank gun hangs over the cargo hold.

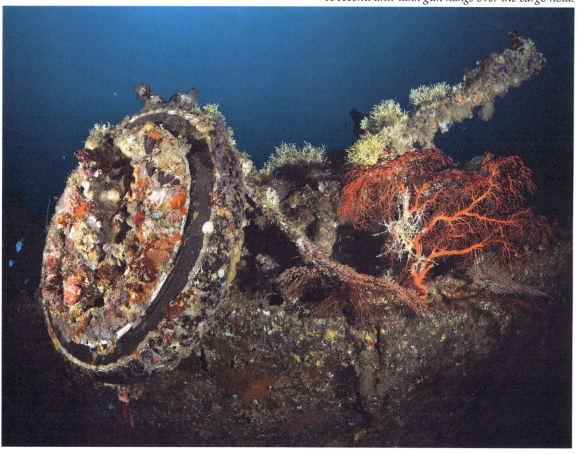

Japanese Type 95 light tank. (Australian War Memorial)

Two Type 95 tanks smashed against each other on deck.

172 FOURTH FLEET ANCHORAGE

San Francisco Maru

The *San Francisco Maru* is one of the older ships in Truk Lagoon and her appearance is very different from the sleek fast ships built in Japan during the 1930's. She is of the Taifuku class of cargo and passenger ships built immediately after the end of World War 1. These 50 ships were the forerunners of the more graceful ships that make up the majority of wrecks in Truk Lagoon. When launched on March 1, 1919, in Kobe, Japan the *San Francisco Maru* was 385 feet long and 5,831 tons. Being coal powered and with only a single propeller she was not especially fast; she was designed to haul bulk cargo over long distances.

San Francisco Maru (US National Archives)

San Francisco Maru entered service on the long haul route between Japan and Western Australia. For three years she steamed between Fremantle and Kobe likely hauling coal and iron ore back to Japan to feed the needs of the industry rapidly growing there. Finally in 1923 the ship was taken out of service temporarily and converted to an oil powered steamship. The age of coal was ending and the age of oil had begun. After conversion she was sold to Kohusai Kisen KK Line and put back in service hauling bulk minerals from the mines in Western Australia back to Japan. All records point to the *San Francisco Maru* serving this route for almost 20 years.

As war grew near the aging *San Francisco* was sold to the Yamashita Kisen KK Line. In 1938 there is some evidence that she was used by the Imperial Army to haul troops and cargo to China. She was getting old, but she could still haul a lot of freight. From this time until she was taken into Imperial Japanese Navy Service it does not appear she was active. The war provided the aging ship a new lease on life and she would render great service to the Empire.

The factories in Japan were desperate for raw materials to turn into planes, guns and ships and most of this had to be shipped in. The mission given to the *San Francisco Maru* was obvious, return to hauling ore back to Japan for smelting and use in manufacture. Obviously the Australia route was no longer an option, so the San Francisco was set to hauling bauxite from the Palau Islands back to Kobe, in addition to coal and phosphate. This was hard and dirty work, but the minerals were in critically short supply. For the first full year of the war *San Francisco* essentially did what she had always done.

Unfortunately for Japan by 1943 the war had begun to go poorly. American submarines were beginning to sink cargo ships at an alarming rate and at the same time ever more tonnage was needed to bring men and supplies to the war of attrition grinding away in the Solomon Islands and New Guinea. The need to reinforce New Guinea finally pulled the *San Francisco*

Ornate traditional pillow in perfect condition.

away from ore carrying duty. In early 1943 the ship was assigned to the convoys that were making repeated runs from Palau to New Guinea carrying thousands of men and tons of equipment. These were dangerous journeys and the ships were subjected to almost constant threat of air attack from ever-increasing numbers of American and Australian planes.

On May 1st, 1943, the *San Francisco* was part of a big convoy of six cargo ships and four escorts that made the run into Wewak on the northern coast of New Guinea. The convoy carried 6,000 men of the 41st Infantry Division and all their ammunition and provisions. On the final run the *San Francisco* and one escort were detached to deliver their men and supplies to the nearby island of Kairiru. This saved her from attack as the convoy was bombed twice that morning as they unloaded. However the air attacks were not successful and the convoy known as Wewak Number 3 was successful in delivering their huge load of men and supplies.

The convoy runs into New Guinea continued to run into more and more resistance and ships were coming back battered and burned, if they even returned at all. This required even more speed from the transports to minimize their time in range of enemy air attack, and speed was not something that the *San Francisco Maru* had a lot of. The critical shortage of minerals for use in the war industry had not gone away and it was decided the old ship would be better used back in her original role of hauling ore. By June 1943 she was back to her old duties.

The fortunes of war would again intervene to put the *San Francisco* in harm's way. By late 1943 it was obvious that the Americans would soon be invading the Marshall Islands and any available ship was needed to haul war material and men to these islands to prepare them for the expected onslaught. *San Francisco* joined these efforts and began to haul things like artillery shells, tanks, mines and ammunition instead of bauxite or coal. These new duties would place her in Truk Lagoon on February 5, 1944, with a convoy carrying supplies to the forward bases. However something went wrong, perhaps mechanical, and the old ship did not leave with the convoy when it departed a week later. This was bad news for the *San Francisco* as being part of that convoy would have saved her, at least for the time being.

Instead the *San Francisco Maru* was at anchor in Truk Lagoon on the morning of February 17, 1944. She was still fully loaded with a huge amount of war supplies when Operation Hailstone exploded over Truk Lagoon. The old ship was not the most lucrative target in the area but she still attracted a constant stream of attackers. She was likely attacked by planes from three different carriers in three different waves on the first day. Not being the most desirable target she never attracted the intense

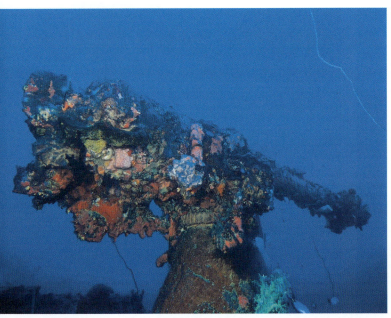

The very clean bow deck gun.

TBF Avenger (US Navy)

attacks directed at big ships like the *Aikoku* or *Shinkoku*, but she was still struck at least once on that terrible first day. As the sun set and the fleet burned the men on the *San Francisco* were battling flames from damage in the midships area caused by a bomb from an unknown attacker.

The morning of the second day the *San Francisco* was still afloat and in fairly good condition. This meant that she caught attention of the first group of bombers of the morning, in this case bomb-armed TBF Avengers from the *USS Essex*. These bombers were each carrying four 500-pound general purpose bombs instead of their usual torpedo. The big planes swarmed with open bomb bays and released their bombs four at a time. One cluster of four bombs hit around the stern causing severe damage both above and below the water line. The ship slammed violently back and forth with the impacts sending cargo crashing all over the place. Barely had she settled when two more 500-pound bombs hit causing serious fires amidships and in the Number 3 cargo hold. The damage to the stern was mortal and the ship was wracked with flames around the superstructure. Luckily for the crew scrambling over the side the flooding in the stern would claim the ship before the flames hit the tons of high explosives on board. The survivors could count themselves lucky, but five of their shipmates had died in the attack.

The *San Francisco Maru* sank in deep water upright and with her cargo almost entirely intact. Diving this wreck requires a lot of experience and to truly see her amazing cargo divers will need technical training. Many experienced recreational divers do explore the wreck, even if only for 12 minutes. Depths here are no joke with the deck being at 155 feet and the bottom being at 210! The average diver will descend on the wreck on the badly damaged superstructure which has seriously deteriorated over time.

Lantern in incredible condition.

SAN FRANCISCO MARU

Japanese beach defense mines. The San Francisco is full of these deadly devices. (US Marine Corps)

Forward of the bridge they will find three Japanese Type 95 Ha-Go light tanks. These are an amazing sight to behold as two of them managed to end up on top of each other when the ship sank. Just forward of the tanks there are the remains of a truck on top of the number two cargo hold. There are more trucks down in the hold and they are well worth a quick peek. Continuing further forward and looking down into the first hold is an amazing scene as it is just jam packed with high explosives. Stacks of beach mines, artillery shells, boxes of cordite and even aircraft bombs are stacked in this hold. On deck just forward is a really photogenic bow gun that has limited amounts of marine life on it. It still really looks like a deck gun and not a coral reef.

It is possible to dive the stern section of the *San Francisco*, but this is rarely done. Depths are still extreme but there is plenty of interesting cargo to find. A short dive on the stern involves dropping straight into the engine room, which is surprisingly open given the appearance of the ship from the outside. From the engine room it is possible to swim into the rear cargo holds where much of the fatal damage to the ship occurred. These holds contain a variety of small arms ammunition as well as torpedoes and depth charges. There is also a lot of damage evident and it seems to get more severe the further aft divers travel. Depths in the holds and engine room will take divers well into the realm of decompression diving with multiple and fairly long stops required. The normal visitor is encouraged to stay on the deck and closely follow their guide and computer if they want to see this deep and incredible wreck.

Well preserved porcelain dishes with clearly visible scenes from long ago.

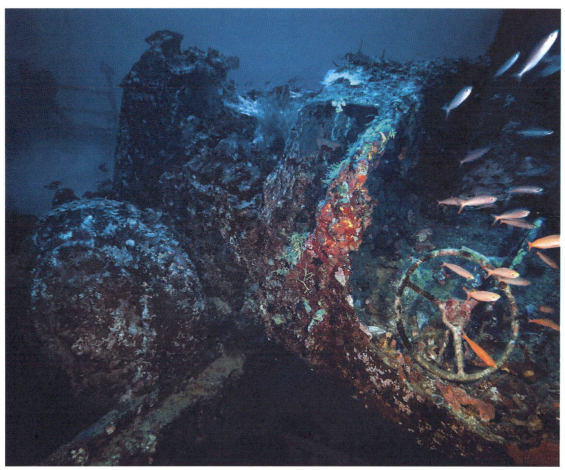

Remains of a truck on the forward deck.

The trip back to the surface is a long one after this deep dive.

SBD Dauntless dive bomber on the attack over Truk. (US Navy)

A torpedo hits the Amagisan Maru; it would be a mortal blow. (US National Archives)

Southwest Anchorage & Aircraft

The Southwest, or Uman Island, Anchorage functioned as a type of overflow anchorage and was not assigned to a specific command. It is often referred to as the 6th Fleet Anchorage, but this is an incorrect label. The 6th Fleet was actually in charge of submarines in this theatre and their base facilities were on the northwest side of Moen/Dublon Island in the Combined Fleet Anchorage. The ships in this area were an ever changing mix of ships and cargoes.

During the attacks of Operation Hailstone the area around Uman Island had a number of big ships at anchor, mostly transports hauling the basic necessities of war. The *Rio de Janeiro Maru* stands out, as she was a submarine tender for a good part of her career; but at this point in the war she was a simple transport just like her neighbors. The *Yubae Maru* is unique in Truk Lagoon as she was still in Imperial Army service when she was sunk. Many ships served in the Army, especially in the late 1930's, but this appears to be the only one to remain so in Truk.

The area around Uman Island was also home to many tenders and smaller craft, especially after Operation Hailstone. The biggest of these is the *Hino Maru* which is interesting as she was sunk during the second carrier raid in April, 1944. There were not many ships to sink when that attack occurred, but *Hino* has the dubious honor of being one of them. Today there are still a number of unnamed smaller craft littering the bottom along the west and northern coast of Uman.

Truk was home to more than just ships during the war. The Japanese Navy was largely responsible for air operations in the area and there were a huge number of aircraft based on the various islands, but these were very ineffective during the battles around Truk. This was due to a very confused command structure in which very few of the planes based in Truk were actually under local command. Instead the planes all had to get their orders from Tinian, Rabaul and even Surabaya in the Dutch East Indies! The Japanese had over 350 planes spread over the airfields of Moen, Eten and Parem; and most were destroyed on the ground.

This volume of aircraft has left a treasure trove of plane wrecks to explore. For bombers there are Jill's, Judy's, Emily's, Tabby's and Betty's (bombers were named after women). The fighters include Zeke's and Claude's; named after men. The planes can be found all over the lagoon and many of them are fairly shallow. There is also a huge amount of airplane parts in the cargo holds of the various ships. Everything from guns, engines, cowlings, landing gear and even propellers can be found with just a little bit of searching.

The ship's bells from Amagisan Maru.

The Amagisan Maru as she lies today.

Amagisan Maru

Amagisan Maru (Mitsui)

The *Amagisan Maru* was a big and fine looking ship, one of the classic interwar cargo and passenger liners built during the 1930's for trade with the United States. Completed at the very end of 1933 she was 450 feet long and weighed 7,623 tons. The *Amagisan* entered civilian service in the distinct black hulled and white superstructure paint scheme of the Mitsui Line and she promptly completed her initial cruise to the Philippines. *Amagisan* was destined for a much bigger job than simply servicing the shorter Philippine routes; she was assigned the prestigious Yokohama to New York route starting in January of 1934. For the next five years she steamed across the North Pacific from Yokohama to the west coast of the United States, where she was a regular visitor to Los Angeles. From southern California she went south and transited the Panama Canal on her way to New York. She was a common sight in New York for many years, but suddenly she stopped appearing in late summer of 1941. Like many of her contemporaries she was being taken into military service.

In the months before the war she underwent conversion to an auxiliary transport; she would now be transporting troops to invade the islands of the Southern Resource Area. She never would return to the cold North Pacific, her fate and future lay in the south. The *Amagisan Maru's* first combat role was to function as a troop transport in the Japanese invasion of Davao in the southern Philippines. For the first time she embarked combat troops destined for a war zone, in this case the men of Kure No 1 Special Naval Landing Force. The overall invasion force consisted of 17 ships and they were able to complete the invasion without incident. *Amagisan* would remain in Davao for the rest of the month before loading up for the next invasion.

Amagisan got her first of many wounds during the invasion of Manado on January 11, 1942. She was part of a substantial invasion force that also included future Truk Lagoon wreck *PB 34*. Her role was the same as the Davao operation, which was to function as an assault transport. For this operation she carried men of the Combined No 1 and No 2 Special Naval Landing Force. These men climbed over the side of *Amagisan* and boarded their landing boats in the pre-dawn darkness and were pushing inland against very light opposition by the time the sun rose. The rest of the morning and early afternoon was occupied with unloading the cargo needed by the troops ashore, but this routine was broken when anti-aircraft guns on the escorting warships began to open fire on three approaching planes. The exact identity of these planes is unknown, but it is likely they were ungainly and obsolete Glen Martin B10 bombers of the Royal Netherlands Indies Army.

Incredible porcelain vase discovered on the Amagisan Maru.

The unusual looking planes roared over the Manado Roadstead and each released four 250-kilogram bombs on the ships below. One of these bombs tumbled out of the bomber and exploded near the *Amagisan* causing only minor damage.

The pace of invasions in the East Indies was rapid and ships that could carry assault forces, like *Amagisan*, were in high demand. Following Operation H, the attack on Manado, the ship continued on to Kendari to the south. By this point she needed to return to Davao to pick up follow-on forces for subsequent invasions. The trip back to Davao was uneventful up until the time the *USS Swordfish* launched torpedoes at the convoy *Amagisan* was travelling in. The men on *Amagisan* only became aware of the attack when a sound like a massive hammer striking metal reverberated through the hull and men were tossed into the nearest bulkheads. The torpedo had hit near the stern and the *Amagisan* ground to a stop in the ocean waves.

Damaged and taking on water the *Amagisan* was a sitting duck. The men on board frantically worked to stem the flooding and to get the engines in operation again, while the escorts methodically worked over the area where the submarine had attacked from. After a couple hours of extreme exertion the *Amagisan* was able to get up steam again and slowly head for Davao. Upon arrival in Davao she was met by the tug and salvage ship *Yusho Maru* and emergency repairs were immediately begun. The damage to *Amagisan* was severe and it would take six months of repairs in Davao to get her in condition to make the slow voyage back to the shipyards in Japan where full repairs and refit could be completed.

During the long months in Davao the war had moved south and east and losses had begun to mount. The *Amagisan Maru* was sorely missed, but she was still in very bad shape and unable to take part in any operations. It would take nearly a month for the big ship to limp north under constant escort, finally arriving in Japan and entering dock for extensive repair work and refit on July 28, 1942. It would take another seven months in the heavy shipyard to finish the work on *Amagisan*; the

The USS Gato had Amagisan in her sights. (US Navy)

Bow deck gun on Amagisan Maru with the forward kingpost in the background.

AMAGISAN MARU   183

View from of the bow showing her severe list to port.

single torpedo had taken a key transport out of the war for over a year. During this time it is likely that *Amagisan* was modified to carry fuel, which was always in short supply. With her new role she finally left Japan in March 1943. She would now be hauling aviation fuel and aircraft parts between the Home Islands and Truk in convoys with other aviation supply vessels such as *Kikukawa* and *Fujikawa Marus*.

The aviation supply convoys lasted well into the summer of 1943 when they gave way to hauling fuel oil from the East Indies to Truk. *Amagisan Maru* arrived at Balikpapan in Borneo in August 1943 and began loading fuel oil destined for Truk. Operations were disrupted during the night of August 14, 1943, when nine American B-24 Liberator heavy bombers of the 380th Bombardment Group came roaring over the oil facilities at extremely low altitude. With a nearly full moon the big bombers swept over the waves and each dropped their six 500-pound bombs in an attempt to skip them into ships, like skipping a stone on a still pond. As the bombs skipped and detonated all around, the men on *Amagisan* were subjected to strafing from the belly and tail gunners on the big planes just above them. The planes were so low the men could feel the heat of their engines as they passed seemingly low enough to touch.

The damage from the air attack was light and simple repairs were made to fix the holes made by the .50 caliber machine guns before the ship left in a convoy bound for Palau and Rabaul. A week into their journey the men of *Amagisan* were again attacked by a submarine, but this time they were not hit.

The submarine *USS Tunny* was not so fortunate as she was subjected to a severe depth charging from the escorting subchasers and was forced to return to base for extensive repairs. The supply mission through the forward bases would terminate in Rabaul, with the *Amagisan* finally leaving there on October 5, 1943. *Amagisan* was headed back to Truk and ultimately the East Indies for another load of fuel when the men again heard the huge hammer blow of a torpedo striking the hull. This time there was no secondary explosion as the weapon was a dud. However the torpedo did strike the number 6 hold with enough force to spring some leaks, but these were easily patched and *Amagisan* would continue on. Her attackers on the *USS Gato* could only watch through the periscope as their juicy target got away.

The remaining months of 1943 and January 1944 would see the *Amagisan* moving cargo across the East Indies and Singapore. She would pick up her final load of fuel in Balikpapan on February 1, 1944, and join a convoy with the *Fujisan* and *Shinkoku Marus* heading for Truk. None of them would ever leave Truk Lagoon. *Amagisan Maru* was hauling a full cargo of aviation fuel in drums and assorted cargo in addition to nearly a thousand aviation ground crew personnel when she entered Truk Lagoon for the last time on February 14. Luckily for the Air Force men they were transferred off the ship before the morning of February 17; but unluckily for the *Amagisan* she was still carrying most of the aviation fuel when the Americans arrived.

The starboard anchor is an impressive and beautiful sight today.

Amagisan Maru burns. (US National Archives)

The *Amagisan* was a big and inviting target and it didn't take long for her to attract a variety of US Navy aircraft on the first morning of the attack. The *Amagisan* had two 3.7-inch deck guns but these were of little use to their crews as nine American carrier planes from the *USS Bunker Hill* singled out the *Amagisan* for their attention. Five burly SB2C Helldivers plunged out of the sky and released 1,000-pound bombs on the ship. One of these bombs dove into the water and exploded just off the port side at the stern. The shock of the explosion brought back awful memories of the first time the ship had been torpedoed. The bomb exploded in the water but the pressure wave tore a hole in the ship and continued on with such force that it actually blew the hull plates out on the starboard side. Warm seawater began roaring into the ship in a flood, but at least there was no fire to set off the aviation fuel in the holds.

Inside the stricken ship the crew barely had time to regain their footing and react when a flight of TBF torpedo bombers unleashed their deadly weapons. The first torpedo in the water dropped cleanly and ran a straight course straight into the starboard side of the ship just forward of the bridge. This caused a huge plume of water to erupt hundreds of feet in the air and tore a relatively small 15 foot tear in the hull. The hole may be small by the standards of torpedo damage, but it was enough to send water roaring into the forward holds. The explosion was also strong enough to ignite the cargo of aviation fuel which began to burn fiercely. The fire in the forward holds would grow and send a column of smoke high in the air visible for many miles, but it would never consume the ship for the simple reason that she was rapidly filling with water. Between the out of control flooding and fire and in the forward holds the crew knew she was doomed and the order was given to abandon ship, leaving three of their comrades killed in the explosions behind to a watery grave. After surviving a number of torpedoes and bombs throughout the war only to survive another day, the *Amagisan* had finally been hit hard enough to send her to the bottom.

The *Amagisan Maru* settled on a sharply sloping bottom with a 45 degree list to port. Overall she went down almost intact as she never fully burned and both damaged areas were below the waterline and relatively small. Thus to this day she continues to strike a very stunning profile and the beautiful lines visible in the old civilian photos of her in the Panama Canal are still very clear today. The clean look of the wreck is helped by the fact that she does not have heavy marine growth, mostly due to her deep depth. The big ship is

This large serving plate is one of the best artifacts discovered.

resting on a slope with the bow gun being the shallowest part at 100 feet and the stern descending into the gloom at 190 feet. The forward end of the bridge is between 120 and 130 and is where most dives begin.

The view forward from the bridge is very impressive and it is very easy to visualize the ship on the surface making her way through the Panama Canal or pulling into New York Harbor. Moving forward over the cargo holds the damage in the third hold is apparent and there are the remains of a car, which is a rare find. Moving forward into the number 2 hold there are assorted airplane parts and these continue into the first hold. The real star of the show is not in the cargo holds but the deck gun on the bow. The 3.7-inch gun is in the stowed position pointing directly ahead, indicating that it was not in action during the attack. Due to the list of the ship it is possible to get under the gun and look up towards the light from the surface 100 feet above with the gun in profile. Swimming just off the bow it is an amazing sight to look back on the *Amagisan* as her huge mass descends into the darkness towards the stern.

The outside of the hull also holds a few interesting items. Upon closer inspection there is a very prominent cable that runs along the hull. This is a degaussing cable designed to demagnetize the ship, which was a defense against magnetic detonators found on mines and some torpedoes. Also on the outside of the hull is the starboard anchor still in the raised position, while the port anchor is extended and the chain heads down to the sandy bottom below. On the bottom along the port side at about 135 feet is the remains of a tanker truck. While the truck is interesting, the view of the huge ship looming above you seemingly falling over is a sight to behold. The stern areas of the *Amagisan* are very deep and not normally visited, but they can be seen while swimming above.

The *Amagisan Maru* is an amazing wreck that is not often visited due to her depth and location at the very southern end of the Southwest Anchorage. There are substantial sections of the ship that are accessible to experienced divers and they make for excellent, albeit short, dives. The depth does pay off in that the ship is still fairly clean and not heavily overgrown. The ship is one of the classic 1930's era Japanese cargo ships and even to this day she retains her amazing shape and lines that make for a memorable dive especially on a bright sunny day.

Forward engine telegraph with bow gun in background shadows.

Gosei Maru

The *Gosei Maru* is a paradox. One the one hand she was a small and very unattractive freighter, but on the other she is an amazing shallow wreck. She is one of a large number of Standard D type freighters produced before and during the war and which served as the backbone of shorter shipping routes across the Japanese Empire. These were smaller and slow coal burning freighters with a small super structure forward and the crew quarters, engineering spaces and stack were at the stern. Attacking pilots described the *Gosei* as, "rusty and unkempt looking". At 271 feet long and weighing just under 2,000 tons she is one of the smaller wrecks in the lagoon but she is an almost perfect size to complete in a single dive and is a great mix of interesting cargo, easy penetrations, incredible marine life and photogenic structure. All this with a maximum depth of 100 feet and a great propeller at only 20 feet makes for a nice bright and long dive.

Gosei Maru (Japanese Archives)

What is known of the *Gosei* begins in August of 1937 at the dockyards of the Tsurumi Seitetsu Zosen at Yokohama. Upon completion the ship began servicing the routes to the Mandated Islands until she was ultimately taken into service by the Navy as a Miscellaneous Auxiliary Transport. In the years before her sinking she occasionally appears in the records hauling various goods between Japan and the main bases at Truk and Rabaul.

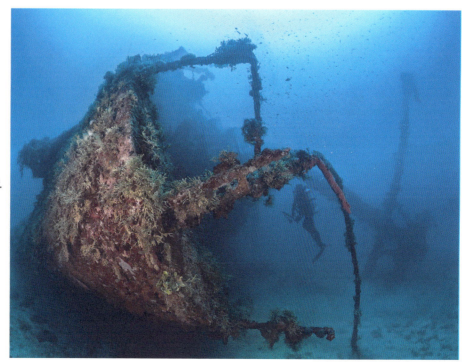

Bow and broken forward mast.

Opposite: Ghostly light in the mess of the engine room.

An example of a typical voyage can be found in October of 1943. That month she left Japan loaded with men and supplies for torpedo boats bound for Rabaul. She made the same trip again immediately after returning to Japan, this time loaded with aircraft parts and bombs. Following the delivery of this cargo to the air units based at Rabaul she joined the badly damaged *Yamagiri Maru* and returned to Truk in a very slow moving convoy. Following this trip she returned to Kure in Japan and loaded aboard her last load of supplies. This time it was torpedoes for the submarines operating out of Truk Lagoon. She entered the lagoon with her deadly cargo of 21-inch torpedoes and anchored just off the eastern shore of Uman.

Unloading had proceeded well and the men on the "rusty and unkempt" ship were preparing to finish the job. All that was left was the cargo of torpedoes in the main hold, but unloading ceased when the first attack wave hit on February 17. The crew on *Gosei* had a tremendous view as the early morning strikes swept in and the lagoon exploded in flame, smoke and shockwaves. From their ship they could watch the ships across the 4th Fleet Anchorage being hit, as well as the terrific pounding delivered to the airbase on nearby Eten. It was around midday when TBF Avenger torpedo bombers from the *USS Bunker Hill* and *USS Monterey* got around to attacking the smaller ugly freighter. The first two bombers roared in and dropped their torpedoes, but both of these malfunctioned and missed. One of them even managed to drunkenly weave its way through all four ships anchored in the area without hitting any of them! The second pair of Avengers from the *Monterrey* had better luck and one of their "fish" ran straight and true, slamming into the *Gosei Maru* just below the superstructure on the starboard side.

View of the stern area.

190   SOUTHWEST ANCHORAGE & AIRCRAFT   *Opposite: Incredible reef life on this shallow wreck.*

Back massager found on Gosei Maru.

The *Gosei Maru* was not a big strong ship like many of the others in the lagoon; she had been designed for mass production and coastal duties. The torpedo blasted a huge hole in her thin side and water filled the ship. She was on the bottom almost before the spray from the blast had subsided on the surface.

The *Gosei Maru* didn't have very far to sink with her stern hitting first on a very shallow reef and the bow resting on a sandy bottom at 100 feet. Upon hitting bottom the *Gosei* eventually rolled over on to her port side and the remaining cargo of torpedoes scattered across the main hold and out onto the sandy bottom. Having come to rest on a shallow reef slope put the *Gosei Maru* in a great location to become a focal point for the local marine life. She has become a key part of the local marine environment and amazingly is still clearly visible as a ship which makes for an excellent dive.

Diving the *Gosei Maru* begins at her bow, which at 100 feet is her deepest point. Looking up the slope from the bow the ghostly outline of the ship and her broken forward mast are often clearly visible. This area is also home to a number of reef sharks and sightings are not uncommon. Moving shallower towards the stern divers pass the empty forward hold before coming on the scene of the torpedo impact that sunk the ship. The area around the superstructure is a total mess of twisted, blasted and collapsing sheets of metal; evidence of the fantastic violence that sent the ship to the bottom so quickly. Beyond the destruction in the bridge area is the main cargo hold which still has a number of the cigar shaped 21-inch torpedoes lying about on the bottom. Some of these show explosion damage from when their high-pressure air tanks burst after long years on the bottom. Continuing on towards the stern the aft superstructure is the last area to explore. The years and constant pounding in shallow water have badly degraded the actual structures, but the inside is fairly open and brilliant shafts of light inside the wreck make for an incredible natural light show. It is possible to work your way through the entire stern structure and exit near the propeller without ever leaving sight of a clear path to the surface. The shallow stern propeller makes for a stunning photo op at the end of a dive.

Glass from a lantern.

Inside the engine room.

Photographer on the rudder shooting the abundant marine life.

Hino Maru No. 2

The *Hino Maru Number 2* was laid down in 1935 as a small coastal cargo ship for Shokuen Kaiso K.K. and was one of literally dozens of "Hino Marus" operated by that line. At less than 1,000 tons and only 200 feet long she was designed for much shorter routes with substantially less cargo then the big Trans-Pacific liners she shares the lagoon with. Despite her small size she has an interesting history and is one of only a few wrecks in Truk Lagoon that was sunk during the second big carrier attack in April 1944.

Hino Maru Number 2   (Shokuen Kaiso)

Hino Maru No 2 spent six years hauling all variety of cargo for her owners before she was requisitioned by the Imperial Japanese Navy in November 1941. The Navy at the time had plenty of cargo ships, but it was in need of patrol craft and harbor defense vessels. The *Hino Maru* was designated as an auxiliary netlayer and was converted to this role during the first month of the Pacific War. This conversion included arming the former freighter with a small bow gun and a variety of net laying gear. Following conversion she spent the first six months of the war laying and tending anti-submarine nets in Japanese home waters and in Formosa.

In May 1942 she received surprising orders that would take the unassuming little ship to the front lines of the war in the frigid waters of the Aleutian Islands. *Hino Maru* departed Yokosuka on May 23 and arrived at Kiska in the far off Aleutian Islands on June 20, 1942. Her time in the Aleutians was hard and fraught with constant peril, her small crew having to adapt to life in a combat zone. Much of the time was spent laying and tending nets intended to thwart and trap American submarines trying to infiltrate the newly captured Japanese bases. By August 1942 the *Hino Maru* had taken a battering in the harsh weather and she was sent home for minor repairs and the addition of a hydrophone to help her detect submarines.

Hino Maru finished her refit and returned to service in October of 1942. Her role was now that of a pure patrol boat whose role was to serve in early detection picket lines out in the open ocean to the east of Japan. On the picket lines the mission of the patrol boats was to simply patrol a small area and be on the lookout for any incoming American ships or planes, in the event they spotted anything they were to radio in before they were sunk. These were tedious and boring patrols that would last three weeks on average; but action wasn't desired as it meant almost certain death for the slow and lightly armed boats.

For a year the *Hino Maru* came and went from a variety of ports to serve on picket lines. Her time in port was spent getting minor repairs and the occasional upgrade such as a depth charge rack and a spotlight. During this year the fortunes of war were rapidly declining for the Japanese Empire and over a million tons of shipping had been sunk.

Opposite: The bow gun has collapsed into the bow.

This led to a chronic shortage of cargo vessels and so the *Hino Maru* was ordered to resume her original role as a small cargo ship. Officially she now became an auxiliary transport, Otsu category. It would take a month to convert her back to a cargo ship.

During the next quarter of a year she spent her time hauling cargo around the Home Islands and occasionally Korea. The attacks of Operation Hailstone hit Truk Lagoon on February 17 and 18th 1944, but at that time *Hino Maru* was well to the north delivering cargo to Chichi-Jima and Iwo Jima. The attacks in Truk would change her fortunes forever, as she was now desperately needed in the south to replace the shipping lost in the attack. *Hino Maru* now began to service a route that led from Japan through the Bonin, Mariana and Caroline Islands ending at Truk. This new route would take her further from home then she had been since Operation AO in the Aleutian Islands two years before.

The *Hino Maru* entered Truk Lagoon during the third week of April 1944. The damage from the massive attacks in February was visible everywhere. Shore facilities were piles of rubble and scorched metal and oil still coated the surface of the lagoon from the recently sunk ships. There were still some signs of resistance though as fighters from the airstrips continued to take to the skies and attack the almost daily bombing raids by American heavy bombers. On land thousands of soldiers were well dug in and new land defenses were beginning to appear in anticipation of an imminent invasion by the US Marines. In this scene *Hino Maru* anchored over the marine graveyard along with several other smaller cargo ships and offloaded her small but desperately needed cargo.

The resilience of Japanese resistance in the area around Truk was well noted by the Americans who needed the base completely neutralized before their forthcoming invasion of the Marianas. The resurgent strength of the Japanese on the islands is evidenced by the fact that nearly 50 Japanese fighters rose to challenge the American bombing raid on April 1, only six weeks after the smashing they took during Operation Hailstone. To put an end to Truk once and for all US Navy Task Force 58 returned on April 29 and 30th, 1944. This time it would be four big fleet carriers and eight light carriers that would hit the islands, their mission being the destruction of shore installations and air facilities. Any shipping would be a bonus, but very little was known to be there. One of these unlucky ships was the recently arrived *Hino Maru No. 2*.

The American planes arrived in force and easily knocked down the Japanese defenders who got airborne to meet them. Things were not so easy with regards to the effectiveness of the anti-aircraft guns onshore. The guns of all calibers opened a tremendous return fire on the attacking planes and many American planes came back with holes and 36 did not return at all.

The bow is the only recognizable structure left.

The Hino Maru burns after being savaged in the attacks on April 29-30, 1944. (US Navy)

The *Hino Maru* drew the attention of 14 American SB2C Helldiver bombers. The Helldivers off the *USS Bunker Hill* had been directed to attack shore installations on nearby Uman Island, but the small freighter proved too good a target to pass up. One of the bombers performed a glide attack, swooping in and dropping two smaller 250-pound bombs that impacted just behind the ship. The bombs damaged the stern area and served to draw the attention of the rest of the squadron. In the next several minutes the doomed crew of the *Hino Maru* could only try and find cover as the big dive bombers performed repeated passes, hammering the ship with their 20-millimeter wing cannons and sweeping the decks with smaller .30 caliber bullets from the rear gunner position. It was reported that the *Hino* was hit by over 1,000 rounds of heavy 20-millimeter cannon fire, leaving her badly chewed up and with various fires starting. Crew casualties must have been severe.

Captain Nagatsuka Tatsugoro (actually referred to as a supervisor, not captain) decided his ship was doomed as more waves of planes began to appear overhead. Amidst the cacophony of battle he ordered the small *Hino* run aground on nearby Uman Island to prevent her from joining the many other ships already at rest beneath the waves. As the ship shuddered from the impact of grounding on the reef her fires continued to burn. She would not get a break as a division of F6F Hellcat fighters armed with 500-pound bombs decided to take a run at her. The fighters bored in at wave top level and attempted to skip their bombs off the water and into the side of the ship, but the bombs failed to skip. Unfortunately for the *Hino* even the near misses caused severe damage when the underwater shockwaves hit the hull and caused the plates to buckle. Water began entering the ship even as the fighters came back for repeated strafing runs, each plane unleashing six .50 caliber machine guns. Finally the rampaging fighters departed, out of bombs and bullets. They left the *Hino* listing and burning badly.

Just as the fighters finished their savage work a single TBF Avenger torpedo bomber appeared and came in for an attack. Expecting a big torpedo to drop from its belly, the surviving crew were surprised to see two 5-inch rockets fly from its wings. The first two rockets hit short, but two more followed and these hit causing even more destruction on the shredded decks. At this point the ship was a near total loss: her hull leaking from the bomb near misses, her stern wrecked from the initial bombs, her decks and structures torn apart from thousands of rounds of heavy machine gun and cannon fire and finally blasted with two rockets. The *Hino Maru* had been hit by every type of attack aircraft flying off the US carriers that day and was aground and burning.

The ruined ship was spared any further attacks the next day, even as land targets nearby on shore were being blasted. Finally on May 3 at noon the *Hino Maru's* stern sank beneath the waves and she was officially sunk.

She had burned for almost five days. The ship settled in very shallow water on a slope, so shallow that the deck gun could be touched from surface. Even the deepest place at the stern is only about 60 feet. When she sank the ship was a total mess and 70 years of storms in the shallow water have not been kind to her. Descending on the wreck only the bow is recognizable, with the deck gun now fallen inside the collapsed area of the forecastle. Behind this is the area that was formerly the cargo hold, which is now a mess of twisted metal which is home to some incredible sea fans. Continuing to the stern, the superstructure area is completely unrecognizable with only a few ribs sticking up from the piles of metal. At the stern amazingly, the propeller can still be found along with an assortment of smaller engineering equipment. This area and the bow with its gun are the only parts of the *Hino Maru* with readily identifiable artifacts. The wreck still makes an interesting second or third dive and trying to piece together the jigsaw puzzle of wreckage can make for a fun dive.

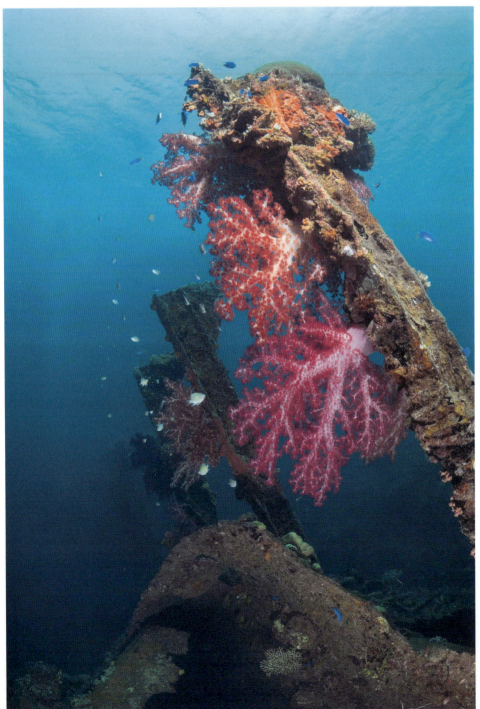

Colorful soft corals adorn some ribs sticking up from the wreckage.

Opposite: Bright yellow sea fans.

The Rio de Janeiro Maru at her finest. (Mitsui)

Ship's bell still looks new.

200   SOUTHWEST ANCHORAGE & AIRCRAFT

Rio de Janeiro Maru

The *Rio de Janeiro Maru* is a classic ship with a storied history and as a wreck is still wowing people to this day. Known simply as *Rio Maru* to the Imperial Navy (also in this text) this ship is a perfect example of the golden age of interwar passenger shipbuilding in Japan. She was nearly 10,000 tons and 450 feet of beautiful lines that spoke to her role as a passenger ship that circled the globe. Her story begins in Nagasaki, Japan, where she was launched on November 19, 1929.

Porcelain cup from the Mitsui Line.

On June 1, 1930, the *Rio* made her maiden voyage for the OSK Line carrying a full load of 1,140 passengers bound for South America. The *Rio* cut gracefully through the waters of the North Pacific heading first to California and then down the coast all the way around Cape Horn and into the South Atlantic before heading north to Santos, Brazil. The voyage would take over two months each way but at least the passengers travelled in comfort and style. *Rio* would make the round trip 13 times during 1930-1937 before she undertook her most celebrated voyage.

In January 1937 Rio left the cold waters of Tokyo Bay and headed south for a trip that would take her around the world. She went first to Hong Kong and then Singapore before turning west into the Indian Ocean. *Rio* stopped in Sri Lanka on her way across the Indian Ocean headed for Durban and Cape Town in South Africa. Then it was across the Atlantic to her old stomping grounds on the South America route with stops in Rio de Janeiro, Santos, Montevideo, Buenos Aires, Belem, Cristobal and Balboa. Her last stop was Los Angeles before heading back across the Pacific to Japan. It was an epic voyage for the big graceful OSK liner and was celebrated on post cards and posters at the time.

Rio would go back to her regular South American route for several more runs before making another around the world voyage in 1939. Following this voyage service resumed on the South America route, and with the clouds of war growing dark over Europe the *Rio* left on another run to Brazil. The passengers on board weren't concerned about the conflict in Europe; their country had already been at war in China for years. They were concerned though when their journey was interrupted by the grinding of metal on metal as their sleek liner collided with the *Kagu Maru*, which had just returned to civilian service after an extended time as a seaplane carrier off the coast of China. The *Rio* was not in any danger, but she did need to be towed home to Kobe for what would turn out to be almost seven months of repairs. Spending extended time in dock was to become a recurring theme for this proud ship. The accident would end the glory days of the *Rio de Janeiro Maru*, she would no longer carry thousands of passengers in luxury across the globe. Instead she left the repair yard and completed only two short trips to China before being taken into Navy service, which sent her right back into the Kure Navy Yard for conversion to an auxiliary transport.

First class dining room. (Mitsui)

First class lounge. (Mitsui)

The conversion would take a month, during which her luxurious accommodations would be replaced by more utilitarian berthing for soldiers. The promenade deck was also rendered substantially less pleasant with the installation of new signal equipment and a pair of twin 25-millimeter anti-aircraft guns. In early 1941 the *Rio* completed several assignments carrying soldiers to battle in China, but her service was stopped when it was decided that like other former passenger liners she should be converted to a submarine tender. In March 1941 she entered the shipyards yet again to have two big 5.9-inch guns installed, along with a range finder to guide them and an anti-magnetic mine degaussing cable. In the cargo holds conversions were made to turn them into depth charge and torpedo storage areas, in addition to space for general goods. In May 1941 she finished her conversion and was assigned to Submarine Squadron 5, which was also the unit where fellow Truk Lagoon wreck *I-169* was assigned.

The beginning of the war saw the *Rio Maru* in Camranh Bay, Indochina, supporting the invasion of the Malay Peninsula. The men on board loaded up all the personnel and equipment for the 11th Submarine Base Unit and steamed with them to their new bases in Malaya and Brunei. With all the excitement of war and her conversion to a fighting ship there was a sense of

The Rio during her around the world cruise. (Asahi Shinbum)

letdown as the initial operations of the Pacific War were simple transport duties. In May 1942 the operations in the East Indies no longer required the submarines of Subron 5, so the *Rio* along with *I-169* were assigned to the next big operation. It was time to end the war by destroying the Americans at Midway.

The *Rio's* mission was to support the submarines that were to head out and intercept the American fleet on its way to Midway, but she never made it past the north coast of Borneo. Late on the night of May 29, 1942, the convoy containing Rio was sighted by the submarine *USS Swordfish*. The submarine submerged and fired two old steam torpedoes out of her stern tubes, which actually functioned during this attack. The *USS Swordfish* was the same submarine that had badly damaged fellow Truk Lagoon wreck *Amagisan Maru* several months earlier. On the *Rio* the ship suddenly convulsed as one of these Mark 14 torpedoes hit her in the forward cargo hold and blew a massive hole in the side of the ship. The crew on the *Rio* scrambled against a raging torrent of water to slam shut the watertight hatches which would isolate the hold and save the ship. The flooding was severe and the ship halted to prevent further damage.

Meanwhile on deck the mighty ship was noticeably down by the bow and the anxious lookouts scanned the water for the submarine hunting them in the dark. Suddenly another fireball bloomed on the water further away in the convoy and seconds later the shockwave from the blast swept the *Rio*. In this case it was the *Tatsufuku Maru* which quickly sank, taking 48 soldiers and crew with her to the bottom. This energized the men on the *Rio de Janeiro* to heroic action.

Intact crates full of sake bottles.

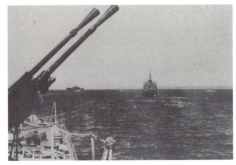
Rio at war; she is to the left. (Japanese Navy)

With the massive 46 foot long hole torn in the first hold and down by the bow, the ship was in no condition to get underway without risking tearing open the hole even more and flooding the rest of the ship. To fix this problem six sailors on the *Rio* volunteered to enter the flooded hold and patch the leak enough so that the ship could get underway. Over several hours' time these brave men jumped into the debris strewn water repeatedly, each time they were able to shore up the damage a little more. Finally they were able to seal the hole enough for the ship to be taken under tow back to Singapore. These six incredible men were given commendations from Admiral Yamamoto himself for their actions.

Rio Maru would remain in Singapore for a month of repairs before being able to return to Japan. During this time Japan had been soundly defeated at Midway and Subron 5 was disbanded. Finally able to return to Japan, the *Rio* was given a brief refitting in Sasebo and reassigned to Submarine Squadron 30 operating out of Camranh Bay, Indochina. On July 21, 1942, she departed Japan for her new assignment, but the *USS Spearfish* had other plans. Less than a day away from entering Camranh Bay the *Rio* was hit again by a torpedo, this time in the stern. In the dark the torpedo blasted into the aft hold and the ship ground to halt, the damage appeared so bad that the crew of the *Spearfish* figured she was done for.

Divers exploring the stern area of the Rio de Janeiro Maru.

Inside the engine room of the Rio today.

They reported the ship sunk and left the scene, but on the *Rio* they were far from finished. This crew had been damaged worse than this before, and before dawn Captain Ohashi had them underway headed to Hong Kong for temporary repairs. The temporary patch was put in place and the *Rio* sent with the repair ship *Yamabiko Maru* to Singapore for more permanent fixes. She spent all of September back in the same docks she was in less than a 100 days prior, finally putting to sea again heading to Surabaya on Java to serve as sub tender.

The *Rio* would spend almost the entire year of 1943 serving as a sub tender and transporting various cargo and men around the East Indies. It was during this seemingly peaceful time carrying out routine duties that the *Rio de Janeiro Maru* would join the ranks of some of the most notorious ships in the history of warfare; the Japanese "Hell Ships" that carried Allied prisoners of war back to Japan. The conditions on these ships was almost beyond comprehension and many thousands of men died on them in horrific circumstances before the war was over. Twice during 1943 she transported Dutch POW's within the East Indies, each time the number of men carried was 2-300 and thankfully for the POW's this leg of their journey was short. Regardless of numbers or length of the journey, joining the ranks of the Hell Ships is a tragic fall from grace for the once graceful passenger liner that circled the world and was celebrated everywhere she went.

The *Rio* would return home to Japan for the last time in December of 1943, where she again entered the docks for some modifications. She left Japan on February 3 full of thousands of rounds of medium ordinance, a large quantity of depth

Decorative object from the Rio.

charges, coastal defense guns, food, sake and mail bound for Truk. Nobody could have known that in just over two weeks' time the still beautiful ship would rest on the bottom of Truk Lagoon. She arrived there on February 11, 1944, and proceeded to unload all the heavy ammunition and depth charges for use on other vessels in the lagoon.

The morning of February 17 found the *Rio* in the Southwest Anchorage off the east of Uman Island. Her men had a splendid view of the entire lagoon and the myriad of ships in it as the sun rose. Suddenly sirens could be heard wailing over the waters of the lagoon and fighters began to scramble off the strip on nearby Eten Island. The crew on *Rio* manned their stations, and the men on deck locked and loaded the 25-millimeter guns ready to sell themselves dearly. They did not have long to wait as the American fighters poured out of the heavens and quickly annihilated the Japanese aircraft that had gotten off the ground. The heavily laden bombers were not far behind them and the crew on deck had a tremendous view as the planes rolled into their dives to attack the ships spread out on the lagoon before the *Rio*. The *Rio* was a big and beautiful ship and her attractive lines demanded attention; unfortunately these same qualities immediately drew the attention of the very first wave of bombers.

A very impressive collection of plates and a tea set.

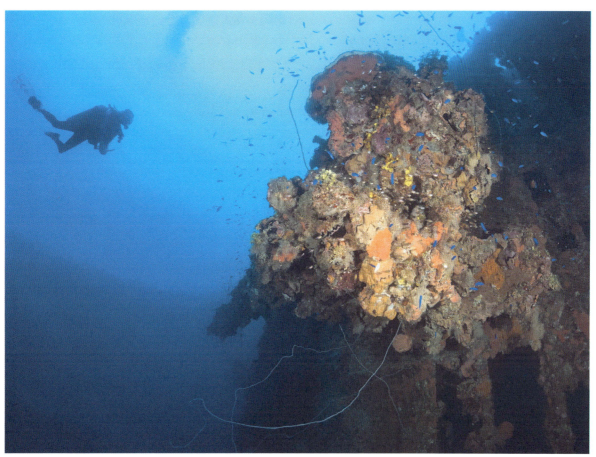

The big deck gun on the stern.

The Rio was carrying a staggering amount of beer and sake.

RIO DE JANEIRO MARU

The first planes to find the *Rio* were very likely SBD Dauntless dive bombers flying off the carrier *USS Yorktown* coming in at low level instead of the usual high altitude associated with dive bombing attacks. On the *Rio* the twin 25-millimeter anti-aircraft guns opened up with their rapid staccato booms sending deadly projectiles ripping through the air at almost 3,000 feet per second towards the attacking planes. On the bow and stern the crews stood by their big 5.9-inch guns, but they couldn't bring these to bear against the swift moving planes. As the *Yorktown* planes roared across the length of the *Rio* their huge 1,000 pound bombs began to rain down causing total pandemonium aboard the ship. One of these bombs dropped into the first cargo hold with a deafening roar which was followed by a constant barrage of secondary load bangs. The men on the forward deck gun dove for cover as the big shells beneath their feet began to detonate blowing holes in the deck from the inside; which can still clearly be seen today.

The fire and secondary explosions on the bow were just starting when a second bomb hit in the rear area of the amidships superstructure. The bomb tore apart the area that once housed luxurious accommodations for globe circling passengers, now just a tangled mess of twisted metal and bodies. The *Rio* was in trouble as she was beginning to burn fiercely and water was pouring in from either near misses or bomb hits right along the water line. Her crew bravely battled the damage, having no time to observe the epic carnage taking place around them in the lagoon. As the battle continued to rage around them another wave of bombers appeared and took aim at the battered *Rio*.

These bombers were the big SB2C Helldivers likely off the *USS Bunker Hill* and they attacked in the traditional fashion of dive bombers, dropping on their prey from high above. The bombs from this attack plunged down and caused more devastation aboard the stricken *Rio*, likely in the area of the superstructure. When they left Captain Kanemasu was dead and the ship was mortally damaged. Despite her crew's best efforts the once glamourous passenger liner turned Hell Ship sank sometime between the afternoon of February 17 and very early morning on the 18th.

The *Rio de Janeiro Maru* came to rest on her badly damaged starboard side at 115 feet. This means that the entire wreck is accessible to recreational divers, and much of it is less than 100 feet. The wreck is a spectacular site and she still captures the grandeur of the liner when she entered service in 1930. Her most famous sites are on the stern, which presents a very clear picture to divers as there is no damage in this area. The highlight of this area, and probably the entire dive, are the two massive propellers hovering in the deep blue water, each blade the size of a diver. These are the same propellers that drove the mighty ship around the world and they have churned the waters of almost every ocean on Earth. Upon coming topside, divers are presented with the huge stern deck gun still in the stowed position but very imposing nonetheless.

Perfectly intact lantern.

Moving forward from the stern structure the first cargo hold encountered is literally stocked floor to ceiling with bottles of sake still in their wooden crates. It is amazing to see the crates still intact after all these decades spent on the bottom, and even more amazing is the quantity of sake that was being shipped into Truk Lagoon. The superstructure area is a mess and the damage in this area is considerable, however it is still possible to enter the engine room through this tangled mess. The engine room is an interesting site and is worth visiting on the way to the forward cargo holds.

Continuing forward the bridge area is recognizable but it is starting to collapse in places. The forward holds are interesting as divers can clearly see the cargo the *Rio* was carrying to Truk. Luckily the big shells and depth charges were unloaded, but the entire setup for a land-based coastal defense gun battery is in the holds. It is hard to recognize at first, but given a moment to look around, the big 150-millimeter guns are clearly visible and the rifling in the barrels is still able to be seen if a light is shined down the opening. The bow area is usually a short visit as this is a very long ship and air will be in short supply at this point. On the bow the most interesting object, the big deck gun, has since fallen to the sea floor so there is little to see as divers make their way back up the hull to the anchor line. The *Rio* was a beautiful ship and she still shows this even after so many years on the bottom. This is a fascinating and popular wreck not to be missed.

One of the massive propellers on the Rio.

Sankisan Maru

The story of the *Sankisan Maru* is a mystery and much has been lost to the sands of time; much like how most of the ship was lost when she sank. Physically the *Sankisan Maru* was just under 5,000 tons and 367 feet long, making her very average amongst the wrecks of Truk Lagoon. There is much conflicting information about her history and even that information is very incomplete. It is likely that she was a relatively new ship launched in 1942. Upon completion she was not immediately taken into Navy service and she spent almost two years servicing civilian trade routes. Dan Bailey does an excellent job tracking some of her movements in his indispensable book World War Two Wrecks of the Truk Lagoon. It is likely that she was involved in hauling rice from Thailand and Indochina back to Japan and carrying various industrial products on the return voyages. Unfortunately for Japan, shipping losses were becoming severe by late 1943 and ships like *Sankisan Maru* were needed for military cargoes. *Sankisan Maru* entered naval service in September 1943.

Sankisan in happy times. (Kaburagi Kisen)

Her first voyage in service of the Imperial Navy was to Formosa. For this journey the *Sankisan* sailed in a convoy with eight other cargo ships escorted by a single destroyer. On September 7 in the inky black early morning darkness torpedoes were spotted coming in from starboard. Amazingly all the ships executed almost perfect evasive maneuvers in the dark and the torpedoes missed, all this while the gun crews cleared their weapons. Immediately orders were given to open fire on the suspected location of the submarine in case it were on the surface. Guns boomed across the convoy and the bright orange arc of shells zipped through the darkness impacting unseen in the gloom. They never did hit anything, but the *USS Pargo* was forced to draw away and make her escape.

Clips for a Nambu machine gun from the Sankisan.

Opposite: Looking up at the clouds and sun.

The convoy got through and the *Sankisan* eventually broke off to deliver supplies to Truk. She would be there until October 26, 1943, when she joined a small convoy of two other Marus and two small escorts to return to Yokosuka, Japan. The following month she would haul supplies south to the Marianas and Bonin Islands before once again heading home to Yokosuka on December 6. The activities during the remainder of December and January are lost to time.

Sankisan Maru entered Truk Lagoon in the second week of February 1944 with a volatile cargo consisting of literally hundreds of tons of ammunition, medicine, trucks and airplane parts. This was a very standard cargo destined for Truk at this time as all these materials were needed for the defense of the islands. She could not have been in the lagoon long before the attacks began on February 17, as it appears almost none of her cargo was unloaded.

Even the events surrounding the destruction of the *Sankisan* are mysterious. What is known is that she was attacked after her neighboring ship *Amagisan Maru* and that the ships in this area were attacked by planes off the *USS Bunker Hill* during the afternoon of February 17. Based on the information available here is a likely story of how she sank.

On the afternoon of the first day of strikes the crew of *Sankisan Maru* could see the planes roaring through the sky above and blasting the airfield on Parem Island and installations on nearby Uman Island. From this vantage they could not see the devastation occurring on the other side of the island, and likewise most observers throughout the islands could not see what was happening in this extreme southwestern part of the anchorage.

The bow kingpost is home to a stunning reef.

SOUTHWEST ANCHORAGE & AIRCRAFT

Medicine bottles dramatically lit up in the hold.

The primary weapon of the Japanese soldier in the Pacific War, the Arisaka rifle.

The torpedo that hit the nearby *Amagisan* would have rocked the *Sankisan Maru*, but they would not have much time for gawking as the dive bombers were already hurtling down on their ship.

One of the bombers aim was true and a great explosion knocked men off their feet all over the ship and killed many instantly as a bomb tore into the superstructure area just behind the bridge. Flames washed over the amidships area and men scrambled to fight the blaze, knowing full well that their ship was stocked full of hundreds of tons of munitions. Following the bomb strike F6F Hellcat fighters roared in with their six heavy machine guns sending thousands of rounds of .50 caliber bullets into the freighter. This just added to the chaos and death on the ship. As the planes departed for the day the men fought to save their ship, just as thousands of others were doing across the lagoon. Nearby the *Amagisan* had already sunk and smoke hung heavy in the air which left *Sankisan* the furthest ship out in the anchorage and not much mind was paid to her.

Onboard the ship the fires continued to rage from the bomb and strafing attacks and some of these fires began to spread into the aft cargo holds. Suddenly there was a cataclysmic explosion as the flames reached the munitions waiting to be unloaded. The explosion was so immense it completely disintegrated the aft holds and most of the superstructure area, while the entire front third of the ship was thrown forward almost 300 feet. The bow area quickly took on water and sank upright on a shallow bottom at 80 feet. The explosion was so strong that the ocean bottom beneath the ship was blasted into a giant crater at least 50 feet deep and well over 200 feet across. Amazingly the extreme stern area with the propeller and rudder survived and it too sank upright but in the much deeper crater bottom at 150 feet. Somehow there is no record of this massive explosion, but the evidence of what happened is indisputable.

Diving the *Sankisan Maru* is an incredible experience as her bow holds are still full of cargo and her shallow depth means that she is absolutely smothered in lush marine life in every color of the rainbow. Most divers begin their dives descending the line that leads to the very tip of the bow, which is an amazing site in the bright clear water sitting perfectly upright and disappearing into the haze towards the stern. The area on deck around the first hold is home to a number of badly disintegrated trucks, but parts of them and the chassis can still be found.

Urinal bottles on the Sankisan and in the museum.

Collection of various caliber small arms ammunition.

Mountains of bullets cover the holds of the Sankisan Maru.

SANKISAN MARU

Radial aircraft engine in the Sankisan Maru.

The bow of the Sankisan.

Opposite: *The kingpost looms behind a wall of color.*

SANKISAN MARU

The whole area is heavily overgrown with soft and hard coral plus a profusion of sponges and whip coral so making things out can be difficult. Descending into the first hold the marine life disappears and huge amounts of interesting cargo can be found.

Gazing around the first hold it is very obvious why the *Sankisan Maru* exploded so violently. The hold is still full of a massive amount of ammunition for infantry rifles and light machine guns. Thousands and thousands of bullets are heaped all about the dark recesses, some of it still in boxes and in clips for the Nambu machine guns. It is almost impossible to describe the amount of ordinance. Heading towards the ghost of the stern divers will encounter several more trucks (these are much easier to identify), engine cowls for Zero fighters and a number of aircraft radial engines. Behind all this there are huge amounts of medicine bottles and jars. These are fascinating to look at as they are a variety of colors and sizes and are present in huge quantities. Exiting the hold is easy and back on deck the twisted ruins of the superstructure area are a sight to behold. Looking at this mess of ripped and twisted steel it is possible to image the massive force of the blast that sank the *Sankisan*.

Finishing the dive on deck is very enjoyable both for the incredible variety of marine life and for the random artifacts that are still strewn all over. The warm clear water, clearly identifiable parts of the ship and huge numbers of fish could occupy divers for hours. Heading back up is best done on the mast which is like a 40 foot tall vertical reef swarming with everything from big jacks to tiny cleaner shrimp and even occasional eels. From the top of the mast it is possible to clearly make out clouds in the sky above as it is only eight feet deep. *Sankisan Maru* is usually done as a second dive and there may be no greater second dive in the world as what remains is an incredible wreck and one of the top five reefs in Truk Lagoon.

One of several trucks in the holds and on deck.

The reef on the Sankisan is almost indescribable in its beauty.

Photographer on the bow deck gun of the Unkai Maru.

Unkai Maru Number 6

Unkai Maru has a great story that begins with the fact that the ship was not named *Unkai Maru* for the first 15 years of her career, nor was she even Japanese! The *Unkai Maru* is the oldest wreck in the lagoon, being built in England in 1905. She was just over 3,000 tons and 331 feet long and her design was from a different era than most of the other ships in Truk Lagoon. She was powered by a single coal-fired steam engine and cruised at a slow 9 knots.

Prior to being sold to Japan in 1921 the *Unkai Maru* was named *Venus* and served with a variety of shipping lines throughout the United Kingdom. In the years following the First World War the economy in England slowed and the empire began to slowly come apart. Simple economics combined

The Venus, before she became the Unkai Maru. (Royal Archives)

with the age of the ship led to the *Venus* being sold to Japan, which had an almost insatiable need for shipping. The *Venus* made her way halfway across the world to Hiroshima and was renamed *Unkai Maru Number 6*.

The *Unkai Maru* fit in very well with the shipping plying the routes to the Mandated Islands like Truk, Palau and the Marshalls. She served these routes hauling basic civilian cargo for over ten years. After this time the ship was requisitioned by the Imperial Japanese Army, which ironically operated their own navy. During her time with the Army the *Unkai Maru* was called Number 15 and she likely hauled men, horses and military supplies to China during the Army's escalation of the war there in the 1930's. After several years of service she was released back to her owners the Nakamura Kisen Line.

The old ship, now rapidly heading towards 40 years of service, didn't spend long back in her civilian colors. Like so many other Japanese ships she was chartered by the Imperial Japanese Navy in August of 1941, claiming the honor of having sailed for England, Japan, the Imperial Army and Navy! The old ship was given the rather unglamorous role of general work ship and set to work hauling cement to the Mariana Islands for use in the construction of military base facilities. However by the time the Pacific War began the Navy no longer felt like they needed the slow old *Unkai Maru*, so they released her back to civilian service.

Back in civilian colors the *Unkai* was showing her age and she likely began hauling iron and bauxite ore, basically she was a rusty old ship hauling rocks. For 1942 and 1943 she serviced civilian routes including one adventurous episode while in a convoy between Formosa and Indochina. During the last week of November 1943 the *Unkai* was in a big convoy of 13 other Marus and a single coastal defense ship for escort when they were set upon by the *USS Bowfin*. The submarine got in the first punch just before dawn with her initial salvo that swept through the scattered ships.

Gas masks are commonly found on all the wrecks; here one from the museum and others still in the hold of the Unkai.

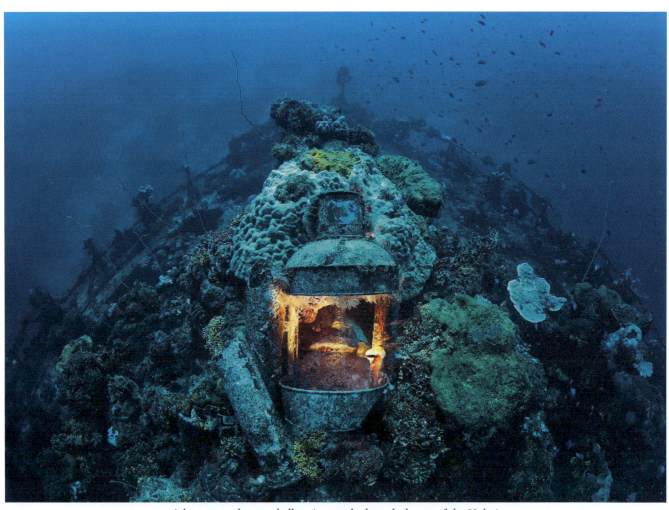

A lantern and spent shell casing on the bow deck gun of the Unkai.

First hit was the *Tonan Maru* which was hit by a single warhead on her starboard side, followed by the *Sydney Maru* which took two hits to the stern which seriously damaged her rudder. The *Sydney* veered wildly out of control before a third torpedo blew apart her engine room. Men on the other ships report her sinking rapidly with a ghastly noise, taking 43 men with her to the bottom. Meanwhile on the *Unkai* the crew on the bow deck gun noticed something in the dark, two torpedoes coming right at them from dead ahead! There was no time to react and the men braced themselves for sudden death; but the shots missed. In relief the men looked up and noticed what had to be the outline of a submarine in the darkness. The ancient deck gun immediately went to work blasting away at the elusive shape with 76-millimeter shells before losing sight of it. At this time the massive *Tonan Maru* lost control of her flooding and sank, taking 84 of her crew with her.

After the adventurous journey to Indochina the *Unkai* returned to a Japan in desperate need of any type of cargo ships to replace losses from submarines. Thus on January 5, 1944, the *Unkai Maru* again entered Navy service as a general work ship. The old *Unkai* sailed for Yokosuka and her crew reported for duty, though they had already been at war. They did not have long to wait before heading to sea in a convoy hauling military supplies such as tanks, trucks, fuel, ammunition, munitions, artillery pieces and all sorts of military gear to Truk. Convoy Number 3120 formed up and left Yokosuka on January 20, 1944. The *Unkai* joined two other famous Truk Lagoon wrecks *Hoki* and *San Francisco Marus* for their collective final voyage. These were all old ships and two of them were former British ships, such was the desperate need for cargo vessels at this time. For *Unkai* it would be her first and last mission in her second bout of Navy service.

Gas mask lit up inside the forward hold.

The deck gun on the bow still has a readable manufacturer mark.

The convoy almost didn't make it to Truk as the waters between there and the Home Islands of Japan were thick with US Navy submarines. These submarines received excellent intelligence as to where the convoys were and what their destination was due to the fact that Japanese Navy codes had been thoroughly broken by US codebreakers in Hawaii. Only two days into the journey the men on *Unkai* witnessed their next combat when a submarine was detected and depth charged by the escort ship *Manju*. Over the next several days the convoy was incredibly lucky as they dodged a large number of submarines, but high command ordered them to shelter at Saipan rather than risk sailing any further.

The convoy would spend several days in Saipan, finally resuming their course for Truk on January 31, 1944. If the convoy had continued to sail on it is very possible the ships would have already left Truk Lagoon when Operation Hailstone hit. Convoy 3120 encountered and depth charged one more submarine before arriving in Truk on February 4. The men on *Unkai* knew they had been extremely lucky thus far; but fate finally caught up with them on February 17.

On the morning of February 17, 1944, *Unkai* was at anchor to the north of Uman Island at the extreme northern end of the Southwest Anchorage. This provided her an excellent view of the majority of the fleet at anchor that morning, and gave her crew a ringside seat to the explosive battle as it unfolded shortly after dawn. That was until the second wave arrived and bored in on the ships located in the Southwest Anchorage. The first to target the *Unkai* were TBF Avenger torpedo bombers flying off the *USS Essex*. These Avengers weren't carrying torpedoes, though, so the pilots took the planes into long glide attacks and released their 500-pound bombs at about 1,500 feet. While most of the squadron was hitting ships in the 4th Fleet Anchorage, one crew targeted the *Unkai Maru*.

The lone TBF began the long shallow dive and dropped a train of 500-pound bombs that exploded in a string along the port side of the ship. The force of the blasts was enough to cause the ship to flood and she began to list. *Unkai* would get no reprieve as the next wave of attackers appeared on the scene shortly after. The first to take a run at the stricken ship were more bomb-carrying Avengers, but these were from the *USS Yorktown*. The planes swooped over and dropped their bombs, two of which were reported as near misses that put more pressure on the already damaged hull. Almost simultaneously SBD Dauntless dive bombers from *USS Bunker Hill* winged out of the sky and released their big 1,000-pound bombs on the ship. One of these bombs blasted the ship just behind the stack causing major damage to the superstructure. Almost immediately fires raged out of control, causing a huge oily black cloud to billow out of the ship. Planes from three different carriers had savaged the old ship that first day, but men on board fought throughout the night and succeeded in keeping her afloat.

Planes from the *USS Essex* returned again first thing in the morning, this time they were SBD's carrying more big 1,000-pound bombs. The pilots found the *Unkai* amazingly still afloat, but with smoke still drifting out of her fire blackened structures. The old ship made an easy target for the dive bombers as they fell on her from 12,000 feet. On board the men could only cringe as five bombs fell on them in rapid succession, two of which hit and three barely missed close off the bow. The force of the explosions was enough to visibly lift the entire bow of the ship out of the water and kill three crew on board. As the planes departed water began to pour into the ship from a large number of leaks in the badly abused hull. It was not long until the *Unkai* took on enough water and began to settle, finally sinking around the middle of the day. The nature of her flooding allowed her to come to rest on an almost perfectly even keel in 130 feet of water.

Pristine beer and sake bottles.

While the *Unkai* may have been an old and unimpressive ship when in service on the surface, she is an amazing as wreck. She sits upright on a flat sandy bottom with only her deepest recesses being beyond recreational dive range. The fact that almost all of her interesting areas to see and explore are around the bow makes even shorter dives meaningful and fun. A lack of heavy marine growth means the *Unkai* is much more of a wreck and less of a reef.

Starting at the deepest point near the stern the ship is intact, but there are no areas of particular interest. Moving forward the area where the first bombs hit is clearly visible and this renders penetration in this area difficult. Further forward around the bridge the *Unkai* is very easy to explore as fire gutted the interior of the superstructure. There is plenty of light as this whole area is only a skeleton, all the wood flooring and partitions were swept away in the inferno that raged in this area. It is the very forward part of the ship where the *Unkai* really shines.

In the first cargo hold there are an impressive collection of artifacts to found. Strewn all about are boots, bottles, gas masks and all variety of personal objects. These are fascinating to find and examine before heading up to the forecastle and the area around the bow gun. The bow gun on *Unkai* is a 76-millimeter field gun made in 1893 for land use and modified for use on the ship. The original manufacturer's plate is still clearly readable! Mostly the gun just needed to make submarines think twice about making surface attacks. Around the gun are ammunition boxes, several shells and even a lamp. There is some pretty marine growth around the gun and hovering over it provides a great view out over the sandy plains surrounding the ship. A good way to end the dive is to head up the mast where a very colorful little reef is growing on the top. This makes a great spot for decompression stops and also provides a really amazing bird's eye view of the entire forward section of the ship. The *Unkai* is usually off the beaten path for most divers but this is a shame as the wreck is in really good shape despite being the oldest ship in the lagoon and in a depth range almost all divers can enjoy.

Engine gauge covers, made in England like the Unkai.

The bow of the Unkai Maru is an incredible view.

Diving the Yubae is like cave diving; here the entrance into the hold.

Yubae Maru

The *Yubae Maru* is a ship from an era before most of the other wrecks in Truk Lagoon, much like the *Unkai* except she was built in Japan. This older style of ship comes from a time before ships were built for specific cargoes, so they tend to be much more basic and all look very similar. She was just over 3,000 tons and 305 feet long and ran on a single coal-fired steam engine that pushed the ship through the water at a relatively slow 10 knots. The *Yubae* was built in 1919 and fully entered service in 1920.

Yubae Maru. (Japanese Army)

The first twenty years of the *Yubae Maru* are a complete mystery. Based on her size and age it can reasonable be assumed that she was involved in transporting basic goods and raw materials in the Japanese possessions in the central Pacific or in close proximity to the Home Islands. Regardless of the specifics, it is likely that the *Yubae Maru* saw many of the major ports and islands of the western Pacific during her long prewar service. When preparations for the coming war with the United States were started in earnest the aging *Yubae Maru* didn't join the Imperial Navy, she became an Imperial Japanese Army ship and entered service on September 22, 1941. To the Army she became Army Cargo Ship Number 780, thus like so many common soldiers, she just became an anonymous number. Before the war began it is likely she underwent some refitting as was common practice with almost every ship that was taken into service.

Her war began in the Philippines when she participated in operations to seize and occupy the many islands of the archipelago. While there are no records of her in the initial invasion forces, by March 1942 she was busy transporting garrison forces to various islands. The soldiers on board sweltered in the rusting holds while the old ship made the slow journey between Formosa and the Pescadores south to Luzon. The *Yubae* made many trips plying these waters, mostly safe from any kind of attack from Allied forces while she delivered men and supplies. These routine assignments continued through 1942 and into 1943, but shipping losses were slowly beginning to mount and the old bulk cargo hauler would be needed elsewhere.

By 1943 the area of operations around New Guinea and the Solomon Islands had become a meat grinder for the Imperial Japanese forces. Ships, planes and men were being chewed up and lost at a far too rapid pace and Japan could not sustain these efforts for much longer. Even the oldest and slowest ships were needed to carry cargo to forward bases, all while under constant threat of air and submarine attack. The *Yubae Maru* appears to have been called into this cauldron in the late spring of 1943 and assigned to transport desperately needed cargo to Army garrisons and bases in New Guinea from the bases at Rabaul and Palau.

Ships on the Wewak run under air attack. (US Army Air Corps)

Wheel inside the twisted metal of the engine room.

Diver illuminating a tea pot discovered inside the wreckage.

Yubae made her first run from Rabaul to Wewak on the north coast of New Guinea in the second week of March 1943 with four other Army transports and two small submarine chasers as escort. The ships made all possible speed and made it safely to the base at Wewak and dropped anchor. Unloading was begun in extreme haste due to fear of air attack. As the men on board strained and sweated in the sweltering equatorial heat their worst fears were realized when suddenly an air battle erupted overhead. Japanese planes were able to get off the ground in time to intercept the attacking planes and the constant buzz and of engines and banging of machine guns gave the crews on the ships extra motivation to finish their work quickly. They worked through the night and weighed anchor in the early morning darkness. The small Army convoy worked up to maximum speed and headed back to Palau. As the men on board willed the slow ships to safety time seemed to stand still and the miles between them and potential attack increased at a snail's pace. Their worst fears were realized when the planes appeared again and launched one final attack on the convoy before it got away. With every available gun shooting as fast as they could the convoy weathered the attack without damage and finally made their escape north.

The white knuckle run to Wewak was just the beginning, things would only get harder as time wore on. On June 21st, 1943, another convoy assembled in Palau with the objective of delivering 5,000 men of the Army's 20th Division to Hansa in New Guinea. This convoy was labelled Hansa Number 4 Convoy and included another future Truk Lagoon wreck, *Nagano Maru*.

Intact glazed storage container. (left)

Face plate written with traditional Chinese characters.

Rudder and propeller on the Yubae Maru today. (below)

As the ships steamed into harm's way all eyes scanned the skies for bombers that seemed even more numerous than the mosquitos that swarmed out of the jungles at night. The convoy arrived early in the morning as dawn broke and unloading began with extreme urgency. Men and equipment poured over the sides of the ships and into smaller vessels waiting alongside, officers shouting a nonstop barrage of orders in an attempt to get things moving faster. Their efforts paid off and the convoy was underway back to Palau before sunset, and more importantly before any bombers could react to their presence. The mission was a complete success, another 5,000 soldiers were now available to battle the approaching Americans and Australians.

Back in Palau there was no time to rest on the laurels of their successful operation; the 20th Division still was short their horses, tanks, ammunition and more soldiers. In the next two weeks all these items were hoisted aboard an even bigger convoy and preparations were made to ship them to Hansa. On July 25 Convoy Hansa Number 5 left Palau and made all possible speed south to the coast of New Guinea. The convoy followed the successful pattern of the previous mission and arrived just as day began to break, and was gone by nightfall. The ships were packed in such a way to allow for rapid unloading, but this also meant they carried much less cargo. Once again the *Yubae Maru* had dodged a bullet in her runs to New Guinea.

Yubae Maru arrived back in Palau after the exhausting mission, and once again the old ship was given no respite. The Yubae was assigned to the convoy Wewak Number 7 with the objective of bringing more desperately needed supplies to the beleaguered base at Wewak. The ships loaded tons of ammunition, aviation gasoline, rice, spare parts and miscellaneous gear for the Army air units bravely battling the seemingly endless numbers of American planes. The convoy left Palau and the men girded themselves for the coming storm. However it seemed the storm had already hit as the convoy returned to Palau due to heavy American attacks on Wewak. The loaded ships sat in the harbor and waited for things to calm down, which they finally did five days later. The old *Yubae* though didn't have it in her and mechanical problems kept the old ship in port for this mission. The crew toiled to get the ship operational again and on September 7, 1943, they stared in shock as the convoy returned. It had been absolutely savaged on the run to Wewak by submarines, P-38 fighters and B-25 bombers. Of the five cargo ships two had sunk, two were severely damaged and the final one had escaped serious damage only due to the fact that the bomb that struck her was a dud. The *Yubae Maru* had dodged yet another bullet.

A view of what the Yubae missed on the Wewak Number 7 Convoy. (US Army Air Corps)

Tea cups like those still found inside the Yubae.

The *Yubae Maru* was repaired, but by no means could she handle another high speed run to New Guinea. Her old engines needed an overhaul so the ship joined a big convoy and returned to Japan in September 1943. The crew enjoyed their time in the beautiful autumn weather, glad for the brief respite from the crushing heat and humidity of equatorial New Guinea. In New Guinea the battle was going very poorly and the Imperial Army was in retreat or cut off. The war in New Guinea was now shifting to the central and western bases along the coast, so the *Yubae Maru* returned to the Philippines to make her next run from there. She made the first of these as part of convoy H-2 to Manokwari in western New Guinea without incident. Thankfully this base was still safe for the time being and the *Yubae* returned to Cebu in the Philippines on November 2, 1943.

Operations to reinforce western New Guinea continued the rest of the way through 1943, but the *Yubae* was never involved in any serious battles. As 1944 began she was tasked to join convoys that were bringing reinforcements to the Caroline Islands and the bases on Truk and Ponape. In February 1944 she was part of a convoy with fellow Truk wreck *Nippo Maru* that brought supplies to Ponape before turning around and stopping in Truk Lagoon on February 10. The convoy began unloading the supplies destined for the defense of Truk. The men on *Yubae* were very skilled in hasty unloading after their experiences in New Guinea and the ship was rapidly unloaded. *Yubae* was empty and riding high in the water at anchor on the morning of February 17. The storm hit Truk Lagoon that morning and *Yubae* would not be dodging this bullet.

Like the other ships in the Southwest Anchorage, the *Yubae Maru* was targeted by US Navy planes flying off the *USS Bunker Hill* during the third strike on the first day. It was around 12:45 when the Helldivers and Avengers winged their way around Fefan Island and began to hit the ships anchored north and west of Uman Island. The old *Yubae* wasn't the juiciest target in the area, but she still quickly attracted the attention of several dive bombers. One of these released a 1,000-pound bomb that hit just off the stern on the starboard side. The bomb appeared to have a delayed fuse and it detonated just below the water releasing a jarring shockwave that tore open the *Yubae's* stern. Water began to flood into the stern and the crew fought to try and save the old ship. Little did they know a TBF Avenger was just then dropping a torpedo that sped through the water and hit the *Yubae* amidships. It was a perfect shot and the blast punched open a massive hole in the *Yubae*. One crew member was killed instantly in the explosion and two others were seriously wounded.

Water rushed into the two gaping wounds and the *Yubae* began to settle rapidly in the water. The crew could only scramble over the sides as the decks were completely awash by the time the bombers finished their attacks. In less than an hour the 24 year old *Yubae Maru* would sink. When she hit the bottom she struck a small hill and rolled onto her back on a mixed sand and reef slope that ranges from 105-120 feet deep.

The *Yubae* today looks like a giant coral encrusted hill with some dark cavern-like holes in it. Those mysterious caves are actually the damage from the torpedo that sank her and the bomb that hit her stern area. Entering inside is a dramatic and disorienting experience, as the blast damage combines with the capsized ship to make everything seem like something out of Alice in Wonderland. There are artifacts still laying around, and these include tea pots and the ever present sake bottles. The old ship was badly hit and exploring the dark, twisted and torn metal can make for an unforgettable dive.

Leaving the dark cavernous inside, divers can head towards the shallower stern areas. These areas are home to plenty of marine life which tends to be especially dense around the propeller and rudder. The single prop that was the focus of all the prayers for speed when she was trying to escape the bombers in New Guinea still makes for a very strong photograph. Along the bottom of the hull, which is now the top, there are many interesting macro critters including nudibranchs and shrimp. Keep an eye peeled as there are often some very big barracuda and several reef sharks that patrol the often slightly murky waters in this area. Seeing them come out of the gloom while on a safety stop is something no diver will ever forget. The *Yubae Maru* was never a glamorous ship and is very seldom visited by divers. Despite this she has a unique story, being an Army ship and the wreck provides some very different types of exploration compared to the other ships.

There is more than wreckage inside the Yubae today.

G4M Betty

The G4M Betty was the primary land-based bomber of the Imperial Japanese Navy in the Pacific War. Officially designated the Mitsubishi Navy Type 1 Attack Bomber, the Betty had outstanding range and carried a deadly payload. Unfortunately the excellent range and speed of the Betty came at the cost of any type of armor for the crew and self-sealing fuel tanks. Like many Japanese aircraft of the era, the Betty tended to easily catch fire when hit. Japanese pilots even began to refer to the plane as the "Type 1 Lighter".

Early in the war the Betty was a stunning shock to the Allies, much like the Zero fighter. Its outstanding range allowed it to sink the British battleship *Prince of Wales* and battlecruiser *Repulse* on the second day of the war when their captains assumed they were beyond attack range. This was the peak time for the Betty, and despite scoring the occasional success, it never really evolved during the Pacific War. There were five main variants of the aircraft but all were essentially the same with the same fatal weaknesses. Between the first flight in 1940 and the end of the war a total of 2,435 Bettys were built.

The Betty had a crew of seven. These men were given four light 7.7-millimeter machines guns and a nasty 20-millimeter cannon in the tail to defend themselves. For a payload the Betty mainly carried a single Type 91 aerial torpedo. If the target was not a ship, then the bomber would carry a single 800-kilogram pound bomb or four smaller 250-kilogram bombs. The aircraft could carry this deadly payload over 1,700 miles at 196 miles per hour cruising.

Flight of early model G4M Betty's. (Japanese Navy)

Opposite: Interior of the Betty looking forward.

Overall the Betty was a big plane being 65 feet long with a wingspan of 81 feet and the fuselage was wide and spacious. There are very few Betty's left in the world and even their wrecks are rare. The wreck in Truk Lagoon appears to be from an aircraft that was attempting to land. The aircraft hit the water at very high speed as evidenced by the tangled mess of metal that is all that remains of the cockpit and nose areas. Further evidence is given by the fact that the impact was so severe it tore the engines from their mountings and threw them over a hundred feet forward. The propellers on the engines show that the engines were not running when the plane hit the water. The exact details of the crash are not known, but it is safe to assume that it was incredibly violent and it likely killed a number of the crew. The wreck itself is amazing as the plane is still mostly intact and sitting upright. It is possible to swim through the fuselage, which is now home to thousands of small fish. On the outside there are many artifacts to examine including seats, toilet and oxygen bottles. This may be the one of the best remaining examples of the Betty in the world.

An incredible school of small fish can always be found lurking behind the former cockpit area.

The wreck sits in a shallow reef so fish are abundant.

The G4M was a big aircraft. (US National Archives)

The propellers are all easily identifiable.

Very few interior spaces remain.

240   SOUTHWEST ANCHORAGE & AIRCRAFT

H8K Emily

The massive H8K Emily was a superb patrol plane. (Japanese Navy)

Officially designated the Kawanishi H8K Type 2 Flying Boat this massive aircraft was codenamed Emily by the Allies. The Emily was a hulking aircraft that bore a striking resemblance to the Pan Am Clippers of the 1930's. The plane was over 92 feet long with a wingspan of 124 feet and it weighed 40,436 pounds empty. With four 1,850 horsepower engines she could reach a top speed of 290 miles per hour and fly an incredible 4,440 miles.

The crew of ten were able to defend the massive plane with a fearsome defensive armament. There were five 20-millimeter cannons and five 7.7-millimeter machine guns. The cannons were capable of inflicting serious damage on even the heaviest armored fighter. In addition to the extensive search range and heavy defensive firepower the Emily could carry two Type 91 torpedoes or 2,000-kilogram of bombs. Just like the other famous Japanese planes of the era the Emily sacrificed protection for speed and range. Only 167 of these amazing planes were produced.

There is a strong oral tradition regarding the Emily in Truk Lagoon. It goes that this plane was the personal aircraft of the commander of the 6th Fleet and he was away at a conference in Palau. Upon his return the plane was attacked by American F6F Hellcat fighters. The pilots desperately climbed to try and get higher than the Hellcats could reach, while the gunners fought back ferociously with their guns. When they were unable to outclimb the fighters the pilots instead dove into a nearby thunderstorm.

An Emily burns after being forced down. (US Navy)

By this point the aircraft had been badly shot up and was full of holes, but the pilots waited as long as they could in the terrific turbulence of the storm. When they finally emerged the American planes were gone, but the Emily was in bad shape. Somehow they managed to nurse the plane back to Truk and even landed it in the water near the seaplane base on Dublon. On board the admiral and his staff prepared to evacuate the moment the plane came to a stop. When the plane stopped it immediately began to fall apart and everyone on board desperately jumped in the water. In the end they all survived and the crew were given commendations for their incredible performance. The Emily itself broke apart and came to rest on the bottom in pieces.

The wreck today is a mess of twisted and bent metal. Fortunately the wings are still intact and the engines generally in place, which gives a good sense of scale. Only on days where visibility is perfect is it possible to see from wing tip to wing tip. Elsewhere the aircraft is upside down and broken up with all types of artifacts strewn about. It is easily possible to find large holes punched in the aluminum from American .50 caliber machine guns. There are only four Emily's remaining in the world.

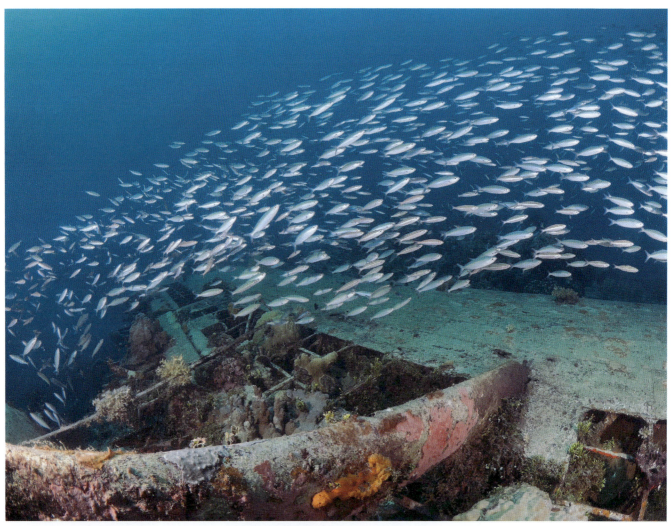

Large school of fish swims over the wing.

A torn float support makes an ideal home for soft coral and sponges.

Emily in flight. (Japanese Navy)

H8K EMILY

A Jill goes down in flames after attacking the USS Yorktown. This was one of the few Japanese planes to get off a counter attack on the US carriers during Operation Hailstone. (US National Archives)

This Jill lies not far off the beach at the Blue Lagoon Resort.

Closeup of the cockpit. It held a crew of three.

B6N Jill

B6N Jill   (Japanese Navy)

Officially called the Nakajima B6N Tenzan "Heavenly Mountain" this aircraft was simply called "Jill" by the Allies. Introduced in 1943 the Jill replaced the B5N Kate as the Imperial Japanese Navy's primary carrier borne torpedo bomber. However, due to the fact that there were so few Japanese carriers left by the time it arrived, the Jill flew most of its missions from land bases. In two years of service there were 1,268 B6Ns produced.

Over its brief life the Jill was known more for constant engine problems and changes than it was for success in combat. The Jill had a crew of three that had two light 7.7-millimeter machine with which to defend themselves. Overall the plane was 35 feet long and had a wingspan of almost 49 feet. It could carry either a single aerial torpedo, 800-kilogram bomb or two 250-kilogram bombs on an external mounting. What is interesting about the Jill is that the bomb rack is slightly off center, as is the tail. This was to compensate for engine torque from the radial engine.

The Jill wreck off the Blue Lagoon Resort in Chuuk is one of very few examples of this plane anywhere in the world. The only other known surviving aircraft is in the National Air and Space Museum in Washington DC. This wreck shows perfect evidence of the constant engine problems and changes associated with the Jill as she does not even have an engine attached! It is likely that it was based at the airfield that was located on the grounds of the Blue Lagoon and then simply pushed into the water at the end of the war. The plane is almost upright and is almost perfectly intact with the exception of the engine. This is a unique opportunity to see an incredibly rare aircraft.

A very late model Zero at the end of the war. (US National Archives)

A6Ms preparing to launch against Pearl Harbor on December 7, 1941. (Japanese Navy)

A6M Zero

The Mitsubishi A6M Navy Type 0 Carrier Fighter is one of the most famous aircraft of all time. Commonly called the Zero, in reference to it being Type 0, the plane was actually codenamed Zeke by the Allies. Introduced in 1940 the Zero was perhaps the most formidable fighter in the world, especially when in the hands of elite Japanese pilots who had been fighting in China for years. The Zero was a perfect fighter during the early war period for Japanese carrier and land based operations as it combined great range, incredible maneuverability and good firepower.

The A6M was 29 feet long with a wingspan of 39 feet. The single engine gave it a maximum speed of 332mph at low altitude, at higher altitude it suffered badly. The single pilot had two 7.7-millimeter machine guns mounted in the nose and two 20-millimeter cannons in the wings. Later versions could carry a single 250-kilogram bomb, which was useful for kamikaze attacks. The Zero would fight in every battle in every part of the Pacific and would achieve lasting fame. 10,939 of these legendary planes were built and a number are still flying today.

When it was first encountered by Allied pilots it ruled the skies, achieving an awesome 12:1 kill ratio. However like all Japanese planes of the early war years it sacrificed pilot protection and self-sealing fuel tanks. Once the Allied pilots got over the initial shock, the Zero began to lose its effectiveness. Another problem with the Zero was that although it went through nine different variants during the war, it was never substantially upgraded. Thus by the middle of the war it was weaker, slower and less well armed than the Allied planes it encountered. Towards the end of the war the best use for these obsolete planes was as kamikazes.

There are several wrecks of Zeroes in Truk Lagoon. The most intact is laying in shallow water just north of Eten Island. The plane is an easy snorkel or short dive and it appears this one was shot down. There is a second Zero off Eten but it is badly broken up in very shallow water, as is a third just off the old runway on Parem. There are probably more as a large number of these planes were shot down on the first day of the attack. Likely the most visited Zeroes are in the cargo hold of the *Fujikawa Maru*. These planes are still in pieces awaiting final assembly on land. There are also a great many Zero engine cowls, propellers, engines and parts on ships all over the lagoon. The *Kikukawa Maru* has a great variety of these artifacts.

Early model Zero preparing for battle. (Japanese Navy)

OTHER WRECKS

HOKUYO MARU

The *Hokuyo Maru* was built in 1937 for use in servicing routes in Northern Japan, Korea and Siberia. She was specially reinforced to deal with ice in the water just like the *Momokawa*. The ship was sunk by planes from the *USS Essex* when bombs caused a secondary explosion that flooded her boiler room. Today she is a deep wreck sitting on the bottom at a little over 200 feet. The ship is upright and makes for an enjoyable technical dive.

KATSURIGISAN MARU

The *Katsurigisan* is probably the deepest wreck in Truk Lagoon. She was a smaller tramp freighter, at 285 feet and 2,427 tons, which serviced routes to China. In December 1943 she was taken into naval service and loaded with war materials bound for the central Pacific. On this first voyage she hit a Japanese defensive mine and promptly sunk. The wreck is very deep at 230 feet and in an area that is subject to currents, thus she is almost never dived on.

Colored lantern glass found on the Katsurigisan Maru.

Nagano Maru

The *Nagano Maru* is one of the oldest wrecks in Truk being built in 1917 for the long haul passenger-cargo routes. At 345 feet long and 3,824 tons she was smaller than the ships that ultimately replaced her on these routes in the 1930's. In the late 30's she served with the Army supporting the war in China, before joining the Imperial Navy in August 1941. She was converted for use as a transport and saw extensive action early in the war, even being bombed in the Philippines at one point. She was sunk by a succession of bomb attacks over both days of Operation Hailstone which caused extensive damage. Today the *Nagano* is deep, with the top of her superstructure at 140 feet and the bottom of the holds at 210. She is upright with a slight list. Inside the holds there is a variety of construction equipment.

Oite

The *Oite* was one of nine Kamikaze class destroyers built during the 1920's. Despite her age she fought in at Wake Island, New Guinea and in the Solomons. Following those viscous battles she spent the rest of her career on convoy escort duty. She was returning to Truk with survivors from the cruiser *Agano* crowding her decks when Operation Hailstone began. Caught in open water in the far northern part of the lagoon she put up a valiant fight, but was hit by a torpedo amidships. The blast blew the ship in half and she immediately sank taking 172 crew and all 523 survivors of the *Agano* down with her. Today she sits at 200 feet in two pieces: the bow is upside down and the after section upright. She is very rarely dived upon due to the great depth and very long trip to reach her.

Ship's bell from the ill fated Oite.

Ojima

The unfortunate *Ojima* was an 800 ton salvage and repair tug built in 1940. Early in the war she towed a number of damaged ships back to a variety of ports for repairs. She finally settled in Truk after the Battle of the Coral Sea and worked with the repair ship *Akashi* on many occasions. On October 7, 1943, she was sent to assist the *Kikukawa Maru* which had caught fire while unloading fuel and aircraft supplies. When the fuel in the aft holds caught fire it created an explosion that literally blew the *Ojima* to pieces. Today her remains are little more than two mangled piles of debris in 120 feet of water. Some recognizable items are visible but it is mostly a scene of total devastation. She is very rarely dived.

Reiyo Maru

The *Reiyo Maru* was built in 1920 for service as a cargo and passenger steamer on the Japan to New York route. She was good sized at 400 feet long and 5,446 tons. After long service on the long haul routes the *Reiyo* was taken into Army service to support operations in China. Unlike most ships that were taken into Army service in 1937-40 the *Reiyo* remained with the Army well into the Pacific War usually moving troops between Japan and Formosa. During this time she survived numerous submarine attacks. It was only right before she came to Truk Lagoon that she was finally taken over by the Navy and her last mission was in the company of the *Momokawa Maru*. She only completed one or two missions before she was sunk by 1,000-pound bombs from dive bombers off the *USS Essex* and *USS Intrepid*. She was carrying munitions and these detonated which brought her quickly to the bottom. The *Reiyo* is another deep wreck with her top structures at 155 feet and her deck at 195 feet. Heavily damaged and very deep, she is not a popular dive site.

Shotan Maru

The *Shotan Maru* was built during the war and entered service in 1943. Her usual duties were to move cargo between bases in the central Pacific, often in the company of other ships now lying in Truk Lagoon. At 285 feet long and 1,999 tons she was a smaller freighter. When attacked she was carrying trucks, ammunition and fuel. She survived the first day, but was sunk by a 1,000-pound bomb dropped by an SBD Dauntless dive bomber off the *USS Enterprise*. Due to her location and orientation it is possible that the crew were trying to ground the ship on nearby Fanamu Island. Today the *Shotan* is upright with her decks around 150 feet and the bottom at 180. The cargo holds still hold much interesting cargo, but she can't compete with the nearby *San Francisco* for divers looking to do only a single deep dive on their visit.

Taiho Maru

The *Taiho Maru* is one of the smaller cargo ships in the lagoon at 321 feet long and 2,827 tons. *Taiho* was a standard Type C freighter and was used as a simple auxiliary transport by the navy starting in October 1943. She was sunk when her cargo of aviation fuel was ignited by bombs dropped by planes off the *USS Yorktown*. The resulting explosion and inferno incinerated most of the forward holds and blew the bow section well away from the rest of the ship. Today she is almost never dived on and is a very difficult wreck to find even though she is in fairly shallow water.

Diving helmet like those used on the Ojima.

Bell from the Reiyo Maru.

Notes on Sources

For historical information on the ships I drew on a variety of sources. Everything, from online forums dedicated to the Japanese Navy to mainstream academic books, were used. The best source on the movements of ships by the Japanese Navy came from the massive amount of data compiled by the website www.combinedfleet.com. Anyone with an interest in the history of the Japanese Navy in World War Two should check that site out. My other main source was a very rare English translation of Japanese convoy sailings during the war. It was tedious work, but combing through that revealed a treasure trove of information on some very obscure ships. My last two sources are well known to divers and scholars of Chuuk/Truk Lagoon. These are the excellent books <u>World War Two Wrecks of the Truk Lagoon</u> by Dan Bailey and <u>Hailstorm Over Truk Lagoon</u> by Klaus Lindemann.

The research on the current state of the wrecks was primarily first hand observations while diving them. I spent many weeks in Chuuk diving the wrecks and have used my favorite dive profiles when describing the wrecks. I also took a lot of inspiration from the two books mentioned above and would often use them to fact check my own information after I had returned home to write. The color photographs are all mine, with the exception of the old shot of the B-24. All the historical photos used are in the public domain. For the Japanese and American photos I checked with each countries national archives (or equivalent) to make sure there were no copyrights on the photos. I did my best to ensure each photo was free to use, if I erred on any of these please let me know. As a photographer copyrights are sacred to me.

The pictures of the artifacts in the museum were shot by me with the assistance of the staff at the Blue Lagoon. Like all other photos in this book they cannot be reproduced without written permission, in this case from the Kimiuo Aisek Museum and Blue Lagoon Resort. I am using these photos with their full permission and cooperation. I drew on many different historical accounts of the war to draw stories and inspiration to fill in the gaps in the ship stories. There are no quotations, direct or paraphrased, from any other works in these accounts.

This book should not be considered an academic work, nor serve as an academic source. I did my very best to make it factually accurate and I spent hundreds of hours doing research and fact checking so it should be very close, but you just never know for sure. For diving this should not be used as a dive planning tool. It should give the diver ideas on what they may want to try and see or find, but use the excellent dive guides and existing wreck guide books for planning purposes.

Finally I hope everyone enjoys the book. The vision I laid out at the bar at the Blue Lagoon has been truly realized in these pages and hopefully you will be interested in the next installment of Legends Beneath the Waves!

About the Author

Andrew is a long-time diver and history buff. He got started diving as your normal vacation diver while living in Washington DC, but everything changed when he moved to Guam. Once on island he ditched his MBA and prior career to become a dive instructor. During his four years teaching diving in the Mariana Islands he introduced hundreds of new divers to the wonders of the ocean; but it was his photography classes that struck the strongest chord. Upon leaving Guam, Andrew hung up his dive instructor hat but he still loves teaching underwater photography.

After Guam, he and his family moved to Beijing, China. This move kept him in close proximity to all his favorite dive locations, but also provided an opportunity for his two daughters to become native Mandarin speakers. During this time he began to enter photography competitions, and his entries were very well received. After an especially good run of winning shots he had his work regularly published in major magazines. This eventually translated into writing articles to go with the photos. Finally he embraced the dark side and became a full time photographer and writer and you can find his stories and photos in publications across the globe.

Currently he still lives in Beijing, but all his work is outside China. Andrew has two blond-haired blue-eyed Mandarin speaking daughters who he is immensely proud of. Keep rocking Elly and EJ! His wife of going on 20 years, Dalice, is a very successful doctor who is practicing in Beijing. She deserves a medal for putting up with his mountains of dive gear and camera equipment that live spread across their apartment. Legends Beneath the Waves Volume 1: Truk Lagoon is Andrew's first book, but there are two more in the works. The Legends Beneath the Waves will continue………

You can connect with Andrew easily online. Here are some helpful links:

Homepage: www.fata-morgana.net
Email: amarriott@fata-morgana.net
Facebook: Fata Morgana by Andrew Marriott

Andrew and Dalice on the last dive of the last shooting trip for this book. This is the very last photo of all the trips and is on the Hino Maru No. 2. One of very few selfies he has ever taken.

Want To See More?

      Is there a specific ship you like and want to see more images of it? Scan the QR Code below to view all the pictures in this book, and many more that there was no space for! The galleries in the link are organized in the same manner as this book. This makes it easy to scan, search and find the ship. Enjoy!

If you can't scan the above code, you can enter the link manually. It is:
https://marriottphotoandart.smugmug.com/The-Underwater-World/Shipwrecks-and-Caves/Truk-Lagoon
or just go to www.fata-morgana.net and follow the links.

Printed in Poland
by Amazon Fulfillment
Poland Sp. z o.o., Wrocław